# THE CHRISTIAN CRITICISM OF LIFE

# THE
# CHRISTIAN CRITICISM
# OF LIFE

By

## LYNN HAROLD HOUGH
DEAN OF DREW THEOLOGICAL SEMINARY

*ABINGDON-COKESBURY PRESS*
*New York* ● *Nashville*

THE CHRISTIAN CRITICISM OF LIFE
COPYRIGHT, MCMXLI
By WHITMORE & STONE

K

To
THE MEMBERS OF MY SEMINARS
*1930-1940*

# CONTENTS

# INTRODUCTION

The man who has lost his past is a tragic figure. Other men use their memories as bricks with which to build their house of hope. They can look forward because they can look backward. The man who has lost his past wanders about, a vague and pathetic shadow, scarcely even a person. Because he has no memories, he has no secure hopes. His childhood is a blank. He cannot remember his parents. His boyhood is forgotten. His early manhood is beyond recovery. He has lost the stuff of which life is made. He does not even know his own name.

If the man who has lost his past is the veritable visible essence of failure, the age which has lost its past represents an even darker tragedy. For an age is made of millions of interlacing memories. History is simply memory made articulate. And the meaning of any age is found in the fashion in which it takes the materials of the past and weaves them into the life of the present. Even when it takes the threads of the past and weaves them into a new pattern, it is dependent upon what has been, as it sets about making what is to be. An idiotic age is an even more startling portent than an idiotic person. It has no memories of the childhood of the race. It has forgotten the youth of civilization. It has lost the sense of the early maturity of the mind of man. Forgetting the tale of man's moral struggle and moral victory, it loses the meaning of conscience itself. Forgetting the tale of man's spiritual adventures, it loses the sense of the life of the spirit. All the meanings magnificently won from centuries of experience are beyond its

reach. The age does not even know its own name. It has
lost its humanity.

That the life of mankind is in reverse is the most significant fact which the men of today confront. It is not merely
what Oswald Spengler called "The Decline of the West."
It is the decline of man. The journey back toward savagery
has been going on apace. The jungle has become the goal
of the human adventure. At first this reverse movement in
human life seemed like a wild and glorious emancipation.
The instincts which had been controlled became the passions
which were controlling. The primitive emerged from the
dark caves of the subconscious to master the life of man.
And with each surrender to the vivid lusts of the jungle
some stable control of the life of civilized man was also
surrendered. The mind itself became the servant of the
body. The intelligence became the slave of the instincts.
Reason was brushed aside by masterful individual and national and racial passions. Now the age which has lost its
past is like a ship which has lost its rudder and is being
driven by a fierce tempest toward the rocks.

If our age is to regain the sense of the meaning of civilized
life, it must recover its past. It must recapture the insights
which it has cast away. It must make its own that vast
body of human experience whose richness it has lost and
whose meaning it has not understood. On the basis of its
intellectual and moral and spiritual history it must build the
only secure future it may construct. The stones which the
builders of our time have rejected must become the foundation of the House of Man. Only so may we find hope for
the age which has lost its past.

From the time when Aristotle wrote his *Poetics* there has
been a central movement in the criticism of literature and
10

of life which is of the utmost importance in that recovery of the past which is the great need of our time. In America this movement has been represented in recent years by Professor Irving Babbitt and Dr. Paul Elmer More. No problem which confronts this bewildered age is foreign to its searching study. Through the disciplines which this movement has introduced, students all about the world have been able to see the age in the light of the ages. Many men who might have made the old mistakes over again because they did not know that they had been made before have been saved from this sort of folly. The experience of the ages becomes vocal in the great masterpieces which the critical humanists study. The standards which emerge when we examine twenty-five centuries of man's civilized life stand out clearly. It is the contention of the present study that all of this is seen at last to come to complete expression in the Christian religion.

The tale of the humanists is one of the great stories of the world. And the tale of that humanism which has sharpened its instruments until they have become more and more critical has its own fascination. That journey of the humanists which has at last come to the great parting of the ways on whose highroad humanism itself has become evangelical is the greatest story of all. The principles of critical humanism come to be an assortment of keys which fit all the locks. It is not by reading about the keys, but by using them to open closed doors, that the student becomes aware of their exhaustless significance. Ten years of teaching these principles have convinced the author of this book that there is no field where it is so easy to have the words and entirely to miss the meanings as just this field which we are now to study. The ordinary student repeats a sharply turned phrase which embodies an important insight, sees no harm in it, in a fashion verbally accepts it, and then forgets all about it. The exceptional student patiently sets about analyzing the phrase, appropriating the insight, applying the principle involved to a thousand situations, and at the end of five years admits that he is just beginning to see its manifold and far-reaching ramifications. Here especially the letter killeth, and the spirit of patient understanding maketh alive. The true humanist constantly practices the fine art of applying his principles to the books he is reading, the situations which he is confronting, and the experiences through which he is passing. So he discovers what these principles really mean. And he is prepared for this subtle intellectual activity by a thorough study of the fashion in which these principles have emerged and the extraordinary way in which they lie embedded in the history, the biography, and the literature of the world. So recovering his past as a member of the society of civilized men, he is ready to have his share in saving the House of Man from the attacks of the barbarians. And after the passing of these bitter years he will be ready to have a share in the making of the House of Man into a statelier mansion than it has been before. He will come to understand the stream of critical humanism as it has moved through the ages. And at the very crisis of his thought he will come to see how humanism finds its best interpretation at last in the Christian religion.

We need to remind ourselves that the man in pursuit of that truth which is the life blood of humanity may use one of several methods, or may use each of them in turn. He may use the instruments of formal logic. This has been done with immense skill by the great philosophers. Such a system as that of Hegel is an example of the monumental quality of the application of this method. The theologian, too, has used this method with his own power. Such a system as that reflected in the *Summa* of Saint Thomas Aquinas is the result. The setting forth of a coherent logical structure of thought interpreting the life of man and his relation to the ultimate reality is a task which has commanded some of the greatest minds of the world. In our own time such conspicuous thinkers as Jacques Maritain and Etienne Gilson have applied themselves to the clarification of these tasks. And with penetrating understanding they have come to do battle in respect of the central matters of life and of thought. Once and again they have said words which deserve the attention of all serious men in respect of the way from the chaos of the contemporary mind back to the cosmos of orderly thought, based upon the great realities which have to do with God and man.

The student in pursuit of truth may use the pragmatic method. He does not now ask about intellectual structure. Perpetually he brings forward one question: Will it work? To him the workable is the acceptable. Such an interpretation as that of William James is the result. Here we need to make a distinction between pragmatism as a method and pragmatism as a metaphysic. As a method by which we test the truth of a position it has very important values. To test the truth of an assertion by its workability is a kind of large laboratory exercise. But to make of pragmatism a metaphysic, to say that the only reality to be found in a conception or a principle is just its workability, is to confuse all clear thinking. The pragmatic metaphysician quite easily incorporates any amount of contradiction in his interpretations. Each is true as far as it is workable, and so the very conception of truth falls apart in relativity. The pragmatist offers us a very interesting and useful method. But he is a bad metaphysician. In fact the philosopher of the flux which goes back toward the jungle likes nothing better than pragmatism as a metaphysic. The jungle has its own pragmatic philosophy, which recognizes the instincts and the biological urges as the commanding realities. Actually, any obsession is workable while it lasts. You must have a higher and more dependable test. The pragmatist offers some significant arguments in the lower courts. But the pragmatist himself must come to judgment before the Supreme Court of coherent thought.

The man in pursuit of truth may use a third method. He may follow what may be called the dialectic of life as it expresses itself in man's history, in the biographies of men, and in the great literature of the world. Here it is seen that the literature of the world contains an implicit philosophy of life which may also be discovered in the experience of man as its tale is told in history and biography. This appeal to experience through the story of the experiences and writings of human beings is the special concern of that humanism which we are to study. The principles which emerge will be seen to have their own place in a coherent intellectual pattern and to be authenticated by the higher pragmatism. So the three methods will at last come together in supporting a compelling interpretation of life.

In the meantime, there are certain advantages in turning to the tale of human experience and of human thought and writing to see what this story itself says to us. This approach has the advantage of a large catholicity. Each of the voices has an opportunity to speak. All the voices are heard. Life corrects logic, and logic is reinforced by life. No Procrustean bed of formal logic pulls the facts apart to fit its

14

demands.  Just when everything begins to fall into formal coherence a voice which has not been heard speaks out loudly and with masterful energy, and the whole pattern has to be reconsidered.  In fact, there is no better discipline for the professional philosopher or the professional theologian than the humanistic studies.  They will perpetually remind him of the fact he would like to ignore.  They will constantly declare to him the difference between formal completeness and vital adequacy.  They will fertilize his patterns of thought by the stream of life itself.

Here we may well speak of a matter whose importance will be emphasized often enough in the pages of this book.  The humanistic studies have to do with man acting, man thinking, man interpreting.  They tell the tale of man the controller of his deeds and of man the controller even of his thoughts.  They tell the story of what man has done with his manhood.

A whole series of disciplines—and the series most popular in our time—tell the story of the world of mechanical interaction which we study in physics and of the vital impulses which we study in biology.  In other words, men of our time have studied things and animals more than they have studied men.  And when they have studied men they have studied those aspects of their lives which belong to the world of things or the world of animals.  They have even tried to interpret personal actions in impersonal terms.  All this has been part of the debacle leading men back toward the jungle.  We must recover the sense of free men if we are to recover citizenship in a free world.  And the humanistic studies will do more than any others to restore our sense of free action as the center of the human life.  Indeed, the humanistic studies tell the story of what man has done with his freedom.

There is no better introduction to this study than the eleven volumes of the first series of the *Shelburne Essays* by Paul Elmer More. In these volumes you see an American of highly disciplined mind as he confronts the richness of man's intellectual inheritance. Dr. More's patient scholarship, his rich and ripe intelligence, and his capacity for seeing everything in the terms of vaster relationships than would ever occur to a less cultivated mind make him an admirable guide as the student enters upon his own intellectual inheritance. The Unity series edited by F. S. Marvin bring to the reader a mass of material not always thoroughly digested or always rightly understood, but the best sort of material for the teeth of the student as he tries to see the meaning of the human adventure. The critical humanist more than most men dislikes predigested brain food, and the assembling of the necessary material loses nothing in fascination when the collecting has been done by a mind less critical than his own. The works of Christopher Dawson are grist for the mill of the critical humanist. His own synthesis of human knowledge is always thoroughly significant and often characterized by an almost final critical acumen. Professor Irving Babbitt, with a fairly bewildering erudition, had a keen scent for the prey the true humanist must follow. His *Rousseau and Romanticism* will do more for the understanding reader than a university education has done for many a man.

But the student must go beyond the interpreters to the sources. Professor Mortimer Adler, at the close of his stimulating and provocative volume *How to Read a Book,* gives a list of a hundred volumes which he conceives to have the

16

root of the matter in them. In truth, every student will make his own list in the days of his ripe fruition. Many books will be found in all the lists the wise men make. But there is nothing hard or rigid about the humanist's library of culture. It must include all the significant voices.

It will be clear enough by this time that the author of this book will claim no small or provincial place for the Christian criticism of life. The first philosophy of history was written by Saint Augustine in the fifth century A.D. It was as spacious as the life of man. It was saturated by a sense of the cosmopolitan significance of Christ. The Christian critic must claim all history, all biography, and all literature as his university. And all study of physical interaction and biological energy must find a place in his ample interpretation of life. It has often been admitted that it is the business of the Christian to keep the soul of the world alive. More and more it will become evident that it is also the business of the Christian to keep the mind of the world alive, to fight for the civilized mind in the face of invading barbarities. And that is only another way of saying what indeed is the central claim of this book, that civilization is Christian, and that when it ceases to be Christian it ceases to be civilization.

# CHAPTER I

## Types of Humanism

MAN'S DISCOVERY OF MAN IS ONE OF THE MOST IMPORTANT matters in the history of life on this planet. Man's misinterpretation of man brings into view much of the tragedy which has directed human life toward frustration and to bitterness. Man's discovery of *things* opens doors to vast realms of knowledge and of achievement. It also is related to a strange matter not often studied or understood, namely, man's curious habit of forgetting his more important knowledge of himself when he becomes engrossed in the less important matter of the relations of things. Alexander Pope, who often constructed a bright phrase capable of bearing a freight he could never put into it, was on the edge of great matters when he wrote, "The proper study of mankind is man." And these matters are all involved in the intricate and checkered history of the word humanism.

The plain man who is not very familiar with the culture of the world is likely to be confused by the various ways in which the word humanism is used in contemporary writing and even in contemporary conversation. Many men drop the word lightly from casual tongues and often from even more casual minds. Clearly enough they use the word with different meanings and in connection with quite different backgrounds of thought and experience.

It is important at once that we come to terms with this vital and definitive word. As long as it is an ever-changing Proteus, we cannot do much with it. If we have to fight until the break of day, we must come to understand its true name and its true nature, and to understand as well why it has been used in so many different ways.

In the United States of America the word is often—in religious circles perhaps most often—used to indicate a group of earnest left-wing Unitarians who have ceased to believe in a personal God and are very eager upon an entirely human level to work out the theory and the practice of the good life. We all owe more than we may understand to the moral energy, the sincerity, and the intellectual rigor and vigor of members of the Unitarian circles of thought. That they have had most far-reaching differences among themselves is in part an indication of their deep sense of the integrity of the individual mind and the importance for every man of complete loyalty to the processes of his own thought. So it happened that those thinkers to whom it seemed that the materialistic sciences of the period just behind us had made it quite impossible to retain faith in a personal conscious deity, found themselves put to it to maintain religion in a really godless world. The matter was complicated by the fact that a universe with no room for a free God left little room for a free man. Not too much attention, however, was paid to this aspect of the dilemma. The positions which were asserted were these: Here is the mathematical pattern of a world of inflexible physical law. Here is man, who must somehow make terms with this world. The life of man must always be man's supreme concern. How can that life be made good in a world of unchanging laws, with no great controller ruling the laws themselves? The dilemma was faced with much earnestness, if not always with consistency. It had to be assumed implicitly that man possessed powers which this impersonal world could not give him.

But at all events a brave attempt was made to teach man how to find and enjoy the good life in a universe of impersonal laws. Since it was man whose problems were studied, and since there was no looking beyond man to find a Great Helper, the proponents of this interpretation of life and conduct felt that they had a particular claim upon the word humanism when they sought a word to describe and represent the central meaning of their position. To be sure, this involved a clear break with the historic usage in connection with the word humanism. But in this republic there have always been brave men who were quite ready to break a lance with historic usage.

Not many years ago, William James gave vast circulation in America to that type of philosophy which accepts or rejects principles or attitudes on the basis of their power to help human life to get on, or their tendency to hinder human life from coming to full achievement and power. Here life—human life—is considered to be more important than logic. Life—human life—has the right of way. That which is friendly to human life is accepted. That which is hostile to human life is denied. Philosophy is just man making the instruments which will plow the fields of his own mind. In England, Professor Schiller of Oxford was setting forth very much the same sort of philosophy as that to which Professor James gave the name pragmatism. But Professor Schiller preferred to call it humanism. Here is a type of thought in which man has the right of way. Unhesitatingly he claims the ideas and the conceptions which will help *him*. Unhesitatingly he turns from the ideas and the conceptions which would lead his life to impotence and frustration. By a kind of right of eminent domain he

21

claims whatever will help on that which is distinctively human. So his philosophy is called humanism.

The American nontheistic humanist and the philosophical humanist of the variety of Professor Schiller differ essentially in their use of the word. It is especially noteworthy that Professor Schiller escapes from the network of impersonal law while the religious humanists of whom we have spoken surrender to it. They ask: How can man live a good life in a mathematically determined world? Professor Schiller asks: How can man best assert his right to whatever beliefs will advance his life? Professor Schiller can rather gaily pass by uniformities which are the be-all and the end-all of the humanism based upon materialistic science.

But the history of science itself is a marvelous tale of human achievement. The scientist is a human being. Even if he works out a materialistic conception of the universe, he the scientist has worked it out. The long tale of science is the story of what man has done in understanding his world. Practical science is the tale of what man has done in using his world. So to a scientist familiar with the full history of the field upon which he is engaged, it may well seem that science is the typical and characteristic human achievement. To him it may very well appear clear that the scientist is the humanist *par excellence*. Science is the great achievement of humanism in the world. If we want to know the possibilities of humanism, we must study the possibilities of science. The man in the laboratory uses human power to penetrate the secrets of nature. Who, then, has a better right to the great word than the man of science? For here two great rivers meet. In America perhaps Mr.

22

George Sarton has been the outstanding representative of this view of science as the real humanism.

It is evident that there are aspects of this claim which will require our earnest attention. At the moment we will content ourselves with the remark that while man using human powers to study nature is indeed in a sense a humanist, man using human powers to study humanity is moving in the genuine realm of humanism. But of this there will be very much more in the pages which follow.

Men are always trying to preserve human values in the world in which they live. No matter what philosophy they accept, they cannot escape the stubborn and ever-present fact of man. And they do not really want to escape this fact, for they are men. So we find earnest thinkers like Walter Lippmann using the word humanism as they busy themselves with the problems of ethics, because they are trying to find an ethic which will conserve the genuinely human values. The weakness of the position lies in the fact that they do not insist on having a philosophy which really makes room for human values. Quite often they hold a philosophy which has no room at all for human values. Then they fasten these values inconsistently on the outside of a philosophy which really contradicts them. With a sort of desperate courage they call themselves humanists, because they are determined to preserve human values, even in an inhuman world.

But there are thinkers who move in precisely the opposite fashion. They inspect human life in its characteristic aspects, and pursue human values to their philosophical roots, and insist on having a philosophy which is determined by just these things. So the philosophy is itself the friend and not the foe of the deepest life of man. Such thinkers inevitably

23

become theistic philosophers, and they may do their philosophical thinking and writing with as much brilliancy and finesse as characterized the work of the Earl of Balfour. Such men have the deepest right to call themselves humanists. Their philosophy of the universe is determined by the human facts and the human values. They use human intelligence as a clue to a universe created and controlled by divine intelligence. They take the controlling intelligence which is the characteristic thing in the limited life of man as the essential matter in the fullness of the divine life. They believe that man is indeed made in the divine image. And they reason back from the image to the deity. They are humanists indeed.

Pragmatic humanists like Professor Schiller take their principles rather lightly, never facing questions regarding the ultimate nature of the universe. Theistic humanists like the Earl of Balfour take their principles very seriously, asking the most penetrating questions regarding the ultimate universe and giving the answers which place the human values in the very nature of reality itself. They have seen that the only consistent way in which a man can be a humanist is by being a theist.

The historic meaning of the words humanist and humanism and their place in the cultural thought of the world are matters of very real importance. The Renaissance represents the first great watershed in the modern world, as naturalistic science represents the second. In the centuries before the Renaissance, men had been occupied with the thought of God. They had been busy with theology. That it is all too easy to underestimate the significance of these theological ages we shall see later on. Now we are calling attention to the fact that at the end of the Middle Ages men went back to the classics of Greece and Rome—especially of Greece—to find a philosophy in these ancient documents. The men who went back to the golden products of the mind of man in the great old culture found themselves dealing with documents always busy with the human. In this very clear sense the writings of Greece were human documents. So the fifteenth and sixteenth century scholars who went back to study them were called humanists. And the interpretation of life they set forth was called humanism. To this day classical scholars often bear the name humanists, though when they are interested in the mechanics of philology rather than in the inner spirit of the classic documents, the name is rather a misnomer.

The Renaissance inaugurated a new period—a period of man's confidence in his own powers. On one side a secular humanism developed, which became an egotism of humanity, a philosophy of humanity cut loose from its roots in God. And so there emerged a false humanism.

The Platonists in Florence and the men who, having gone back to Greece to find out what man meant, went back to Israel to find anew what religion meant, saw the humanistic sanctions against the background of the divine. They moved in the central stream of humanism.

But men of this age were also going back to nature directly to study that life which man's body shares with beasts and things. They entered upon processes of thought which tended to release all those lawless energies which come to their true meaning only when under intelligent control. This world of impulse was found in man's body as well as in the bodies of beasts. In a sense it also was human. So there began to develop the false humanism of

25

the body in control of the mind, against the true humanism of the mind in control of the body.

It was a vital, glorious, tragic, potential age. At the central point one mighty insight stood clear: The world of the human is the world of intelligent control by the mind of man.

But long before the word was thus used, the thing now called humanism existed as a power in the world. When thinkers in fifth century Athens turned from a study of things—of the material world—to a study of the mind of man—of thoughts and ideals and quick-moving intelligence, humanism was born. For humanism first of all is based upon a distinction between life lived on the level of human intelligence and life lived upon the subhuman level of appetite; and between a life concerned with thought and a life engrossed with things. This distinction between a material world to be controlled and clear-eyed intelligence to do the controlling is the fundamental matter in the classic humanism of the world.

We have followed this seminal word on many trails through many obscure places. We have by no means exhausted the tale of its manifold and strange vicissitudes. But we have seen at least the characteristic ways in which it has been used by various types of thinkers, and we have come right upon the classic, central stream of humanism as it has moved masterfully through the world.

When we turn to the world's literature, we see the very richness of the forest in which the tree of humanism grew. Man has strange experiences in coming to self-consciousness and in finding his way in the world. He is aware of his impulses before he is aware of his thoughts. And the literature of many a religion is the varied tale of the deification of the impulses of men. When man begins to feel the passion for unity, there is very early a desire to find that unity in the world of impulse rather than in the slowly growing world of thought. So the tropical jungles of impulse begin to find a pantheistic monism of their own.

Always there is the battle of that which man shares with the world below him with that which is characteristic of the distinctive life of man. Slowly but surely the sense of man the controller emerges. Slowly but surely experiences and struggles and some light from beyond reveal the principles by which man the controller is to guide his craft through the perilous seas. At last man has lifted his head. At last the true Odyssey of man has begun.

Throughout the history of man, that which was meant to be subordinate has tried to be dominant; that which was meant to be subsidiary has attempted to be controlling. And once and again that which is true but irrelevant to the central matter has tried to impose itself as the one really important matter. Those who think they are educated but have only received a degree in pseudo education are the thinkers all of whose erudition amounts only to a brilliant capacity to misread culture, to put the incidental in the place of the essential, and altogether to miss the meaning of intelligent control. The classic humanists have found a clue to guide them through the vast labyrinth of life. One clear vision of intelligence controlling the world of impulse for high ends, and we are able to put our feet on the true road of humanism. We have found a cause. And we have found weapons for the fight.

## CHAPTER II

## *The Humanism of Greece*

"IF A THING BEARS THINKING IT IS GREEK," DECLARED A MODERN Cambridge scholar with a gift for trenchant speech. It was one of those pardonable exaggerations which point straight to the heart of a great truth. One can put it in another way by saying that until you have understood Greece you cannot understand anything else. And one may add that when we misread the meaning of Greece we are sure to misread everything in the modern world. With Greece in the background, everything in our troubled era can be seen in its true significance. With Greece taken out of the background, we confront the chaos without a clue. If it be objected that if we have the religious experiences of Israel in the background we can understand everything else, we will admit that Athens and Jerusalem must meet, and that when they do meet Jerusalem will have the last word. But it remains true that as far as we are civilized men, we are all Greeks. And it also remains true that only as members of the community of civilized men can we offer the most understanding allegiance to Christ. In a sense, Israel offered the world salt to save it from decay. Greece offered the world light in the midst of its darkness. Jesus said, "Ye are the salt of the earth." He also said, "Ye are the light of the world." There is a good deal to say for the contention that essentially the Greek spirit came to flower and fulfillment in Him. We know how deeply moved He was when the Greeks in Jerusalem said, "We would see Jesus." Of all this there will be much more later on. Now we are content with the affirmation that in Greece man discovered his humanity. And this is one of the most important discoveries ever made by the mind of man.

In the first period, Greek speculation was busy with a study of nature. In the second, it was occupied with the mind of man. First it dealt with things. Then it dealt with thought. In the earlier period, Thales, for instance, tried to find one physical substance to which everything could be reduced. He declared this principle to be water. Heraclitus thought of this principle as fire. Later the four substances, earth, air, fire, and water, were suggested. The Eleatics discussed substance; Heraclitus considered change; Democritus advanced an atomic theory. But in general, such thinkers were engrossed with the material world, with things.

It is a curious phenomenon that while the Greeks began with the world of things and rose to the mind of man, nineteenth century scientific thought, reversing the process, began with the mind of man and went back to the world of things. It may be that this reverse movement in scientific thought had something to do with the reverse movement in civilization itself. At all events, the Greek thought of things before he thought of himself. He thought of a material principle in various forms. He thought of stability. He thought of change. The man who believed in stability found it difficult to account for change. The man who believed in change found it difficult to account for stability. The reconciler found the stability in atoms, and the change in their successive relationships. So the mind of man, unconscious of its own powers and of its own meanings, was busy with the world of things. You might have thought that these uncritical early Greeks were nineteenth century scientists. Then came the Great Divide. In the commanding period of Athenian speculation, the mind of man came to its own. Protagoras declared that man was the measure of all things. Socrates examined and charted many activities of observing, thinking, masterful intelligence. Aristotle made the activity of the logical mind the subject of full study and classification. Plato made the world of ideas the ultimate reality. This tremendous achievement of fifth and fourth century Athens stands alone in the history of the intellectual life of man. It was this achievement which made the Greek a Greek. And it was the lack of it which made the barbarian a barbarian. The discovery of the mind powerful and effective in the midst of the world upon which it acted put man at last on the right road. Without it he had been, was, and would be in wandering mazes lost. Always the first question to ask about any thinker is this: Has he made the Greek insight regarding critical intelligence his own? Without this insight he will fall into all sorts of confusion and probably come at last to the curious state where he thinks of things as secreting thought, or of spirit as an aspect of the life of matter. The panpsychist is a thinker who has never understood the central critical achievement of fifth century Athens.

Here, at all events, the air begins to clear, and the fogs begin to lift. Man has become conscious of his mind at last. He has turned from the world of things to master the ways of thought. He has begun to examine the instruments by means of which he studies and classifies and uses what he finds in the natural world.

It is not strange that the method of critical intelligence did not come to be understood and used earlier. Man at the beginning was so busy with what he saw that he did not attempt to formulate a philosophy of sight. He was so busy with the things about which he thought that he did not analyze the processes of thought by means of which he dealt with the world of things. But once his attention was turned to his own mind, everything was bound to be different. Once he began to contemplate the processes of his own thought, new vistas opened in every direction. For the great fact of life on this planet is not that there are things to be understood. It is that there has emerged in the very world where things exist a mind which can perceive them and classify them and understand them and use them. When the physical philosophers were succeeded by the philosophers of the mind of man, humanity had at last come of age. Something had happened which was to be fundamental for every further age and for every future civilization. Man had risen from the tyranny of things to view himself and to become aware of his own powers. Now he saw that he could not express the distinctive meaning of his own life by saying, "I am a body." He could express the distinctive meaning of his own life only by saying, "I am a mind."

The use of the Socratic irony marks a new stage in the life of civilized man. An infinitely agile intelligence belonged to this shrewd, ugly, serious man who hid such profound purpose under his gaiety, and who in effect asked every man he met, "Have you learned how to use your mind?" Everything he saw depended on that. How he reduced pompous and self-conscious ignorance to obvious fatuousness and futility! How he reduced pretentious and uncritical thought to self-contradictory absurdity! Back of the chuckle and the mirth was always the great moral

passion. This strange creature man possessed a mind. If
he misused it, confusion would follow. If he used it perversely, all would be lost. He simply must be taught to use
his mind clearly and honestly and wisely. The distinctive
human quality was intelligence. Man must be taught how
to make the most of his humanity.

It was more than philosophical activity, however. It was
in Greece that man—the everyday man—emerged as man.
It was in Greece that he stepped out of the clutter of the
natural world. It was in Greece that there emerged a sharp
sense of nature to be controlled, and of man to do the controlling.

This sense of controlling human intelligence is the basal
matter in genuinely civilized life, in ethics and aesthetics
and religion. If in man you come upon a power which can
study and analyze and understand and master nature, here
you have something of fairly startling significance. If human intelligence involves a use of that reason which can
master things and control impulses, you begin to have a
new sense of the significance of life. For this intelligence
can detect distinctions. It can erect standards. Without
this, mental life has no meaning. Without this, the moral
life would go down. Without this, aesthetics is emptied
of significance. Without this, religion in any lofty sense is
impossible.

Unless the human mind can distinguish between truth and
error, thought itself becomes a meaningless make-believe.
Unless the mind of man can distinguish between good and
evil, morality is reduced to the absurdity of asking men to
live in the light of distinctions they are incapable of making.
Unless man can see the difference between beauty and ugliness, all talk about beauty becomes incoherent and empty.

32

Unless the mind of man can give clarity and definiteness to the difference between the divine and the human, religion is bound to lose its transcendent splendor and to become a subtle form of self-worship at last. So this discovery in Athens of a mind capable of making distinctions relates itself, not to one thing, but to everything. The essential battle line of humanity has to do with the integrity of the mind of man. If this is lost, all is lost. Here in every age humanity must gather its weapons for its ultimate fight. And because man's battle for his own humanity began in Athens, that fair city above the shining sea is immortal. It is of all cities most truly the city of man.

Right principles can quickly work a revolution in the thought of man. In time fifth century Athens was not far from barbarism. In thought it had made that vast journey which lies between a cipher and a figure one. And the difference between zero and one is infinity. To see Aristotle working out the possibilities of logical and coherent thought for all the centuries is an amazing spectacle. Once the mind of man is turned upon the right subjects and given the right method, the speed is rapid indeed. To see Plato mounting the stairs of his dialectic by means of his doctrine of ideas to a universe of perfect intelligence is one of the completely astonishing experiences which falls to the mind of man. All this so near to the age of barbarity. All this because men's thoughts had been turned from matter to mind. All this because man's intelligence had been turned from things to thought.

It is a sobering consideration that, if the forward movement is rapid when once man's intelligence has been given the proper object and the proper method, the backward movement may be equally rapid when men lose the insights and the techniques of critical intelligence. Professor Arnold Toynbee has made a remark to the effect that we are familiar with the pathetic fallacy which consists of treating inanimate things as if they were persons, but that our time has witnessed the apathetic fallacy of treating persons as if they were things. This, of course, though Professor Toynbee does not go on to say so, means that the journey back from civilization to the jungle has begun. And that journey may be so rapid that it fairly curdles one's blood to think of it. That this journey has been taken with a speed no one could have foreseen, events all about the world have made completely evident. The totalitarian state is erected upon the ruins of man's belief in his own humanity.

Thus we begin to see the extent of our debt to—even as we perceive the precariousness of our hold upon—that humanism which emerged in Greece long before the word humanism had become a part of the vocabulary of man. And it is important to realize that this sense of man as the possessor of kingly intelligence emerges in Greek feeling long before it is given sharp and formal expression. It is implied in much of the writing of Homer. It peers around all sorts of corners in the tale of the wrath of Achilles, and it is woven all through the fabric of the tale of Odysseus. Indeed, it runs like quicksilver through all of Greek literature, both before and after the great days of philosophical achievement.

A few years ago I assigned to one of my students a close and intimate study of the Greek tragedies. It was a rather daring assignment, for neither by environment nor by training had he been fitted for such a task. And he was a good example of the type of American young man who is rather innocent of any especial sense of the beauty or allurement of

34

great literature. However, he applied himself not only diligently, but with hearty enthusiasm to the task. He secured as a background the knowledge of Greek history, of Greek thought, and of the Greek spirit which would prepare him for an appreciation of Aeschylus, Sophocles, and Euripides. Then he immersed himself completely in the writings of the Greek tragedians. He came out of it all having experienced in the world of culture something like the equivalent of a religious conversion. The brilliant humanism which is the soul of Greek tragedy had become an essential part of his own life. He entered upon the study an amiable barbarian. He emerged from it a civilized Greek. Of course, years were required to bring to flower what had so notably begun. But the Greek spirit had made another captive who rejoiced in his liberating chains.

The sense of the meaning of human life becomes a matter of taste in Greek literature even before it becomes a clearly held principle. It is a fascinating subject for contemplation. It enables man to face his universe unafraid. Perhaps it is the first sharp contrast between Europe and Asia, between the Orient and the Occident. The Greek has such a sense of human dignity that his very gods are only glittering immortal Greeks. He reveres them. But he speaks to them politely, with a sense that he can dare to look them in the eye. The Oriental falls flat in the presence of the sense of divine mystery. The Greek stands erect in the presence of whatever gods there be. We shall see in later chapters that the Oriental had his own contribution to make. But this sense of man as man is of the utmost importance. Upon it, we can now say, everything most characteristic of our modern civilization rests.

All of this came to most splendid flower in Athens. Never

before had the human mind played so brilliantly with seminal words in fascinating conversation as when fifth century Athenians talked together about all the things which can engage the attention of curious and eager intelligence. Never before had a language been built into such a stately edifice for the expression of profound thought and of every aspect of man's experience. Architecture and sculpture attained a serene and harmonious loveliness. The sculptor learned how to make the very body of man as he represented it in marble the expression of deep inner meaning and of lofty and regal intelligence. In the battle with Persia it seemed as if there were visible and symbolic expression of the conflict of the kingdom of man's mind with the vast and impressive kingdom of man's body. And it was the kingdom of man's mind which won. That this discovery of the kingliness of man had far-reaching moral meanings was seen when Socrates refused to escape from the judicial action which required him to drink the fatal hemlock. In the very hour when man discovered himself, he discovered something above himself to which he must be loyal. In *Antigone* it became the law eternal in the heavens. And so the loftiest word of Greek tragedy made the same music as that which rose when Socrates died. We shall see later that humanism at its highest is always looking beyond itself. This is conspicuously true in Plato's doctrine of ideas. Far beyond the intelligence of man he has moved to that realm of intelligence on the throne which is the universe itself. Here a man finds the city of his ultimate loyalty. And as in Plato's last writings the eternal ideas become the perpetual thoughts of a conscious deity having their very life in the life of God, we may say that even in Greek thought on its highest summit, humanism finds the secret

36

of its life in the life of the deity. So the city of man is seen at last as the city of God.

All this points implicitly if unconsciously far beyond Plato to a fulfillment which is the goal of all the thought of this book, just because it has been the true goal of all the humanism of the world. At the moment, we only indicate this distant summit in its far and cloudless splendor. For only centuries of experience and the coming of a great Word beyond the words of the Greeks would prepare men for these far heights.

Essentially it was the genius of the Greek to discover the meaning of humanity. And he discovered that meaning in free intelligence investigating and controlling the world and the inner and outer life of man.

That all Greeks did not appreciate the quality of this insight goes without saying. The undertow of man's thinking is always pulling away from the high insights in every land and in every culture. And it was conspicuously so among the Greeks. The Athenian could be brilliantly wrong as well as splendidly right. Greek thinkers took all the paths of illusion and confusion and took them with exquisite finesse. The Stoics and the Epicureans created a world without freedom in which the mind of man was to function and the life of man was to be lived. They used the mind of man to create a world of thought in which that mind could not have come to be. They mixed flashing insights with denials of the very conditions of the best life. Hedonists misused freedom, and misanthropists misunderstood virtue. Even the greatest thinkers were like ships coming to port with barnacles, interest in which might make men on the wharves forget all about the treasure the ships carried as cargo. A man with a genius for the true but irrelevant may easily misquote even Plato.

But it remains true, eternally and gloriously true, when all these things have been admitted, that in Greece man did indeed discover his humanity. It remains true that in Greece man turned from things to thought. It remains true that in Greece man first understood the meaning of free intelligence. And as our ship on the sapphire sea comes within sight of the distant Acropolis, we will lift our eyes and fancy that we see again the light flashing on the shield of Athena above the town which has given the best gifts to the mind of man, and pride in citizenship in the good city of men will glow in our hearts while we gaze on those far heights.

# CHAPTER III

## The Humanism of Rome

THERE ARE THOSE WHO WOULD SAY THAT EVERY GREAT ROMAN got his mind in Greece. This is one of those large generalizations containing more truth than falsehood, but a bit misleading for all that. Greece did provide the university at which Rome matriculated, but we must not forget that Rome brought something to the university. When Rome became a great empire, the city on the Tiber controlled a vast population of a hundred million persons all about the Mediterranean Sea. The Roman was less speculative and more shrewd and practical than the Greek. The typical Roman was an engineer or an administrator. The typical Greek was a man of letters or a philosopher.

The Roman inherited much from the Greek civilization. He liked to believe that he had inherited the best. But he put the inheritance to his own purposes. They were the very practical purposes of men of affairs. The building of great roads—indeed, all the various feats of engineering— gave unadulterated joy to the Roman. He had a hard sense of facts. And he liked to show his mastery by fitting the facts together in his own way. He discovered that this could be done only by a strict and unfailing regard to the nature of these facts. If you ignored the real character of a fact in fastening it to another in building some structure, the result would be that the structure would fall apart. The Greek played with ideas so skillfully that sometimes he thought he could change their nature through the bright agility of his own quick mind. The greatest Greeks did not do this. But the smaller Greeks were all the while substituting cleverness for profundity. They were inclined to dance irresponsibly in the moonlit field of their own phantasy.

There was a solidity about the Roman mind which well supplemented the Greek agility. The Roman was a born governor. He knew how to persuade the most varied sorts of people to live together in some sort of mutual toleration and order. The Greek never made a great governor. At his best he was too busy following truth to its ultimate meanings to be able to make the practical compromises of the great ruler. At his worst the play of an ingenious mind took the place of the rule of a powerful purpose. In a sense he was too puckish to be a potentate. If the typical Greek had a keener mind than the typical Roman, the average Roman had a more dependable character than the average Greek. In all ages the intellectual has been tempted to think that his mental facility delivered him from moral responsibility. It is a fatal blunder. And it has ruined men and nations. In many centuries the man of character has been so afraid of the misuse of intelligence that he has distrusted intelligence itself. That, too, is a devastating blunder. And it is a blunder which the Roman sometimes made. We can see, then, how Greece and Rome supplemented each other. Each offered to the other something which that other did not possess. And each had the cure for the other's vices.

In a man like Cicero you have a synthesis of characteristic Greek insights with characteristic Roman sanctions. The subtler critical understanding is clearly set forth by Cicero when in *De officiis* he emphasizes the distinction

40

between the parts which make up the human mind, one "part" being appetite, the other "part" reason. When Cicero contends that it is an element of the very fitness of things that reason should command and appetite should obey, he is expressing in his own way the profoundest insight of Greek thought. Here the humanism—which in Rome, as in Greece, is a fact without yet having a name—comes to fine flower. And it is exquisitely diffused through the writings of Vergil, conspicuously through the *Aeneid,* which is a sort of handbook of the spirit of Latin humanism. If Greece represents the civilized mind thinking, Rome represents the civilized mind acting. And in each case the civilized mind is disciplined intelligence which has reached a place of control. The Oriental monarchies on the whole had represented grim power ruling. It was always the purpose of the Roman that his empire should represent intelligence ruling. And to a remarkable degree he achieved his purpose.

The sense of a law which grows out of the very nature of human relations was characteristically Roman. And here humanistic insights are moving over farther areas. To be sure, the Stoics, who said much about such matters and of whom we will be speaking a little later on, drew their law for man from a law of nature; and as their nature was held in the clutches of a rigid determinism, their thinking was cursed by an inner inconsistency. They never dreamed of the distinction between the law for man and the law for the thing. Still the Roman was coming to see definitely, if at first dimly, the meaning of a law of human relations as wide as humanity itself. Practical experience and clear thinking combined in the building up of Roman law. The code of Justinian is a vast body of experience in human

41

relationships reduced to statutory form. In a sense it may be called a crystallization of humanistic sanctions. Its freedom from the hard rigidity of impersonal relationships gives to it that human quality which makes all the difference. That which comes from experience alone may be only an incoherent chronicle. That which comes from thought alone may easily become a piece of hard logical dialectic. That which comes from experience guided by thought, and thought fertilized by experience will have that quality of a living dialectic which is the very genius of humanism. This Roman law possessed, and this has given it a powerful purchase upon the mind of men century after century. It is in this sense that our best legal thinkers are always Romans.

The practical experience in dealing with men all about the wide Empire led the Roman to be a pragmatic humanist even when he used no terms, and felt the need of no terms, to define his attitude. The Roman was a great and successful practical politician—perhaps the first example of a politician whose interests widened to the edges of civilization. Now the politician may be an ignoble person. But at least he is dealing with human relations and not with relations between things. So all the while he must be considering all those curious and evasive matters which have to do with man's free mind and his darting intelligence, with his choice between alternatives and his capacity to follow a course he chooses among many. The politician may be far from a moralist. But he lives in the world in which moralists live. Both have to do with choices. The politician may be thinking of securing expedient choices, or choices which will further his selfish ends, but of choices he must think. The moralist is thinking of good choices. So once and again he may be the fierce foe of the politician. But just because each is concerned with the free choices of men, they live in one world. The politician deals with the elements in human nature which are of concern to the moralist.

If the politician sometimes teaches men how to misuse their freedom, as indeed the Roman politician did once and again, it is important that we should see that freedom can be misused only in a free world. The story of the decadence of Rome tells the tale of a very low type of politician. The manipulator of human beings for sordid ends is a very ugly person. But in a sense his very existence is the tribute which vice pays to virtue. It is an understandable and a pathetic fallacy—but a fallacy for all that—which leads a man disgusted with the misuse of freedom to find comfort in the impersonal order of a nature which goes right just because it is never tempted to go wrong. Disgust with the politician who misuses the sanctions of freedom ought to lead us to seek and to follow the politician who uses freedom nobly. The sins which are a by-product of freedom ought not to lead us to idealize the uniformities of tyranny. All this lay deep in the experience of the Republic and the Empire. Things of the utmost importance to mankind were being worked out. But Roman law at its best was a law for free men and not a law for slaves. It was the product of clear and practical intelligence, and not the product of grim tyranny. The Pax Romana was a peace for human beings, and not a peace for driven oxen. Indeed, the sense of the value of a man as a man penetrated so deeply into Roman thought and became so potent in Roman administration that one is constantly surprised at its pervasive influence.

Even when the Roman was an engineer, he was using human intelligence to control the features of the natural world. He was the sort of man who could plan and construct viaducts. He was the sort of man who could build such roads as the world had never seen. Such an architect as Vitruvius was a master of the materials he used for building. He extorted their secrets as he considered weight and pressure and all those stabilities whose free use makes a strong and fine building. In all these ways the Roman felt that he lived at the place of far-reaching power where control is exercised. The engineer controlled things. The Roman governor controlled people. So an apprehension of man as the controller made up a good deal of Roman experience. You can understand Rome only as you examine this implicit and characteristic humanism.

To be sure, both Stoicism, of which Epictetus was so distinguished a representative, and Epicureanism, which Lucretius set forth in so fascinating a fashion in *De rerum natura,* rested upon a philosophical foundation of determinism which ruled out freedom in the exercise of intelligence and tended all the while to pull the Roman down from the place where he saw the meaning of life in the clearest perspective. But he was constantly practicing freedom and control, even when his philosophy led him to deny in theory what was the very foundation of his action. There is something tragically amusing about the spectacle of Marcus Aurelius, that noble emperor, year after year using in unselfish activity for the good of the empire a liberty of action which the sanctions of his own Stoic philosophy denied him. He was a better humanist in his action than he was in his thought. If this inner conflict in the mind of the Roman prevented his coming to a secure position in respect of the control exercised by reason over the appetite, and of man over nature, that he might otherwise have attained, he was neither the

44

first nor the last of those men whose practice has become better than their formal theory. In many centuries the lofty control advocated by humanism has been practiced by men the nobility of whose lives contradicted the central tenet of their speculative philosophy. Spinoza was not a Roman, but he was very much like some of the great Stoics in this regard.

This dilemma of a theoretic determinism which would have struck the essential humanistic position to the ground, and a practical activity which expressed the very genius of free and noble choice, emerges again and again as we try to appraise Roman thought and Roman action. It will emerge again and again as we go on. It seems a ghost which is never successfully exorcised. Even at this early point in our thought, we may begin to have grave suspicions of a theoretic position which must be contradicted the moment we enter the world of action. The humanism of the Roman deed is more important than the determinism of the Stoic thought.

But we must go farther. If we turn from the Latin Stoics to the Latin Epicureans and consider especially Lucretius, we will find that the determinism which in the Epicureans as well as in the Stoics contradicted that belief in the free man upon which humanism insists, had a very interesting psychological—shall we say pathological—origin. We must never forget that these thinkers lived in a world of arbitrary and irresponsible deities. You could never be safe from the malice of some lawless god. The Greeks were often enough better than their gods, and the best Romans put many of their deities to shame. The tension and even the agony of living in a world where you could never be safe from the ugly whim of a god without a character is something which it is very difficult for us fully to understand, and the emotional tragedy of which it is quite impossible for us adequately to appreciate. Any method of striking at these lawless gods seemed to promise better things for men. A universe moving dependably according to impersonal laws was a vast improvement over a universe dependent upon the caprice of almost endless deities who spent much of their time in unlovely struggle with each other, and who tragically and bitterly and unjustly complicated the life of man. The determinism of Lucretius was an escape from a universe of lawless gods. Here, at least, you had a universe upon whose order you could depend, a universe without malice, a universe without spite.

But unwittingly Lucretius proved too much. If you had no free gods, you had no free men. The trap of necessity captured everything and everyone. If spite was banished from the universe, nobility was banished too. If you deny freedom for the sake of abolishing the vices which liberty makes possible, you also abolish the virtues which can exist only in a world of freedom.

Even in Greece and Rome there were loftier thoughts of the gods, and outside the world of classic thought and action there had already arisen the conception of one God who is righteousness alive. If that insight ever became a part of the classic tradition, it was only a step to the conception of the laws of nature as the freely chosen habits of a righteous God. So freedom and order would meet in the character of God, and would become the ideal for the life of man. And so the menacing bitter problem of Lucretius would cease to be.

But if Rome was caught in the clutches of a certain speculative confusion, its practical witness rose high above the tension of its speculative dilemma. At its best, Rome held high the banner of reason acting in loyalty to permanent sanctions. The discovery of these sanctions over the widest areas of human experience, and their codifying for human use and for the purposes of government, produced the noblest achievement of the Latin mind. This was Roman law. The Roman was always a humanist—an exemplar of the noble use of rational freedom—when he was acting up to the level of his most characteristic ideals. Often he became confused when he tried to relate this practice of the free man controlling thought and action to the processes of philosophic dialectic. We will do better by finding an explanation of life which interprets what he did, than by accepting those elements of his thought which would confuse our sense of the significance of his noblest action. And the Roman reverence for fact will help us here. The free man acting nobly is the most significant part of Roman history. We will remember this fact, and refuse to pay too much attention to the philosophical determinism which the Roman was fond of erecting as a wall between himself and the threat of the malice of lawless gods.

We need not say too much of Roman decadence. The history of every people is a matter of warning as well as of inspiration. Sometimes there is more warning than inspiration. Sometimes there is more inspiration than warning. This, however, we may note. And this we may declare with all possible emphasis. Every evil which came upon Rome in any one of its dark and tragic periods was the result either of the loss of freedom or of the misuse of freedom. When tyranny robbed men of their political freedom, evil days came upon them apace. And when men misused the freedom which they possessed, they brought tragedy upon themselves. Every black tale in the life of Rome bears witness in an inverted way to the glory of liberty and to the necessity of its noble use if the very freedom for which men strive is not to betray them at last. In one of his brilliant plays, Ben Jonson reproduced the atmosphere of decadent Rome. Every page of that powerful play is a cry for freedom. And every element of crisis in the life which it describes is a call for a noble use of liberty for the furtherance of the good life for man. From the story of tyrants we can extort the watchwords of freedom. And from the tale of decadence we can see as perhaps we have never seen before the necessity that liberty shall justify itself by noble loyalty to noble standards.

The city on the seven hills has had many vicissitudes. Sometimes it has hidden its face in the shame of inhuman philosophies and of evil deeds. Sometimes it has lifted its head and has stood in calm loyalty to freely chosen standards of the good life for man.

At times Rome has seemed to have a curious capacity for surrender to standards which would corrupt the world. Far enough from the Roman Republic, and far enough from the days of the Caesars, is the Rome which has surrendered freedom in the name of efficiency. This Rome has had its share in declaring that democracy proves so incapable in a crisis that only a dictator can be trusted to organize a nation for forceful activity in the modern world. If there were any truth in this contention, the reply would be that what you lose when you surrender liberty can never be made up for by any skill in organization. If you have lost the cause for which you fight, even the most brilliant victory is a barren victory. Liberty is the cause of humanity. And liberty lies slain in the totalitarian state.

# The Humanism of Rome

As one walks among the ruins of classic Rome, he will remember other voices. He will hear the voice of Cicero in his powerful orations against Cataline. He will see the free spirit of Rome triumphant over the power of skillful but lawless conspiracy. And he will cherish the hope that Rome may yet be free.

A checkered tale it is, this tale of the free man making choices in this difficult world. And Rome has made such contribution to the understanding of the human values and to the practice of the human virtues that it deserves a place all its own in the history of humanism in the world. In Greece man emerged. In Rome man acted as man over ever-widening areas. And once and again the Roman found for man a life worthy of his manhood.

## CHAPTER IV

## *The Middle Ages*

YOU LEARN SOMETHING DEFINITE ABOUT A MAN IF YOU CAN persuade him to tell you what he thinks of the Middle Ages. If he brushes them aside with a few flippant remarks about a period when men debated as to the number of angels who might poise on the point of a needle, you know at once that he has had no firsthand contact with the rich heritage remaining from this era, and you begin to suspect that he has never learned to survey the material coming from other centuries with a clear and critical mind. On the other hand, if his eyes glow with a strange nostalgia and he speaks of the Middle Ages with a spirit of ineffable satisfaction, you can at once be sure that his tender spiritual romanticism has prevented his facing the hard and ugly facts of life. If he speaks of the Middle Ages as one of the seminal periods of the world, you begin to listen to his words with respectful attention. If he tells you that in this period many things good and many things evil were engaged in a strange struggle in the womb of time fighting to be born, you listen with more watchful earnestness. And if in the light of all this, he begins to discuss masterful and magnificent achievements which at last characterized the medieval period, you settle into the receptive attitude of one who listens to an interpretation which must be understood and mastered and then judged in the light of a vast body of facts which often seem to contradict each other, but which all go together to make up the heritage passed on from the Middle Ages to us.

Henry Osborn Taylor's *The Mediaeval Mind* is an inevitable book for anyone who is not making the Middle Ages the preoccupation of a scholarly life but for all that really wants to understand the period. Mr. Taylor himself is literally saturated with the mind of the Middle Ages. He writes with disciplined understanding. And he lets the sources speak for themselves. He captures the very voices of the Middle Ages and carries them to the modern reader. From the stately volumes of Taylor the reader can go on to the writings which give characteristic quality and characteristic distinction to the period. And his mind will be the richer for the experience to the very end of his life.

It is frequently said, and said by very eminent scholars, that during the Middle Ages men were preoccupied with God, and that in the next period they turned their attention once more to man. To such thinkers the medieval period is a time of theology. The period which follows is a time of humanism. The Middle Ages thought of the divine. The ages following thought of the human. There is much truth in those statements. But it is by no means the whole of the truth. And if the contrast is made with the idea that it is complete and definite and final, it requires a good deal of qualification.

Perhaps no book was more popular during the Middle Ages than Boethius' *Consolation of Philosophy*. And the very significant fact about this famous piece of writing is that while its author was a Christian, its whole texture is that of the classic humanism. The fact that it was read all about Europe with appreciation and with no sense of incongruity reveals to us the fashion in which the Christian thoughts of the Middle Ages were given a classic setting. When we get to the heart of the matter, we will see that it was a mind given to the world by Greece which appropriated the revelation which came from Israel. More directly a study of the massive work of Saint Augustine reveals the extent to which humanistic influences entered into the making of the greatest theologian of the earlier part of the Middle Ages. Augustine was a humanist before he was a Christian. And his central achievement was just the making of his humanism Christian. The very texture of his mind had been made by the classic intellectual forms. To change the figure, we may say that these were the molds into which he poured his Christian experience and his Christian faith.

Saint Anselm was a great saint and a great statesman and a great thinker. Every utensil he brought to his work as a thinker was the gift of the classical experience in respect of the intelligence in Greece and Rome. His religion gave him the materials of his thought. His humanism gave him his logic.

When we come to Saint Thomas Aquinas, the greatest thinker of the Middle Ages, we find that his *Summa* is a perfect synthesis of Christian content and classical method. He is a kind of transfigured Aristotle. Indeed, we may say without hesitation that the great humanist, Aristotle, gave to the most commanding theology of the Middle Ages its complete intellectual frame. Here humanism and revelation meet and work together for the building up of a great interpretation of life.

All this shows how difficult it is to make those hard and fast distinctions regarding the forces dominant in particular periods of time of which we are so fond. The thinkers of the Middle Ages were preoccupied with God. Yes, but they thought of God with the intellectual instruments provided by their humanistic training. Indeed, the very conviction that the reason can be applied to great tasks, which was the fundamental attitude of the Christian thinker of the Middle Ages, is itself the outcome of an attitude created by the classic humanistic studies. The questioning and appraising mood which is the essential quality of the thinking and the writing of Abelard is the product of his training in essentially humanistic studies. You get more than a hint of the Socratic irony in his *Sic et non,* and his theory of the atonement sees its power in its capacity to speak directly in the terms of human experience. The large classifications which make up the substance of the *Sentences* of Peter Lombard rest down upon a dependence on the validity of the work of the classifying mind, which the author of the *Sentences* consciously or unconsciously learned from Aristotle and his followers. You cannot think of the characteristic activities of the mind of the Middle Ages and leave the sanctions of humanism out of account.

When we come to Dante, who put every thought and feeling and action of a thousand years into *The Divine Comedy,* and whose popular title—"the voice of ten silent centuries"—expresses the actual truth about him, we find the very synthesis of humanism and revelation so characteristic of the life of the time. It is not merely that Dante tells everything. Everything comes together in him. He is the very incarnation of the qualities represented by the medieval synthesis. At once we are confronted by the fact that Dante is escorted through Hell and Purgatory by Vergil. The great Latin humanist is not only guide. He is also interpreter. He explains to Dante the meaning of everything

53

which the Florentine poet sees. And Vergil represents human reason unaided by divine grace. The mind of man surely comes to its own in the great poem of Dante. When the climax comes and Dante goes beyond the region where the human mind unaided by revelation is competent, his guide is Beatrice, the representative of theology, of divine truth set forth in the forms of the ultimate reason. And even here we are conscious that we are dealing, not with the repudiation of human intelligence, but with the transfiguration of human intelligence by the divine grace. Humanism itself comes to flower as the reason of man is lost in the glory of the divine reason, as the mind of man finds its fulfillment in the mind of God. Indeed, we are now anticipating before the proper time in our argument the final thesis of this book regarding humanism and theology. But so much must be said in fairness to the Middle Ages. And indeed it is not the purpose of history to fit into the neat dialectic of modern thinkers, however much the clever Hegelians may like to believe it so.

But speaking of the humanistic elements in medieval thought, we must refer to one other important matter. Professor Whitehead has declared in memorable words that the very beginning and growth of modern science depended upon that sense of logical structure which was the gift of the scholastic thinkers to the world. Without this sense of logical structure, the amazing achievement of modern science would have been impossible. But this very sense of logical structure was the gift of Greek humanism to the scholastic thinkers. So once more through critical insight and analysis humanism comes to its own.

We may say with all assurance that the man who tried to write the history of the Middle Ages in thought and, we may add, in action as well and left out the humanistic sanctions would be attempting an impossible task. The medieval period received its mind from Greece. It received its soul from Israel.

With all this, however, it is clearly God who is of first and final importance in the thought of the Middle Ages. The supreme intellectual endeavor is not to see all things in man. It is to see all things in God. The shining glory which captures the imagination of the thinker of the medieval period is the nature and the moral and spiritual quality of God. It is not man's world. It is God's world. God is the creator and sustainer, the redeemer and the glorifier of man. To think God's thoughts after Him is man's greatest privilege. To do God's will in joyous obedience is man's supreme responsibility. God is indeed the first word and the last word and the important matter in all the words between. Man has no dignity which God has not given to him. He has no glory which God has not made possible for him.

Here we come upon a tendency which is of the utmost importance for our study. Often—all too often—we find a repudiation of this natural life and its characteristic experiences which is a movement straight away from that appreciation of man and his powers which is so notable in Greek thought. The more rigid asceticism of the Middle Ages is, to be sure, no essential part of the synthesis of humanism and revelation which is the profoundest characteristic of medieval thought. But it is so important a part of the medieval interpretation of life that we cannot pass it by. Gilbert Chesterton has somewhere a series of brilliant paragraphs in which he describes the cleansing of the mind of Europe after the debauchery of classic decadence. It is a frightful picture of nature itself made unlovely through the ugly power of a corrupt imagination. And it is a keen analysis of a situation where the very mind of the world had to be cleansed before the white stars could once more shine in stainless beauty in the sky. When we think of it all, we may see that the last fearful price the world pays for decadence is a grim reaction where the very beauty which has been poisoned by evil thoughts and practices is repudiated, and the very natural powers which have been misused are thought of with hard distrust and ugly hostility. In a sense the decadence of Greece and Rome had almost covered the natural life of man with slime. The asceticism of the Middle Ages represents the process of cleansing by which the world found its way back to a consciousness of redemptive truth and stainless beauty. But for all its service, asceticism was a psychopathic experience. If a thing has been misused, it ought to be rightly used and not to be despised. Because a thing has been misinterpreted, it ought to be rightly interpreted and not repudiated. Asceticism, whether in the Middle Ages or in Puritanism, is the cry of a hurt child who has had a bad fall and is afraid of healthful exercise lest another fall may follow.

We cannot deny, however, that this very repudiation of the natural life led to the emerging of types of beautiful and ethereal spirituality which are a part of the glory of life on this planet. And a long journey through the wilderness of asceticism is rewarded when we come across one of these translucent and transcendent saints.

But even at this point there is more that we must say about the Middle Ages. For, as we have already said, many things which seemed to contradict each other emerged in this singularly rich and fruitful time. As I write these words, I think of a lovely summer day at Chartres, where the sunlight made a shining glory of the glass in the windows one journeys across the world to see, and the whole building seemed to be telling anyone who could understand, how the material can be made the vehicle of the spiritual. Here is no repudiation of the material world. Here is a mastery of the material world for the purposes of moral and spiritual meaning. The whole cathedral shows how the material may be taught to wear the livery of the spiritual, how the temporal may become the very vehicle of eternal meanings. Here the ascetic is swallowed up in the sacramental.

We must not forget that these glorious matters which are the subject of the investigation of the historian of art and of the student of the subtlest thoughts of men belong to a world where the masses of men lived in ignorance and where for them life was precarious and difficult and often cruel. For all the enthusiasm of Henry Adams—whose classic volume I found on sale at a stall in front of the cathedral at Chartres—we suspect that he might have had hesitations about living during the Middle Ages had he had the choice. The word sanitation had not been born when Chartres was built. And the common man had not lifted his head to be a person of privilege and power in these middle centuries. Yet—yet—these cathedrals did belong to common people as well as to kings and princes and scholars. And such stories as the tale of the dancer who had only his rhythmic motions to offer to the Virgin and had his reward, and such other stories as that of the converted gladiator who carried a heavy child across a swollen stream and found that he had carried Christ Himself, belonged to this period. Perhaps in every way it was richer than our too

57

dull eyes and too dull ears and too irresponsive minds have understood.

To go back to central matters in the stream of thought, the typical scholastic owed the structures of his mental processes to humanistic sources. But the content with which he dealt was more and more transcendental. His confidence in the mind of man, however, was little less than amazing. The dinner of a king was so incidental to Saint Thomas in a mighty tussle of thought that when at last the process of dialectic became clear, he forgot king and courtiers and brought his fist down on the table in sheer delight in victorious mental battle. Saint Anselm wanted to live a few days longer in order that once and for all he might solve the problem of the being of God and the Trinity. These giants of the Middle Ages knew very well the irksomeness of man's limitation, the tragedy of his selfish cruelty and his lawless lust; but for all that they believed—how they believed! —that the mind of man was created for the loftiest flights. They preserved humanism at the heart of a transcendental religion.

We may seem to have made rather free use of the word humanism in dealing with this period when the word was not yet in existence. But the thing for which the word stands did exist. And that is the important matter. There are ages rich in words and poor in meanings. Such ages become very artificial as empty words go staggering about with no rich and vital contents. There are ages so rich in meanings that it is hard for the words to catch up with them. It will be enough for us that the humanistic sanctions were busily active in the Middle Ages. In time the word would be found. So there is no harm in our sending the word back to do service in a period before it was born, if we do this in full knowledge of the history of the word itself. We must remember, too, that in formative periods distinctions are never seen so sharply as in later periods when the process of critical definition has been carried on. But these periods are all the more interesting as one looks back on them from the vantage ground which later analysis provides.

Henry Osborn Taylor has helped us to see what glorious things were going on during these centuries. If we admit that these things happened in the minds of only a few people over great areas of space and great stretches of time, it will remain true that to think of the period between the fall of Rome in A.D. 476 and the fall of Constantinople in A.D. 1453 as pure waste would be to make the greatest sort of mistake. Man's mind was busy about mighty matters. And when Anselm and Aquinas are at their best, you would have to journey far in any century to find as skillful or subtle or effective use of the powers of disciplined intelligence.

There is a logic in the historic movement of the mind of man. But there are many roads. There are many fascinating bypaths, and the following of the central logic through all the richness and even the confusion of thought is a difficult and rewarding enterprise. In his important little book, *The Classical Heritage of the Middle Ages,* Henry Osborn Taylor has reminded us of some of the many gifts the Middle Ages received from Greece and Rome. These gifts from classic humanism were often used without too close an analysis of their sources. Without these gifts, however, the mind of the Middle Ages would have been something far different from the mind we study as we go back to the sources which have been preserved through the centuries which lie between that time and our own. We may put it all in a sentence of summary and of final assertion. The instruments which the medieval thinkers used in analyzing and interpreting the Christian religion which they so gladly received as a revelation from God were the contribution of that Greek humanism without which there might have been a gospel, but without which there could have been no Christian dialectic.

So much in connection with the argument of this book at the stage which we now have reached. At once, however, we must add that the central interest in that high argument which the age conducted had to do with God and that which infinitely transcends while it includes the ways of human life.

If one is tempted to say that this inrush of theology interferes with the normal unfolding of the humanistic sanctions, one must also say that it is the fashion of revelation to break in upon human life; only the medieval thinkers would have added, not to deny the meaning and the power of human intelligence, but to complete and fulfill it in the glory which is in Christ. The scholastic thinker at all events would have said that moral evil has not so corrupted the mind of man that he is unable to seize upon divine truth when it is presented to him. Indeed, he would have declared that man can build the truth God revealed to him into a structure of thought not entirely unworthy of the God who has not remained silent but has spoken to men.

# CHAPTER V

## The Renaissance

WE WHO LIVE IN THE PERIOD OF THE DECADENCE WHICH HAS
followed the Renaissance may well find it difficult to appreciate the warm brightness and exhilaration of that marvelous morning of the spirit of man. If we accompany Sir
Walter Raleigh when he visits Edmund Spenser in Ireland
and persuades that fine poet to bring the work he has done
on *The Faerie Queene* to the court for the inspection of
Gloriana herself, we are aware at once of a new quality in
the very air we breathe. If we read the logs of the men of
the sea who sailed with Drake, we discover that something
had happened even to the minds of sailing men which
caused their ordinary records to burst into crisp and racy
and vital speech. If we try to experience one of the plays
of William Shakespeare with eyes and ears and mind such
as were brought to the play when it was first produced in
the Globe Theatre, we know quite well that the Middle
Ages have passed and that the breath of some new life has
come to England. The language itself has become the kingly expression of kingly minds. The exploration of the human spirit by a mighty interpreter of the ways of the
thoughts and acts of men has itself become a royal thing.
When we go with Christopher Marlowe to follow the tale
of the passion for power in *Tamburlaine,* the passion for
wealth in *The Jew of Malta,* and the passion for knowledge
in *Dr. Faustus,* we behold a series of studies of the very in-
flation of man through his own exhaustless energies. When

we peruse the pithy and ornate and distinguished writing of Francis Bacon, we behold a patrician of the mental life interpreting man as the master of the forces of nature, and so—as Bacon all too uncritically believed—as the maker of a prosperous and happy world.

All this, of course, is when the Renaissance had come to England. Erasmus, whom we shall be meeting again, is of course the great figure on the Continent. Caught in chains which might have crushed the life out of him, he emerged to be a kind of incarnation of the new mind in Europe. His laughing criticism—always sharp with the keen mirth of the intelligence—goes everywhere. For the first time in centuries Europe looks into a mirror and chuckles at what it sees. Ironic laughter may turn out to be mightier than an army with banners. It is an amazing day when the old paganism gives the new religion instruments by means of which to conduct its enterprise of self-criticism. For Erasmus, the lord of the wit of the Renaissance, had a predecessor. And that predecessor was Lucian.

When Marcus Aurelius was busy fighting to keep the Empire intact in the second century A.D., Lucian, the last master of Attic Greek, was writing those dialogues which set the fashion for all time of that corrosive and devastating wit before which pompous make-believe and pretentious sham must go down. A long chapter could be written about wit as the raillery of humanism. It is the pebble which the young David of humanism hurls at the Goliath of barbarism. Only when man is conscious of the rights of his own mind can he become a wit. And when Erasmus becomes another Lucian in another age, the weapons of man are indeed burnished and sharpened for a new warfare of the mind.

62

# The Renaissance

It is in Italy, of course, that the Renaissance springs like another Athena from the brain of Zeus. Even when the Roman of the Middle Ages became a barbarian, the stones of an older culture were frowning upon him as he went about his lawless ways. And when, after the fall of Constantinople, the Greek scholars came to Italy with their manuscripts, something strange and magnificent began to happen in the mind of man. Petrarch felt the blowing of a new air from the heights. Boccaccio found the secret of a new enthusiasm which at moments almost turned him from a sensualist into a man. Pico della Mirandola saw a glittering vision of the glory of man. Men like Leonardo, the Florentine, studied the body of man as if the gods were dead and God Himself were a distant dream. Italy was flooded with artists who captured every color and cadence of man's life. The Florentine Platonists tried to keep the soul alive in this new Renaissance body fairly bursting with the lust of life.

Some such thoughts as these come to us as we try to live over again those startling and vivid centuries when it did indeed seem that man as man had been reborn.

Let us now remember a few of the things which are all the while said about the Renaissance. Each of them is partly true. Each of them has its significance for us as we try to obtain a deeper knowledge of the period. The Renaissance, we are told, turned from the supernatural to the natural. The Renaissance turned from theology to the Greek and Latin classics. The Renaissance turned from a study of God to a study of man. After centuries of darkness, now man emerges. Confidence in life returns. Confidence in man appears. A fascinated interest in nature allures men's minds. Ethical other-worldliness is changed into virile and vivid this-worldliness. Man ceases to be afraid of life. He loves life. He loves nature. He loves human experience. He loves all of human experience. The richness and glow of springtime, with all the promise of summer and abundant harvest, have returned to the world. This new joy of life commands the brushes of artists. It whispers secrets to the pens of writers. It sends sailors all about the seven seas in daring voyages of desperate adventure and dauntless discovery.

Such sentences as the above in a varied and gregarious fashion do describe a good many things which actually went on during the Renaissance. But when one analyzes them with a really judicial mind, one is forced to say that they miss the essential distinctions which give character to the thought of the period. They miss its most important insight. They do not see the nature of its deepest tragedy. Let us try to look at the matter a little more critically. Let us see if we cannot put the truth, about the edges of which these general statements have been playing, in a fashion which will set forth sharply the permanent distinctions which are involved.

At its best the Renaissance represented a new consciousness of the power of man as man. It began to understand his critical intelligence. It saw with eyes in which a dawning terror gleamed the menace of his sinking below the human level. It understood the glory of his rising to apprehend that which is above the human level. It saw clearly that—as Robert Browning made the Pope in *The Ring and the Book* say— life's business is just the terrible choice. Joseph Wood Krutch—of all men!—has put the matter succinctly in *Five Masters* in these words: "Humanism, the name which we give to the most characteristic

64

philosophy of the Renaissance, during the period of its highest development, was not, essentially, either the revival of classical learning, or that materialistic scepticism with which it has been connected, but rather an attempt to realize the implication of the fact that life is lived on two planes—the human and the natural—which intersect but do not coincide." Here is a sentence which is worth more than pages on pages of the brilliant and graphic writing of Symonds in his monumental study of the Renaissance. For with all his intimate and sympathetic knowledge, Symonds has a way of allowing his emotions to take the bit in their teeth and run away with his intelligence. Probably no one will write about the Renaissance for many a year without being indebted to Symonds. But no one will write adequately about the Renaissance without transcending Symonds. This, indeed, Joseph Wood Krutch has done. Pico della Mirandola put the matter clearly in his *Oration on the Dignity of Man*: "Thou shalt have power to decline into the lower or brute creation. Thou shalt have power to be reborn into the higher or divine according to the sentence of thy intellect." This is the vital matter in humanism. It was the most tremendous matter in the Renaissance. As scholars went back to the classical writings of Greece and Rome they found something infinitely more important than grammatical forms to study—though modern masters of Greek and Latin philology have not always realized this. They found the most remarkable products of the intellect of man. They found man exercising his intelligence on high levels. And because they found man in these great old documents, they were called humanists. And because these documents gave a unique view of the dignity of man, they were called the humanities. And the view of life which inevitably grew out of these studies was called humanism.

At last the great word had emerged. The thing for which it stood had existed in the world and had been expressed, sometimes brilliantly, sometimes in a sporadic and fragmentary way, for over a thousand years. Its implicit existence had been quite as important as its explicit assertion. But now it emerged like a strong young giant ready to run a race. Man the thinker, man the controller came to his own place.

Centuries of life had prepared for this golden moment in the history of man. Long and bitter experience of the temptation to dabble with and then to surrender to that which is below the level of intelligent human control had left many a bitter mark in the life of man. And the appeal of the jungle of sensations and desires below the level of kingly reason had by no means lost its allurement. But one man who rose above the flux was enough to establish a new standard. And there had been many such men. Alfred the Good and the Great—of precious memory to all Englishmen—was a living example of humanistic sanctions in action without the slightest suspicion of a clear or coherent humanistic philosophy. And whenever man's thought sharpened to a sense of the significance of human intelligence using its powers of reason in thought and life, a new standard was set for interpretation. This had happened again and again in Greece, in Rome, and during the Middle Ages. And now, as the best men of the Renaissance went back to the great old writings, they found not simply a lovely literature dripping with the graces of noble speech. They found man. They found man the thinker. They found man the writer, king over his thoughts and words. They found man the lord of action, king over his own deeds. And so beholding man they had to find a word. The reality refused to exist any longer without being given a place in the vocabulary of the speech of men. So out of the birth pangs of the mind of the age, a new word came. And the word was humanism.

The spectacle of these scholars and thinkers of the new age reaching their great insight and making a monument for it in the language of men is one before which to pause. The lonely scholar with his ancient manuscripts was not content with working out "the doctrine of the enclitic *De*." He rose from the subtleties of classic grammar to the splendid figure of the classic man. Far off on many seas men were to walk the decks of adventurous ships with new gay confidence because of *his* discoveries. Far off in many lands writers were to dip their pens into the ink of a new inspiration because they had received from the humanist the last will and testament of classic humanity—the exhilarating doctrine of the victorious man. Far off in other centuries men in manifold laboratories were to conduct their experiments with a new confidence because humanism had taught the doctrine of nature as a realm subject to man's knowledge and to man's control.

The day of man, then, had actually dawned. The night of pessimism had passed away. Where man had made mistakes, he could correct them. Where he had done wrong, he could face about and do right. His powers were made for the understanding and the mastery of the world. The world had been made for the lordship of his understanding mind. Man the controller had come to his own.

So much in the way of appreciation. But we must admit

that the period was not always clear in its definitions or lofty in its practice. When humanism was the expression of high and permanent sanctions and appreciated and embodied the true essence of Attic principles and of Attic taste, it was a glorious and upbuilding thing. But there was a pseudo humanism which surrendered to the lower nature of man, crowned his appetites, and let loose a reign of moral lawlessness. So the Italian Renaissance especially sank to its lowest depths.

It is easy to see how this came about. The humanist was the prophet of man. But man had a body as well as a mind. He had appetites as well as intelligence. He had what we would now call biological urges as well as the passion for intellectual perfection. The life of sense had been sternly denied by those who represented the ascetic aspects of the thought of the Middle Ages. But if man's mind had rights, his body had rights too. If he could claim as his legitimate portion the use of that clear intelligence for which his mind was made, could he not also claim as his legitimate portion those sensations which are inseparable from the functioning of the bodily life? Had not the ascetics made cowards of men? Must they not rise and claim their rights in the world of sense? The best thinkers of the period saw in the body something to be used and guided and controlled—not something to be hated, but something to be mastered in the name of higher sanctions. And they represented the central stream of humanistic thought. But the pseudo humanist used the great watchword of the period in the name of that world of sense which must always be the servant and never the master in a well-ordered life. The cult of the body became the cult of vice. And vice became perverted and abnormal vice. And—steep and quick is the path to Avernus—abnormal vice became what we would now call sadic cruelty. Its fruit at last was that orgy of murder when, if you had a sword or knew how to use a poison, human life had no dignity or worth which caused you to pause. The pseudo humanist became a skillful and brilliant murderer. The cult which had begun with the dignity of man ended with the utter indignity of man to his fellow. So pseudo humanism plunged that part of Italy and of the world which listened to its siren voice into decadence and moral chaos. The *Autobiography* of Benvenuto Cellini tells much of the tale with unblushing frankness.

More slowly but with a queer inevitability the Renaissance tended in another fashion to miss its way in thickening mazes lost. The study of nature was a notable achievement of the mind of man. But it was possible for the student of nature to become so busy with the nature which he was studying that he forgot the nature of that human mind of his which was conducting the investigation. It was possible to become so busy with what he found in nature that he forgot his own critical intelligence observing, summarizing, classifying, analyzing, and controlling. At last he could come to think of reality as exhausted by what he discovered, and to forget that there would have been no discovery without the clear intelligence which he was now quite leaving out of account in his interpretation of the world and life. So it was easy for his view of life to become subhuman and impersonal. It was easy thus for his science on the philosophical side to lose the insights which would have given a clue to the nature of reality itself. If the scientist forgets the free mind which makes scientific investigation possible, he parts company with that

69

very humanism without which science itself could not exist, and he comes at last to have a philosophy which will first ignore and then deny the humanistic sanctions. We shall have much to say of this debacle in a later chapter. Now we merely point out the fact that it was implicit in an uncritical following of that path back to nature to which some of the ablest men of the Renaissance so zestfully called their followers. When you study nature, you are safe as a critical thinker only if all the while you keep studying the mind which investigates as well as the material upon which it turns its investigation. It is all too easy for the scientist in ways of his own to become a pseudo humanist.

Renaissance thought is sound in its sense of the place of man's controlling intelligence. On the basis of this principle you gladly accept and use the richness of the life of the body, but always subject to that guidance and that control which master the physical in the name of that which is beyond itself. On the basis of this conception you study nature most eagerly, but with a clear understanding that the clue to the ultimate meaning of life is to be found rather in the free intelligence of man than in the uniformities of nature.

Indeed, at its very highest the Renaissance went a step farther than even this central and potent principle. The Florentine Platonists were constantly aware of something beyond the human to which the human is akin. The ideas whose possession is a distinctive characteristic of men are related to that world of ideas which is beyond the transient life of humanity. And the mind which holds the ideas which men make their own is akin to that ultimate mind in which the final ideas of the universe have their existence and their home. So the Florentine Platonists turned their eyes to the light which is beyond the stars. And so, even in the highest humanism of the Renaissance, you begin to get a hint of that ultimate watchword of Christian humanism: "Man under God controlling nature." To all this in due time we shall come.

In the meantime, we have attained some sense of the richness and variety, the glory and the tragedy, of the Renaissance, of the penetrating power of its central insight, and of the fashion in which that central insight could be—indeed was—betrayed.

Charles Kingsley's *Westward Ho!* has been called one of the best boys' books ever written. If it is so, it is because it recaptures that joyous and courageous sense of expectation which is one of the best things about boyhood, and which was a happy characteristic of the very living spirit of the Renaissance. In a fine sense we may say that the Renaissance restored the joyous expectation of youth to the world because it made manhood a thing in which you could believe, to which you could look forward, a thing of glorious power and of almost illimitable potential achievement.

We shall see later that even the central insight of the Renaissance requires a critical examination which we have not yet attempted. It is enough now to say that the understanding of the pivotal place of man's controlling intelligence is essential to any interpretation of life which does not break apart into disintegration at last. If we are to be saved from a view of existence which ends in futility, we must never forget the place of man the controller with his free intelligence in the midst of the bewildering jungle which we call life. And in this insight we may all well be glad to call ourselves children of the Renaissance.

# CHAPTER VI

## The Protestant Revolt

WE HAVE ALREADY SEEN THAT THE CHRISTIAN CHURCH BE-
came an important factor—indeed, the outstanding and
dominant factor—in the life of the Middle Ages. We have
also seen how profound was the influence of the humanistic
sanctions upon the making of the very fabric of its intellectual life. We must take a look at the Church of the
Middle Ages at its highest peak before we turn to inspect
the Protestant Revolt. When a notable Catholic writer
describes the thirteenth as the most wonderful of the centuries, if our knowledge of the period is superficial, we may
be inclined to smile indulgently, admitting his right to pay
tribute to a great epoch in the life of his own communion.
When a skeptical thinker like Henry Adams devotes every
power of his brilliant mind to an exposition of the glory of
the thirteenth century, we begin to feel that the period
must be taken more seriously than we had supposed. The
truth is, of course, that the thirteenth century was one of
the great epochs in the life of man. And it was a period
whose life and thought were dominated by the Christian
Church.

The great Pope Innocent III gave intellectual force and
moral and spiritual dignity to the Holy See. It became
the central political power in Christendom. And that
power was exercised for far-reaching moral and spiritual
ends. The intellectual life of the age centered in the
Christian Church, and its most significant product was the

*Summa* of Saint Thomas. The brilliant dialectic of the *Summa* was turned into stone in the matchless glory of the Gothic cathedral. And all of this was related to the human experience of a thousand years and set forth with something like literary perfection in the lovely music of Dante's *Divine Comedy*. And what had expressed itself in political power and intellectual vigor and literary grace became the beauty of saintly character in Saint Francis of Assisi. One cannot pass Saint Francis quickly by. The most human of the saints and the most saintly of the human beings of many a century, he has captured the imagination and won the heart of the world. Shortly after the seven hundredth anniversary of the death of Saint Francis, I found myself in the little hill city of Jerusalem. One day I went down to the reputed site of the Garden of Gethsemane. Here the Franciscans had built a church in honor of their patron saint. A bright-eyed and kindly Franciscan brother showed me about. We talked a little, in spite of linguistic difficulties, concerning Saint Francis. And the face of the modern brother of the medieval order began to shine very warmly as he learned that I, too, loved the little brother of Assisi. When I turned to go, he went to a bush growing in the garden of our Lord's suffering and, plucking a flower from its branches, eagerly presented it to the alien heretic with whom he had been speaking. So powerful was the spirit of Saint Francis after seven hundred years.

Altogether, in gracious and loving piety, in keen and highly articulated intelligence, in a great splendor of literary achievement, in political leadership on lofty levels inspired by great spiritual ideals, and in an architecture which made the wonder of the period perpetual in stone, the

73

thirteenth was indeed an amazing century. And as many people have pointed out—Henry Cabot Lodge significantly in his introduction to Henry Adams' *Mont Saint Michel and Chartres*—the essential characteristic of the age was its unity. Since the thirteenth century the world has been falling apart. In the thirteenth century it achieved this remarkable oneness. And the harmony of the organization of thought centering in a great loyalty was the creation of the Christian Church.

It was from this lofty height that the Church of the Middle Ages fell upon evil days. And so came about the moral and spiritual and political debacle with which the Catholic Reformation, consummating in the Council of Trent, and the Protestant Revolt tried, each in its own way, to deal. We need always to remember—and especially in this age when the spiritual powers of the world are forced by the very tragic nature of events to stand together against the invasion of a brutal materialism—that the differences between Catholics and Protestants are differences within a common tradition. I remember how one day in Geneva I was talking with one of the most eminent of the representatives of the Barthian movement. He had said something about Saint Thomas which annoyed me, and I replied rather sharply. Quickly an almost tender smile came to his face and he said: "Oh, do not misunderstand me. Of course I know that my quarrel with Saint Thomas Aquinas is a *family* quarrel." We must remember that, even when we are dealing with much graver matters than any which could separate us from the angelic doctor.

When we reach the sixteenth century, we confront a great new stream of experience and thought and action. When we pass by the abuses which both Catholic and Protestant reformers wanted to bring to an end, we come to a fundamental difference of principle. The old church made the corporate life of the Christian organism the great matter. The Protestant made the individual soul the great matter. The relation of humanism and the humanists and of humanistic principles to all that went on in the great struggle is a subtle and fascinating study.

On the spiritual side, the Protestant movement was based upon an individual and personal experience of the grace of God. It was in the heart of the old church and under its guidance that Luther—for instance—came to this experience. It gave him the profoundest sense of God dealing directly with the individual soul. But, under the pressure of events, he drew corollaries from this experience which a thinker whose circle of thought was determined by the old church would never have drawn. To a devout Catholic, an evangelical experience was subject to the judgment of the church. Luther came to believe that on the basis of an evangelical experience he could judge the church itself. This is what he meant when he used the words, "Here I stand and I can do no other." So gradually emerged the principles: No church can stand between a man and God; no church can stand between a man and truth; no church can set apart a group with sole responsibility for the spread of religion. Or, to put the matter in another way: Every man his own priest; every man his own prophet; every Christian an evangelist taking the message of Christianity to other men. To earnest thinkers in the old communion all this more than savored of anarchy. And so the two groups became set in battle array.

It is easy to see that in its emphasis upon the individual the Protestant movement could claim vital kinship with certain fundamental humanistic sanctions. When it turned from what it was ready to denounce as ecclesiastical tyranny, it needed and welcomed support from many quarters. Here the humanistic emphasis on the dignity of the individual man was of the greatest assistance. The tyrant confronted a foe in the humanist whether the tyranny was ecclesiastical or secular. But the Protestant Revolt was a most complex and many-sided movement. The appeal to reason and to the individual judgment which the Protestant was forced to make when he repudiated the papal authority and the authority of the church over the mind of the individual was one for which the whole humanistic position had profound significance. The reformer at this stage found that all the while he was using humanistic weapons. And the appeal to the Scriptures was one which a great humanist could heartily endorse and make his own.

This is not the whole of the story, however, and a closer inspection will throw light on many things. There is the matter of the personality of Luther. He was one of the great peasants of the world. Rude, vigorous, virile—at the center desperately sincere, at the periphery capable of strange compromises—he did battle with God as truly as did Jacob at Jabbok. And, just as truly, at the end of the battle God touched him and he got a new name. This shattering transforming sense of the grace of God is the defining matter to Luther. Before God, he is humbled to dust. By God, he is lifted to the heights. Forever he will bow before God. But there is a sense in which he will never bow before anyone else. In the very hour when he discovers the God of grace, he discovers the independent man. But it is a man made independent by the grace of God. A man of the old church could have—again and

76

again did have—this evangelical experience of the grace of God.  But he never dreamed of extracting from it the doctrine of the man who could judge the church.

Now humanism came to have its own doctrine of the independent man.  But the independent man of a secular humanism was a man independent in his own right, and not a man made independent by the grace of God.  So there came to be a type of humanism which was characterized by a sharp consciousness of human self-sufficiency, and which turned with proud distaste from the doctrine of the divine grace.  With this humanism the reforming leaders were sure profoundly to disagree; and, indeed, the spiritual leaders of the old church were sure to be suspicious of it too.  We need to remember that this attitude of more or less self-conscious assurance belonged to one type of humanist rather than to the essential genius of the humanistic sanctions.  But it was moving about, a subtle and pervasive presence, in much sixteenth century humanism.

A good deal of the tale is told in the life of Erasmus, that prince of the humanists.  In the battle for reform, Erasmus was with the group who became Protestants.  His *Praise of Folly* undoubtedly was influential in preparing the way for the spread of Protestantism.  Indeed, his influence was so important that more than once he may have saved Luther's life.  Erasmus wanted the Bible to be circulated among all people, as did Luther.  His plowboy reading the Holy Scriptures is a famous figure.  In the fight against tyranny, in the struggle for intellectual emancipation, and in the appeal to reason, Luther and Erasmus were inevitably allies.

But Erasmus had no such profound ethical struggle and no such dramatic experience of spiritual freedom as had

Luther. He was more an apostle of well-bred wit attacking evil, than the apostle of a burning spiritual evangelism. He wanted to laugh evil practices out of existence by making them absurd. Luther came with the rush of a devouring spiritual fire. Erasmus distrusted Luther's hot impetuosity. He doubtless distrusted the habit of mind which made Luther increasingly ready to put his judgment against the existing solidarities of the world. Luther distrusted Erasmus' clear and disdainful intelligence. And so the break came.

The very sense of an intellectual tradition which was so dear to humanism made the humanist hesitate about a complete break with the past. Erasmus preferred to attack the abuses of the old order from within rather than to make an assault upon them from without. He never left the old church. And while its leaders were not without suspicion as to some of his tendencies toward rationalism, they had some genuine understanding of his importance and value to their own cause. Indeed, it must be said in all fairness that the Latin communion has always maintained a significant and important humanism as a part of its own life.

It must also be said that the great evangelical leaders continually owed a profound debt to humanism. Calvin was a humanist before he was a reformer. And it is the disciplined urbanity of the humanist which gives to the *Institutes* much of their intellectual power. Melancthon was a humanist with the heart of a reformer. And the deeper tides of humanism had possible relations to the Protestant type of evangelical religion which even Erasmus scarcely suspected. The two movements were always meet-

78

ing in processes of cross-fertilization even when on the surface they seemed to be opposed to each other.

The Protestant Revolt was itself so curiously involved a movement that we can by no means claim that it always maintained the level of its loftiest spiritual insights. Sometimes it was caught in political and social entanglements which dulled the sharpness of its vision and confused its spiritual witness. Luther could not get away from the principle of social solidarity. He had to depend a good deal upon the support of benevolent princes. His relation to the bigamy of Philip of Hesse is not an agreeable episode for the reader of sensitive conscience. And his relation to the Peasants' War represents something more than an episode, which Protestants with a clear sense of social ethics would like to wipe off the map. Here there entered into Lutheran Protestantism a quality which was to run through its life century after century. The tendency of contemporary Lutheranism to regard Hitler as a divine visitation to be accepted humbly rather than as a moral incubus to be thrown off goes back to the very beginnings of the German Protestant movement. Luther had a real sense of spiritual independence. He had little sense of political and social autonomy. So the new church began to have problems within its own organic life not too much unlike those it had attempted to solve by ecclesiastical revolution. There is very little humanism in the Lutheran doctrine of the relation of church and state.

Broadly speaking, however, both the humanists and the reformers were seeking a free man. The humanist did not always see that man finds his ultimate freedom through the grace of God. But there was nothing in the genius of his position which prevented his rising from the thought of a man free in his own manhood to the thought of a man whose real freedom is in God. On the other hand, sometimes the reformer was tempted to express his loyalty to God and his apprehension of God's supremacy in terms which crushed man to the very earth. That tendency has persisted and has found contemporary expression in some extreme forms of the Barthian movement. The humanist exercised a good influence in keeping a sense of man's inherent dignity alive even where it was necessary to admit that man had trailed that dignity in the slime. The two movements interlace in the profoundest fashion. And we cannot understand the Protestant Revolt without understanding humanism.

There is very much more to be said, however. The old church which had been the repository of the intellectual life of the world for over a thousand years is by no means to be thought of as casting its intellectual inheritance aside. In fact, there have been times when the stream of classical humanism was much more visible in the Latin communion than in some of the Protestant churches. The very structural relation of the *Summa* of Saint Thomas, which became authoritative for the theology of the church, to the logical humanism of Aristotle kept the contact between the Latin theology and humanism clear and sure. The fact that the countries speaking the Romance languages remained loyal to the old faith gave added assurance that the humanistic tradition would be kept alive in the Latin communion. For the literary tradition in France, Italy, and Spain was essentially that of classical humanism.

Thus it becomes clear that there is a sense in which intellectually humanism is a bridge between the Protestant tradition and the central theological assertions of the Catholic faith. In Protestant countries like England, men like Milton, with their ripe and rich humanism, spoke a language which their Catholic contemporaries understood, however sharp the differences may have been regarding many matters. And the maintaining of a certain spirit of urbane humanism at Oxford and Cambridge has always meant that there has been a vocabulary which distinguished and disciplined Protestant scholars held in common with their Catholic contemporaries who were steeped in the same historic humanism.

In our own time, the coming of the neo-Thomists with distinguished representatives like Jacques Maritain and Etienne Gilson has made it clear that there is a great corpus of Christian thinking which Protestants who still represent the central stream of the classical Christian thought share with their contemporaries of the Latin communion. When in Protestantism we have really worked out in our own thought an equivalent of the neo-Thomist movement, it will become increasingly clear that over large areas we have a common front. In respect of the personality and ethical perfection of God, in respect of the personality of man and his pivotal position at the place of dangerous but necessary choice, in respect of the deadliness of sin, in respect of the entrance not only of the glory of God but of the God of glory into humanity in Jesus Christ, in respect of the far-flung significance of that deed on the cross whose moral potency carries with it the power of redemption, in respect of the new life the Christian leads by the grace of God, in respect of the incredible richness of the divine life as a social organism of unselfish love, in respect of the suffusion of all life with the glory of the Christian sanctions, in respect of the immortal life with its clarification of all

81

moral issues and the eternal penetration of the life of man by the glory of God—in all these things there is a high tradition which the neo-Thomist and the neoclassic Protestant hold in common. And it is at point after point a characteristic aspect of this tradition that it is rich with the fertilization of a noble humanism.

At the very moment when the world is breaking apart and the historic values in every field are being cast aside, it is a matter of good augury that the mighty branches of the great tree of the Christian faith are seen in so notable a fashion to be bearing a common fruit. We need not ignore our differences. And each can be loyal to that which is definitive and distinctive and precious in his own tradition. But with this great corpus of thought in common, we need not waste time in fighting each other which ought to be given to fighting a common foe. When Athens and Sparta became locked in unfraternal strife, the death knell of Greek independence was already sounded. We can afford no Peloponnesian War in the modern Christian world with the fierce cries of the barbarians already heard just outside our gates.

As we pursue the dialectic of humanism in the chapters which follow, we shall see in more profound fashion the goal of humanistic study, of humanistic criticism, and of experience on the truly human level in a corpus of thought— an interpretation of life—which ecumenical Christianity can hold as a common treasure, and which must be maintained against a common foe.

But there is another matter of genuine importance. The man who pursues his studies of the Christian communions since the days of the Protestant Revolt will discover that each has a distinctive contribution to bring to the full

Christian witness which devoted men are to make before the face of God. That logic of life—of the vast and varied experience of men—with which the true humanist is so deeply concerned, expresses itself in the history of the Christian communions as well as in all the avenues of the secular experience of men. To listen to all these voices is to discover in each an expression—sometimes one-sided, sometimes harsh and overemphasized, but an expression for all that—of something significant for the whole life of humanity and for the whole Church of God. That great orchestra which interprets the music of God for the ears of men will need all the instruments men have constructed if the music is to be complete.

And though this carries us farther than the theme of this chapter, we may take one more step. The great ethnic religions are not without significance for the spiritual life of man. True, there is many a religion whose distinctive insistence tells the story of the man who has lost his way. But even these aberrations, clearly understood and criticized with penetrating intelligence, will help to clarify the Church's apprehension of the actual relationships of its own sanctions. But deeper than this in every ethnic faith there is some shining of that light which there is high authority for saying lighteth every man that cometh into the world. It is precisely the man most securely anchored to the essential sanctions of the Christian religion who, with that keen curiosity which Christian humanism inspires, can learn most from the ethnic faiths.

But there is a central stream. And there is a corpus of interpretation which is essentially Christian. This corpus of belief, as we shall see in the ensuing pages, is found at the place where humanism and the Christian revelation meet.

83

# CHAPTER VII

## The Modern World

THE SEVENTEENTH CENTURY—ESPECIALLY IN FRANCE—SAW THE appearance of a pseudo classicism which we may well call a pseudo humanism. The reign of Louis XIV was a period of glittering magnificence. It was characterized by exquisite standards of taste and of expression. It was said of the Grand Monarch that he even played billiards like a great gentleman. There were many notable and distinguished writers. And whether we are thinking of Racine or Moliere, we must admit the presence of gracious gifts used with clearly disciplined intelligence. It was an age of superb pulpit oratory, when the church itself achieved a royal speech. Massillon and Bossuet are still names with which to conjure in the history of the pulpit. The life of the court itself moved to the stately music of a sophisticated taste. Those who were at the heart of things believed that it was indeed an Augustan Age, and that Louis XIV was a new Augustus.

Yet there is something the matter with all this splendor. A modern visitor to Versailles walking about the gardens at sunset on an evening when the public is not admitted may come upon a sudden sense of a magic hard to put into words as the light from the artificial lake is caught up in a hundred windows of the palace. The statues in the gardens may seem to walk about, each speaking in his own tongue the inevitably right word which he has to say. The Grand Monarch may in imagination walk right out of the palace with the historic figures of his court. The experience is fairly breath-taking. But it is magic rather than reality. And somehow there is a touch of make-believe about it all. Very brightly polished brass may look like gold, but the gay sparkle does not insure the presence of the true metal or quite hide the presence of something which, though glowing, is not gold. Even the pulpit eloquence is often splendid rhetoric rather than the piercing cry which comes from the very soul of man as he does business with the eternal. The funeral sermon—repeated at the request of the court, and a tremendous emotional success even in the hour of repetition—sounds that note of the dilettante which mars the glory of the period. This is only part of the truth, for much which was profoundly real and much of permanent significance belonged to seventeenth century France. But too often it wore the livery of a grandeur which it did not really possess.

Coming to the heart of the matter, we may say that the false humanism of the seventeenth century substituted conventions which were often petty for standards which were permanent, and offered to the incidental and unimportant a loyalty which belongs only to the essential, to that which is not overthrown by the onslaughts of time. This attitude of giving first-class loyalties to second-rate distinctions is a recurrent characteristic of decadent classicism. The seventeenth century believed in standards. And the best men of the period attained to an understanding and a practice of high standards. But the undertow of the life of the time was constantly at work. And at its worst it tempted men so to give passionate loyalty to mistaken standards as to discredit the good standards upon which civilized life depends. The artificialities of the conventional

period are always used to cloud the importance of the realities which belong to periods of true and honest loyalty.
Men who saw through to the emptiness and even the corruption which they too often found at the heart of the
polite life of the seventeenth century were sometimes tempted to despair of civilization itself. All too often the vocabulary of moral grandeur was used to give dignity to a life
of mere social pretense.

The reaction against all this was brilliantly expressed by
Jean Jacques Rousseau. He professed to turn men away
from the conventional to the real, away from the artificial
to the natural. And one would not want to deny that as
a voice crying in the wilderness of a decadent classicism
he was a figure of very real usefulness. But the right way
of escape was from an artificial classicism to a true and
real classicism. It was not through the door of a gregarious
romanticism. In Jean Jacques Rousseau the apostle of unleashed and undisciplined emotion came to the throne.
Impulses became powers to be obeyed and not energies to
be controlled. Those wild horses of hot emotion which are
so useful when they feel their master's hand and so devastating when they break away from all mastery were ideal-
ized as if freedom from all moral restraint were the only
emancipation which made life worth living. The rush of
imperious energies held in check by no noble control became the central matter of experience. Instinct grew bitterly angry at the presence of rational criticism, and emotion
threw intelligence out of the door. Back to nature meant
back to impulses uncriticized by the reason. The real
with complete moral confusion of thought was identified
with the primitive.

And so the most corrupting currents which have played

86

upon modern life began moving all about the world. The creative spirit was conceived to be the spirit bound by no laws and checked by no deathless standards, rather than the spirit freely and deathlessly loyal to eternal principles. At this point unleashed romanticism, striking hard blows at rigid classicism, seemed to have a very great advantage. Warm vitality proudly swept by cold correctness. It was widely believed that to be cramped by any standard was to become formal and impotent. Men were ready to believe that the only true standard was to have no standard. So would the creative spirit be restored to the world. The dilemma was of course a false one. For the true contrast is not that between a rigid and decadent classicism and a warm and human romanticism. The real contrast is between a classicism radiant with vital energy and a romanticism which knows no control of its own hot impulses. Vitality without discipline may indeed seem to be better than discipline without vitality. But it is in a disciplined vitality that the true way of life is found. For true emancipation is achieved when we have attained freedom in law, and not when we have set about the wild ways of freedom from law.

It is not surprising that the romanticism of Rousseau became a theory of education as well as a way of life and a way of art. And here again the infusion of a fresh vitality into the educational forms of a decadent classicism was all to the good. But Rousseau was not content with criticism. Here, as elsewhere, he wanted revolution. And the perverse influence of Rousseauistic principles upon educational theory and practice has set many a young victim traveling away from the world of civilized life toward the barbarism of undisciplined emotion. That there is a place for the spontaneous, no critical student of education would want to deny. But to suppose that you can obtain the spontaneous only through the lawless is to make a fatal mistake. The truly educated man is the person who is able freely and happily to appropriate the wisdom of the ages. He is the man who is able to set the disciplines of the civilized life to music. He is not the man who repudiates the disciplines of civilization for the sake of the mad anarchy of unleashed desire. When education becomes a training for the jungle, you can expect to have a turbulent world. Our foes are indeed within our own household when the processes of our education unfit us for the stern but splendid disciplines of rational life.

As time went on, naturalism took many forms. Sometimes it bent the principles of scientific measurement to its own purposes. It accepted a mechanistic materialism as a philosophy which covered all of reality. And it began to rewrite its criticism in the terms of this impersonal mechanical formula. In France a scientific naturalist like Taine created a criticism answering to this new absorption in the subhuman. Literature, instead of being one of the most important fields in which we can discover what man has done with his freedom, was regarded as a kind of chemistry become conscious of its own necessary and mathematical relationships. What seemed to be personal was regarded as the product of mechanical and impersonal forces. Taine felt that if you knew enough about the soil and climate of England, you could account for Shakespeare. Literature became as impersonal as the study of crystals. Freedom vanished. Consciousness became only man aware of his slavery to forces he could not control. Writing was only an inevitable verbal formulation of quite impersonal ideas. The strata of thought and expression were completely determined. Literature was as hard and fast a science as geology. Just how in this world of predetermined literary forms Taine achieved the freedom which he exercised so nimbly and with such spectacular skill the reader was never told. The naturalistic materialist always has to use powers which, according to his own philosophy, he could not possibly possess. Occasionally a critical reader sees this and smiles a sardonic smile.

Men like Sainte-Beuve were humanistic in their spirit even when they were tempted by materialistic sanctions. In one way the reading of the *Causeries du lundi* of Sainte-Beuve is like taking a course in adequate and disciplined humanism. He has all the good manners of the accomplished literary humanist; and when for a moment or a succession of moments he forgets the naturalistic obsessions of the time, he has plenty of humanistic insight too. It is as a humanist that he thinks. It is as a humanist that he writes. And then the dark clouds of naturalism blow up to confuse and to baffle his mind. Today a man cannot be a well-trained literary humanist without studying Sainte-Beuve and spending with him untold hours of brooding contemplation of the riches of our intellectual inheritance. But a man cannot be a humanist emancipated from materialistic obsessions without criticizing Sainte-Beuve with unhesitating rigor.

The obsession with naturalistic materialism of course did not go unquestioned as decades and generations went by. There were flashes of splendid insight, as when Emerson declared that there is one law for man and another for the thing. Indeed, the necessity for dualistic distinctions as a real and permanent part of a unified interpretation of

89

life became increasingly clear to critical thinkers. A universe which contained only things reacting according to the laws of impersonal mathematics could never account for man with his free intelligence and his power to control the world of things. Yet the freedom of man must always be seen in a world where things do act and react according to the formulas of mathematical law. The two series of facts were not reached through speculation. They were a part of living experience. The things with which we deal do have their existence in terms which can be expressed in impersonal law. Man does have a freedom and a power of control which can never be expressed in such terms. Therefore Emerson's pithy and potent declaration that there is one law for man and another for the thing.

But, as has been pointed out again and again, Emerson was a man of thoughts rather than a man of thought. And his thoughts by no means always agreed with each other. He was always a provocative thinker. He was by no means a coherent thinker. And so, as grateful as we are for his flashing insight, we can by no means claim that he created a philosophy to support it.

Matthew Arnold put the same great insight into a sharp phrase when he wrote, "Man must begin, know this, where nature ends." And Arnold might well have spent a lifetime amplifying and interpreting this phrase. Here is nature, with its mechanical reactions. Here comes man, with his free intelligence and his practical control. He is able to analyze the uniformities of nature. He is able to use them for his own purposes. He begins where nature ends. Arnold saw this. He said this. And so he takes his place among those to whom golden insights of humanism became splendidly real. But he never quite understood that here was a trail which might well be followed to the top of the mountain. He never went through all of his thinking to test it and to remake it in the terms of his high humanistic insight.

Surveying the activities of scientific thought in the period before his own, Stuart Sherman wrote, "The great revolutionary task of the nineteenth-century thinkers, to speak it briefly, was to put man into nature. The great task of twentieth-century thinkers is to get him out again." Here again was a quick insight into that dualistic distinction which is essential to true humanism. And there were days when it seemed that Stuart Sherman would spend his life fighting for the humanistic insights which he had learned from Irving Babbitt and Paul Elmer More. But the stream of contemporary gregariousness became too much for him, and he allowed his banner to float away on its rather muddy waters. But he had known—if he did not retain and make defining in his thought—the difference between that nature which man controls and man as the free controller. He had understood that we must get man out of nature if we are clearly to understand either nature or man.

We will not write in this chapter of Irving Babbitt or of Paul Elmer More. Each is to have a chapter to himself later on. We have said enough to make it clear that the humanistic insights simply would not down even in periods when humanism itself was not on the throne.

As the nineteenth wore into the twentieth century, the tendency to interpret the human in the terms of the sub-human went on apace. Great poetry was written, sad with the sense that humanistic values in their historic meaning had passed from the world. Hardy's *The Dynasts* sees a world of conscious puppets helplessly doing the bidding of impersonal forces over which they have no control. One wonders what Hardy thought when he took journeys on railroads which illustrated man's very obvious control over the impersonal forces of the world. Great novelists—and Hardy belonged to this group, too—interpreted life as a drama from which freedom and responsibility had departed. Philosophies which left no room for freedom or vital control obsessed the minds of men. From the days of Spinoza to the left-wing Hegelians, man freely used his mind to deny the presence of freedom in the world. There was always hope in the suicidal inconsistencies of these systems. Just because you cannot deny freedom without implicitly affirming it, the day was not lost even when freedom was most brilliantly denied. To readers of subtly critical intelligence, there was something ludicrous—something laughably absurd—about the thinkers who in effect cried to the world: "Sons of men, let us use the intellectual freedom we do not possess to convince the free and critical intelligence which you only think is yours, which indeed is quite illusory, that there is no such thing as freedom in the world." When a puppet argues with a puppet to prove that he is not free, there is not much significance to the argument. By the same token, you cannot deny control without assuming it and implicitly affirming it. And all about you are the endless inventions of man which prove the presence of the control in which you do not believe. The skyscraper shouts it. The ocean liner declares it. The radio makes it articulate all about the world.

As a matter of fact, there were always voices crying out in the name of a view of life which explained the lower in the terms of the higher, and refused to try to explain the higher in the terms of the lower. At one period when Herbert Spencer had become the prophet, priest, and king of an impersonal philosophy, in America that brilliant dialectician Professor Borden P. Bowne became the most corrosive and audacious and destructive critic of an impersonal philosophy. Indeed, Professor Bowne's personal philosophy has the very philosophic essence of humanism in it. Men became restless in their intellectual slavery to the subhuman, and here and there all about the world voices were lifted in protest. They were often wiser in their detailed thinking than in their general principles. There was a type of neo-Hegelian who was a most effective administrator of detailed criticism to impersonal systems, who became all too vague himself, once he launched on the sea of his monistic logic. Clearly a new battle regarding the relations of the "one and the many" loomed on the horizon, when once men appeared with weapons which would properly fit them for the strife.

Gradually it became clear to really penetrating minds that critical humanism has no more subtle victory than that which it obtains over those who try to deny its central sanction of free intelligence and find themselves caught in a net of confusing contradictions as they try to persist in the denial.

The central intellectual dilemma of the modern world is related to a persistent tendency to deny the major premise of human freedom, and then to use that premise every hour of the day in respect of every sort of practical problem. The critical humanist has risen to assert that you cannot have it both ways. You can deny freedom and abide by the denial. Or you can use freedom in every practical situation and then create an interpretation of life which gives it an authentic place. Your intelligence cannot be a slave in its presuppositions and free in all its actions. That way lies civil war. And in the end freedom is sure to win.

# CHAPTER VIII

## Humanism and Science

THE SCIENTIFIC MIND AND THE SCIENTIFIC METHOD HAVE HAD a distinguished place in the modern world. The scientist has collected and classified the facts of the physical world and of the world of animate life. He has been a kind of detective, always on the trail of the undiscovered fact. Charles Darwin, voyaging about the world in the Beagle and amassing facts which are to give him the data for twenty years of study, is a typical scientist. The forces of nature have been scrutinized, understood, and mastered by the constant and curious investigations of scientific intelligence. And science has developed a code of morals of its own in the processes of conducting its investigations. That code has centered in the attitude of humble acquiescence in the presence of the stubborn fact. To tell the truth, the whole truth, and nothing but the truth about all his investigations is the demand which his conscience makes upon the scientist. Century after century, he has stood in battle array against all the powers which would prevent his carrying on his research and experiment. He has claimed what in better days Germany made a great watchword: "Freedom to learn and freedom to teach." He has been very angry at the presence of any dogma which interfered with his unhampered investigation. Ironically, if not a little spitefully, he has referred to those days when certain avenues of research were blocked, and across the road was a large sign reading: "No thoroughfare. Moses."

95

He has particularly disliked any sort of dogma which would interfere with his activities.  In brilliant and biting sentences, Andrew D. White has told the long tale of *The Warfare of Science with Theology*.  The scientist has recorded the tale of a company of martyrs of his own.  They are those who have suffered for the sake of truth, the truth men were unwilling to hear.  The sad story of Galileo and the inquisition has been recounted again and again, until it has become a sort of bedtime story of the young scientist.  In a sense the processes of objective study have become a religion to many a man of the laboratory.  The truth about things as they are is his deity.  And he is the sacred priest at the temple of that god.  The cult is all very touching and not without a certain authentic beauty of its own.

The story is not quite so simple, however, as the acolytes of science would have us believe.  Dr. Robert H. Murray has told us another tale in his very significant volume, *Science and Scientists in the Nineteenth Century*.  Here, page after page—with full documentation—we are told the history of dogmatic scientists shutting their minds against new truth in their own field, so that the proud young discoverer of a truth unknown before was almost made a martyr, by his own scientific colleagues, before they recognized the significance of his work.  And then he, at last welcomed by the powerful scientists of his time, helped to form a scientific orthodoxy which made life difficult for the other young men who were seeking a brave new world of truth through constant and daring processes of discovery.  The story has a sad familiarity to theologians.  And perhaps they may be pardoned in the possession of a little sardonic joy in their discovery that among the men science has canonized there have been a good many miserable sinners against the laws of the unselfish pursuit of truth just as there have been among the theologians a good many sinners against the laws of unselfish love.

All this, however, has to do with spots upon the sun. And the sun of science still shines. It has brought light to countless dark places. And that light presents much of the illumination in which the modern man lives. Science has studied the world. Science has mastered the forces of nature. Science has made man king of nature and not its slave.

But the whole matter deserves a closer and a profounder consideration. Professor Norman Foerster has said: "Whatever science can do for us, it cannot give us standards." It would be most difficult in a few words to find a more final or unhesitating challenge of the claims of what we must call pseudo science. For a great number of people have claimed that the realm of science is the equivalent of the whole realm of reality. That which cannot be subjected to science they would say is not real at all. This is a claim which critical humanism cannot for a moment accept. We must now discover why this is so, and we must seek to find just what are the true relations of humanism and science.

We may put the matter briefly by saying that science has to do with the measurement of every thing which can be measured by instruments of precision or their equivalent. Here we have opened before us a vast field in which science works with indubitable right. But at once we must correct an uncritical use of the word science which has characterized this chapter so far. In common with contemporary votaries of the scientific cult we have said: Science has done this; science has done that. Of course, strictly speaking, we have referred to an abstraction as if it were an actuality. As a matter of fact, science is not an entity which thinks things and does things. Science is not a superperson who goes about the world surprising us by his amazing activities. It is the scientists who observe. It is the scientists who classify. It is the scientists who achieve. We are entirely too much inclined to use the word science in an unreal and improper and indeed in a false fashion and to forget the very concrete achievement of the scientist. And now we simply must insist that you cannot adequately study science and leave the scientist out of account. Science consists of the impersonal laws which the scientist discovers. The scientist brings the free mind which does the discovering. And of this scientist with his free mind you must say just the things and all the things which the humanist says about man.

Now we begin to see flashes of light upon a very abstruse and difficult subject. For as we observe the scientist, devising instruments of precision, determining the method of their use, and applying them to the tasks of measurement, it is clear at once that his critical intelligence cannot be subjected to these instruments. A man of free intelligence can create instruments of precision. But instruments of precision cannot create free men. Indeed, the scientist must transcend these instruments in order to construct them. And once constructed, they cannot work by themselves. The scientist must preside over all the processes of investigation which he conducts. You cannot put the scientist into the formulas of physical or biological science. These formulas may be related to some aspects of his existence and his life. But you cannot get his free mind into them. They are the formulas of determined activity.

They never can be used to measure freedom. For in the scientific sense freedom is immeasurable. Critical intelligence in its free moving activity is not subject to the instruments of precision or their equivalent. It constructs these instruments in order to deal with the impersonal and determined aspects of existence. It cannot be guilty of the self-stultification of subjecting its own freedom to slavery to those formulas which it has created in order to deal with the unfree aspects of existence.

Science properly defined deals with the subhuman. It cannot deal with the distinctively human aspects of experience. It can deal with those aspects of the human organism which belong to the world of things. It can deal with those aspects of the human organism which are animate but not intelligent. It cannot deal with that free intelligence which is the distinctive characteristic of man. Science deals with mathematical relationships. It cannot account for the mathematician. Science deals with determined relationships. It cannot touch that which transcends the determined aspects of existence. Only by means of freedom can the scientist do his work. But, as we have seen, freedom cannot be measured by instruments of precision. Its essential quality is just this transcending of the determined aspects of life, so that, though it measures, it is immeasurable. That darting free intelligence with whose presence human life begins to have significance is the essential characteristic of the scientist. It is necessary for the existence of science. But it cannot be subjected to the tests of science. The true scientist is a humanist studying the subhuman.

But all too frequently the scientist forgets that he is a humanist and remembers only the subhuman which he is studying. It is important that we should see just how this happens. The scientist enters the laboratory. Here he is surrounded by the instruments of precision which he has devised. And here are all the materials which he is to investigate and study and analyze. He must forget himself as he studies these things. He must forget his own free mind as he studies that which is not free. And as he extracts from this impersonal material the mathematical laws of its determined relationships and its determined activity, he quite loses sight of his own freedom and thinks only of the forms of necessity which he is studying. As this goes on year after year, it is easy for him to become completely engrossed with the laws of that determined world to whose study he is giving his life. And so at last he may come to think that nothing is real which is not determined. He may come to believe that nothing is actual which transcends the measurement of mathematical law. In other words, he may become a scientific materialist.

But when he does this, in effect he denies his own free intelligence. He denies the existence of the very powers which made his scientific activity possible. He is guilty of the strangest sort of self-stultification. There is no more curious spectacle than that of a materialistic scientist greatly annoyed when he is reminded of the presence of that free intelligence by means of which he has conducted every experiment which he has carried on. He has made his mind an instrument for the grinding out of the laws of the mathematical relationships of the subhuman world. And at last the habit is so strong that he becomes incapable of analyzing the free processes by which he conducts his investigations. Darwin confesses that as years went by he became incapable of enjoying Shakespeare. The great literary humanist of the English Renaissance, always dealing with what men do with their freedom, became an enigma to the man who year after year studied those aspects of existence which can be reduced to the formulas of impersonal mathematics.

The truth is that if the scientist is going to be a philosopher interpreting all of life as well as an observer turning his instruments of precision upon the measurable aspects of existence, he must all the while find time to look in upon his own free mind classifying, as well as to look out on the uniformities which are the subject of his scientific investigation. If every day he spends some time considering his own free intelligence as well as some time using that intelligence to measure the uniformities of nature, he will maintain a full-orbed mental life. It is not without significance that the brilliant criticism of materialistic science which has come from Whitehead, Jeans, Eddington, and Dampier has all been the work of minds which passed through the discipline of sound humanistic training. An angry and obscurantist physicist once exclaimed to me: "I will not read Eddington. Why, I would have to study philosophy in order to understand him!" He was ready to accept with complete complacency the atrophy of some of the organs of his critical intelligence.

By this time we ought to see that whether the scientist knows it or not, he himself is the definite and final answer to a materialistic philosophy. For while that philosophy can do many things, it cannot provide the scientist without whom science would be impossible. There is tremendous power in this humanistic argument against materialism. The day was when the argument was conducted in a transcendental fashion. You analyzed the nature of that transcendent person, God, and in the lofty transcendent

101

realm you found perfect freedom. So you struck blows at the grim materialists of this little world. It was a high argument. It was a worthy argument. And it was a sound argument. But it had the practical disadvantage of taking you away from this immediate world of actual experience. The materialist could reply with a shrewd plausibility: "You are dealing with a world of transcendental moonshine. You can have that world. I profess to know nothing about it. I work in the world of the immediate and the actual. And in that world the determined relationships of impersonal cause and effect work everywhere. You can be lord of the world of transcendental speculation if you leave me in peace to work at the world of hard actuality."

To be sure, the critical thinker had a reply. But it required an intelligence trained in the subtlest processes of the dialectic of the mind to see how devastatingly adequate that reply was. Very often the materialistic scientist simply did not know what the idealistic philosopher was talking about. And so he pursued his way in complacent and unconscious arrogance.

The humanist has a more immediate attack. He says to the materialistic scientist: "You work in the world of the immediately actual. So do I. You do not want to climb to some cloudland of far-flung speculation. Good, I shall meet you on your own ground. I will not ask you to go to God to prove the freedom of man. I will ask you to go to man. I will ask you to go to a particular man. I will ask you to go to the scientist. I will ask you to go to yourself. When I watch you observing phenomena and classifying facts, I find that at every step in practice you are using the freedom which you deny theoretically. When I watch you making instruments of precision, I observe you doing that which only free intelligence can do. When I see you using these instruments, I discover that they would lie helpless without your free mind to guide them. When I hear you saying: 'This is true, that is false'; 'This is right, that is wrong'; 'This is an error, I will correct it'; 'This is a right insight, I will test it,' I find that all the while you are a perfect example of free intelligence in action. I do not have to go to God to produce a doctrine of freedom. I have only to go to you. You are my document. You are my source material. As long as you the scientist live, I cannot deny the presence of a free man in the world. And I must say in all frankness that you have no right to ask me to believe in a universe which would make you impossible. In fact, when I watch your free mind dealing with the interactions of a determined world and turning them to its own purposes, when I watch you living at the place where freedom and necessity meet, I begin to suspect that your free intelligence controlling necessary relationships may be the clue to the most far-off things. Indeed, there are terrible moments when, as I watch you, the human controller, mastering the world, I suspect that you may make it necessary for me to believe in a divine controller over all the vast material order. You in your laboratory may at last make it necessary for me to believe in God. You in your laboratory are a kind of human God turning things to his own purposes. And as I watch your relative intelligence doing such astonishing things with the material world, I am haunted by the thought of a perfect intelligence making and sustaining the world with which you deal, making that world to fit your mind, and making your mind to fit that world. And so you—of all men—a scientist may force me to be religious. I will not go to God to prove your freedom. Inspecting your freedom in action, I may in spite of myself be driven to go to God. In any event, you have made the case for freedom clear and indubitable. You have made the case for intelligence transcending physical uniformity finally triumphant. When I am tempted to descend into the slough of the despondency of the man who has lost his belief in free minds controlling vast issues, I will follow you into the laboratory and all my joyous faith will return. You, my great unconscious humanist, are my best and completest and most immediate evidence against that materialistic determinism which has obsessed your mind."

We can now go on to see that all the pseudo sciences come into existence when we try to apply instruments of precision or their equivalent to that which by its very nature cannot be measured. As long as science works in its rightful realm, it is a lofty and powerful instrument of the human mind. But when the attempt is made to apply it to fields to which it has no rightful relation, it becomes both arrogant and pathetic. Just as science itself would be impossible apart from those powers of the human mind which transcend human analysis, we must be prepared to find that many of the most significant matters in life can be understood only when we pass beyond the realm of mathematical measurement.

Humanism deals with precisely those powers of the human mind which cannot be subjected to measurement. Man's capacity to establish standards and to set about living in loyalty to them belongs to that free world which science cannot analyze but without which science could not exist. Scientific formulas do not become aware of themselves. They can only be constructed by free intelligence. And no formula can be turned against the intelligence without which it could not exist. And when we move into those great disciplines which lie beyond the field of science, the same truth holds. The attempt to reduce morality, art, and religion to terms of mechanical measurement always fails at just the point where these disciplines and experiences transcend mechanical measurement. Morality has to do with what man does with his freedom in the ethical realm. Art has to do with what man does with his freedom in the aesthetic realm. Religion has to do with what man does with his freedom in the spiritual realm. Even politics has to do with what man does with his freedom in the realm of human relationships. And if reality were the equivalent of the measurable, not only would morality, art, religion, and the political activities of free men be impossible, but science itself would become a dream without substantial foundations. All the things that make civilization would go down together. The attempt of the pseudo scientist to reduce life to terms in which the scientific method would make science itself impossible is one of the most astonishing of the recurrent vagaries of human thought.

It all comes to this. You enter upon a path of complete confusion if you try to discuss science and leave out the scientist. And the scientist constantly transcends those instruments of precision which he constructs and those formulas of uniformity which he works out, and so effectively uses. Only humanism can account for the scientist. And in a sense, only humanism can account for science.

All this, of course, has the most far-reaching implications in respect of the life of our own time, and all of its intellectual activities. For in our time pseudo science has sat arrogantly, if not grandly, upon the throne. The study of literature has been reduced to philology, because philology deals with the measurable. The study of society has become an endeavor to reduce free human relationships to impersonal laws. History has become a collecting of facts rather than an account of free men in action. One does not deny that in all these ways important contributions have been made. For in all these fields there are areas which are below the level of free intelligence. But in every one of these disciplines, the important matters arise when free intelligence begins to work. And pseudo science has confused when it has not denied outright the distinctive quality of the humanistic studies.

Education itself has been prostituted by almost endless vagaries as it has lost hold of the central humanistic clue to the meaning of life. For the true process of education is just the study of what man has done with his freedom in order that he may learn how to use his freedom wisely, and the study of the fashion in which free intelligence has met and may meet and control the world of necessary relationships in order to turn them to its own reasonable purposes.

The last significant fact is this. Quite apart from theory, quite aside from speculation, we do actually live in a world where freedom and necessity meet and where freedom turns necessity in directions of its own planning. Every time a machine is made, necessity secures its dependability, and freedom plans its structure and its use. Every time a skyscraper is built, all the laws of physics secure its stability, while free intelligence plans and erects the building in conformity with those laws. Every scientific formula is the charting of a necessity in order that it may be used by freedom. No other fact is so important for us as this fact,

106

that we live at the point where law and freedom meet.
With only law, there would be no human achievement and
no civilization. With only freedom, there would be anarchy
and frustration and futility and tragedy. When law and
freedom meet, you have the world where free intelligence
takes its place in a dependable world, to understand and to
use nature, and to achieve the good life for man.

## CHAPTER IX

### *Humanism and the Machine Age*

SOMETIMES WE BEGIN BY LAUGHING. FOR A LONG TIME WE go on laughing. Then the thing at which we were laughing ceases to be amusing. At last we look at it with startled, disconcerted, even tortured eyes. The thing at which we laughed has become bitterly tragic. Long ago Samuel Butler published his brilliant book *Erewhon*. It was a devastating criticism of the machine age. Machines, it declared in effect, were man's worst enemies. Machines must be destroyed. It told of a civilization where a man's life was in danger when he possessed so much as a watch. For a watch was a machine. If you used a watch you might become fascinated by the evil thing. Then you might use other evil mechanical devices like it. Your friends might do the same. And so by slow stages the evil might grow until the machine age would come back again. And that was something which simply must not be allowed to be.

*Erewhon* no doubt inspired endless scornful mirth. For the machine age with all its spectacular triumph was moving on apace when he published the book. Was not the machine the best evidence of man's power? Was not the machine the most important example of man's achievement? Did not the machine prove that man had become master of his world at last? Rudyard Kipling was one of the gifted men who were inclined to become lyrical as they surveyed the achievements of the machine age. He never outgrew the sense of man's power which the inspection of an intricate, effective machine brought to him. Here was a masterful and definite accomplishment in the hard world of facts. You might become disillusioned about anything, or perhaps everything else. You could not become disillusioned about man the maker of machines.

The song of the machine may not have been sung by means of very great poetry. But decade after decade it was sung with lusty enthusiasm. The steam engine had remade the world. All the processes of agriculture and all the processes of manufacturing were transformed by machinery. Old civilizations had been based on human slavery. The machines were to be the slaves of man in the new age. And since machines were the unconscious and impersonal inventions of man and had no minds and no souls, there could be no question of the oppression of machines, and there could be no question of the uprising of machines to declare their rights. At last man had invented a method by which you could have all the benefits of slavery without the moral problems which slavery had involved. In the United States alone, Stuart Chase told us, two billion mechanical horses waited to bear the burdens and to do the work of men. As you stood in a great manufacturing establishment and listened to the whir of belts and watched the revolving of wheels and looked upon the raw material when it was put in charge of the mechanical devices and saw the finished product when it came forth at the end of the process, there was something about it all which kindled your imagination and renewed your faith in man. As you watched steam shovels lowering hills to the level of the plains, you were reduced to awe by the power you saw in action. The telegraph seemed to abolish space. The telephone made the miracle more dramatic. And the radio at last seemed to make "everywhere quite the same as everywhere else." The typesetting machines and the steam presses made the production of a newspaper almost a more wonderful thing than the news which it contained. Indeed, the machine was actually often more wonderful than the purpose for which it was used. The story of the airplane from the days when it was an impossible dream to the period when it was a commercial necessity and the time when it became the world's most dramatic destroyer is a part of the same magnificent saga, though here, indeed, a minor note begins to be heard which at length becomes a note of tragedy. Even the automobile transformed human life by making it so easy at any time for man to be in another place rather than where he was! Surely out of all these materials a brave new world could be made. Surely the machine age brought Utopia within man's reach at last. Human complacency increased. Human arrogance grew. It was clear that only a perverse mind could question the overwhelming glory of the machine age. Samuel Butler's *Erewhon* was remembered only with sardonic amusement. Sheltered by the power which their machines gave them, men continued to laugh.

They even gave the messianic cult of the machine an almost classical intellectual foundation. Those of them who still used libraries could bring from the shelves the works of Francis Bacon, whom they naturally regarded as one of the master thinkers of the modern world. In training, Bacon had been given all the advantages of the bright humanism of the Renaissance. His language when he spoke and when he wrote had all the clear and pungent and vital luminousness of the Elizabethan period at its best.

110

His intelligence always outran his character, and his distinction of mind and royal powers of expression made it possible for him to give a certain lofty dignity to everything which he said and to everything which he wrote. He was by all odds the most powerful of that group of Renaissance thinkers who went back to the study of nature, believing that if you could control the forces of nature you could quite simply and naturally produce a completely good life for man. He never saw that a world in which man had controlled the forces of nature but had never learned the meaning of human control in the name of moral and spiritual sanctions would surely become a tragic place. And it is more than a parable that it was the weakness and indeed falseness of his own character which led to the utter downfall of Francis Bacon at last. He was brought low by the forces whose meaning he had ignored and whose importance he had never understood.

But the reader of Bacon in the golden hours of the machine age thought only of the polished phrases in which he had described man's reign over nature, and of the new, good world which that control would make possible. Already character was beginning to seem less important than the power to control the natural world. The man of the machine age who read with unadulterated delight the words which expressed the ideal of a naturalistic Utopia as it dwelt in the mind of Bacon was likely to take a sly delight in the shrewd cynicism of the more Machiavellian passages of Bacon's essays.

So the years went on, and the years became centuries. The dynamos did their work. The wheels revolved. The new city made by machinery and fed by machinery and haunted by the darkness of its terrible slums came into

111

being. The new ship, which was like a little city as it was driven across the ocean, with every luxury which even decadent human taste could desire, went magnificently from port to port. And the age of mind's and heart's desire of which powerful Utopian thinkers like Francis Bacon had dreamed and for which they had planned *did not come*. Men achieved a control over the forces of nature quite beyond the range of any sixteenth or seventeenth century thinkers. But every invention proved to be the occasion of the release of forces which could be used for good or could be used for evil. The machine controlled by one man and doing the work one hundred men used to do raised the very practical problem of work for the ninety-nine men whose hands were made idle by the busy machine. The new chemistry produced nitrogenous by-products which, used in the processes of fertilization and with the aid of irrigation, might make the desert blossom as the rose. But this same new chemistry produced of the same elements explosives and poison gases which could destroy cities, and which, dropped from mighty airplanes, would give a new horror to warfare. Indeed, mechanized warfare changed the whole theory and practice of war and the whole problem of securing peace in a world where men of bad will could secure the use of such powers. And from the nation controlled by gangsters to the gangster working in a land still civilized, the same kind of problems emerged. The automobile enabled the gunman to make a quick escape, and the automatic made his weapon a more dangerous and deadly instrument. The machine age put almost divine powers into the hands of the worst of human beings.

Even from the standpoint of material prosperity, the

machine age quite failed to fulfill the promises of the messianic dreamers. Mechanized agriculture produced a plethora in one region and left another starving. Francis Bacon would have been bewildered could he have lived to witness the spectacle of farmers destroying their crops in the name of social planning in one land while men and women and children were starving for lack of these very products in another. The age of the machine has become an age of chaos. Even from the side of material prosperity it has seen devastation come to the world. In a sense of which Emerson never dreamed, "things are in the saddle and ride mankind" on ways leading to tragedy and destruction. The subhuman is destroying the human.

The men who laughed at Samuel Butler's *Erewhon* would find themselves in a strange situation were they alive today. The mirth would choke in their throats. The bitter words of Samuel Butler have ceased to be amusing. They cut too deeply into the quick of reality. Today men do not laugh. They look out on their machine-made world with grim and anxious and tragic eyes.

Critical humanism faces the whole situation with cool and clear intelligence. From the very beginning it has refused to fall down and worship the machines. It has seen in the midst of the moral confusion of machine worship that machines are the product of man's intelligence and that they must submit themselves to moral and spiritual control. The intelligence which constructed them must be their master. The critical humanist is not an ascetic. He gladly accepts the achievements of the inventors. He is ready to put to good uses the mechanical devices which they have constructed. He understands the pessimism of Samuel Butler. But he feels that this pessimism is a pathological

113

state induced by a knowledge of the terrible fashion in which machines can be misused. He is not ready to give up the battle and to destroy the machines because they can be put to bad uses. He understands Mahatma Gandhi who would like to take India back to an age before the coming of machinery. But he does not believe that Gandhi's solution is the real answer to the difficult questions put by the machine age. An age without machines would still have the desperate problems presented by the existence of men of bad will. And men of good will can solve the problems the machines present. It is in men that the real problem lies. And it is in men that the real solution must be found.

From the beginning, the critical humanist has seen that good as is man's control over nature, it is easy for it to become a good which is the worst enemy of the best, and it is easy for it to turn into a veritable evil. When you are so engrossed in controlling nature that you forget the control of human nature in loyalty to permanent standards, you are likely to produce a series of Al Capones with machine guns instead of the society of comfort and good will for which you hope. And you are likely to produce a nation inflamed with a lawless lust for power and controlled by a super Al Capone named Hitler whose wild career of mechanized warfare threatens the life of civilized man. The control of all the vast and varied forces of human passion must parallel the control of the forces of nature, or our inventions will destroy us at last.

It must be admitted that the tragedy as well as the magnificence of the machine age represents the sort of achievement possible only to creatures possessing the essentially human powers. And here the critical humanist must face

114

the element of tragedy in his own philosophy. If man in his distinctive life lives perpetually at the place of "either—or," and if the *either* represents good and the *or* evil, it is always possible for him to choose the evil. In a subhuman world you can never have moral tragedy. But in a truly human world, just because a free man can make evil his good, you have the possible emergence of the darkest and deepest moral tragedy. The free man can use his freedom for the highest ends. He may so use his freedom as to destroy every good thing. And when men who make evil their good have the potencies of mechanized peace and of mechanized war at their disposal, you will come upon evil days indeed.

A machine age, of all the ages, is just the time when critical intelligence acting in loyalty to permanent standards must be set before all men as the consummation of their lives. It is the central matter in education. Any educational theory which denies it simply courts disaster. The biography of Francis Bacon is an epitome of the history of the modern world. He gave himself to the working out of a philosophy of the control of the forces of nature, and he ignored the necessity of the moral control of the forces of his own character. So his life went down in ruin at last. The modern world has busied itself with the control of nature. It has all too frequently forgotten the matter of the moral control of the controller of these forces. And so it is in danger of a collective ruin like that which engulfed the individual character and life of Francis Bacon.

The master of the machines must not be allowed to live in a world which consists of machines and of machines alone. If he does, the machines will take the bit in their teeth and run away with the men. Machines belong to that subhuman order which is safe for mankind only when it is mastered and controlled by clear intelligence. Power without intelligence is always a menace to the life of man.

But we must drop the figure and analyze the matter more profoundly. For while it is all very well to put machinery over against intelligence as a dramatic method of emphasizing the importance of the intelligence, the truth is that it is a perverse intelligence misusing machines which threatens the life of man. A brilliant French writer does excellent execution on a certain level when he writes of the revolt of the machines. It is a perfectly legitimate literary device for helping us to see that something above the mechanical must control the world. But as a matter of fact, machines never do revolt. Machines by themselves never do anything. It is the men who make and use the machines who do the good things which help the world and who do the bad things which hurt the world. It is intelligence in reverse which misuses the machine and breaks mankind. The problem is really a human problem first and last and all the time.

For man's discovery of man choosing among alternatives is not only the discovery of a possible glory. It is also the discovery of a possible tragedy. The machine age gives man his most complete opportunity by a perverse use of his intelligence to bring brutal tragedy to the life of the world.

But human control can be used for high and noble purposes. And so the man who has made the machines may use them to advance the purposes of good for all the children of men. He can—and he must—use them to increase human prosperity. For every advance in the control over nature may be used to increase the comfort of the physical

116

life of man. But the man who controls the machine must seek something far more profound than prosperity, though of course he will keep the problems of a sane prosperity before him. The prosperity itself can be won and made secure only through loyalty to moral standards beyond the material aspects of life in which prosperity is found. And even when we have achieved controls which prevent the machine age from being a menace to prosperity and actually use them to secure prosperity and to make it permanent, the greatest questions of all confront us. How can all this prosperity be harnessed to moral and spiritual tasks? How can men possess prosperity without being suffocated by it?

A full stomach is not enough. A well clothed body is not enough. A house in which to dwell is not enough. The whole ensemble of material well-being simply ministers to a body without a soul unless the moral meanings of life are seen and its spiritual values are understood and appropriated. The machines must be made the servants of intellectual insights. They must be made the instruments of moral understanding. They must be made the vehicles of aesthetic sensibility. They must obey the behests of spiritual sanctions.

And the secrets of all these things lie in the deeper experiences of that strange creature, man. In our time he has bowed down before the machines which he has made, and he has called them his gods. But his ritual has been interrupted by the wild sounds of a world in conflagration and the smoke and flame of the fire which consumes civilization. Now man the idolater worshiping the machines which he has made must recover his human position. Once and for all it is necessary that we see that he must, at the cost of all that is precious in his life, be lord of his creations and not their slave. For this worship of the machine always turns out to be the worship of the lower and more beastly and more cruel forces of his own nature. The machine becomes a symbol of that beast in his own nature which would conquer the man. And even when the beast is slain, there is the menace of a subtler worship of the lower self under cover of the worship of the machine. For the machine becomes in a way the embodiment of those physical energies which move so smoothly according to their own laws that they constantly lower the demand upon the intelligence. A mechanically perfect toy leaves less to the creative imagination of the child. The complete and radiant beauty of the modern cinema at its best leaves less to the living faculties of men's minds than the production of one of Shakespeare's plays with the meager stage environment of the Globe Theatre. There are even those half gay and half anxious cynics who suggest that with facts and news and drama coming to us over the radio, and the rapid approach of the age of the radio picture as well as the radio word, we may reach the time when we will not consider it important to know how to read or write. Georges Duhamel, in his *In Defence of Letters,* has some important observations to make along these lines. It would be a curious thing if man used his brilliant inventive capacity for making labor-saving and intelligence-saving devices in such a fashion as to banish intelligence from the world. The truth is that man has always to fight for the distinctively human aspects of his life. There is a deep and constantly active tendency in man to revert to a level below the human. So it may happen that when the machine has been snatched from the control of the beast in man, the next fight of humanity will be with that law of inertia to which a mechanized humanity might so easily surrender. Man must conquer the beast. He must conquer the thing. A man begins to die when, after having used many vital powers of intelligent activity for the attaining of a competence, he comes to the day when he allows his income to support him, and gradually becomes incapable of exercising the very creative intelligence by means of which he won his wealth. So when a man who owns an automobile fails to take enough exercise to keep his body fit, one has a symbol of that surrender to the machine through which the thing conquers the man.

The warfare of creative intelligence is a perpetual conflict. And thus the greater the mechanical civilization, the more important it is that the voice of the critical humanist should be heard speaking in the light of the wisdom of the ages. That wisdom is the tale of human choices century after century. And the man who is perpetually feeding his mind on the tales of human decisions can never be content to surrender to the state of lethargy in which he becomes incapable of choice.

119

# CHAPTER X

## Humanism and Social Change

THE HISTORY OF UTOPIAN THOUGHT IS A CURIOUSLY INTER-esting and sometimes a very fascinating study. Century after century men have turned to their quickened imagination for a picture of a land of heart's desire which was often a land of mind's desire as well, for a type of life which would satisfy the demands of justice, intelligence, and good will, and would lead in the amplest fashion to human fulfillment. From Plato's *Republic* through Campanella's *City of the Sun* and More's *Utopia* and Bacon's *New Atlantis* to more modern constructions of an ideal human world, the glowing imagination of gifted thinkers has made its way.

During the last century, Utopian thought has completely left the region of literary dream pictures and has become a fierce demand for practical action. A powerful group of thinkers whose most masterful mind was that of Karl Marx attempted to put Utopian thought on what they would have called a scientific basis. In the case of Marx the principles of the Hegelian philosophy were given a twist and a turn which made them fundamental for the brilliant dialectic of *Das Kapital*. And all this became not merely powerful thought but the most practical of practical politics. Without too much exaggeration or too large a resort to metaphor, we may say that *Das Kapital* became the Magna Charta and the Bill of Rights of the Socialist Soviet Republics.

120

## Humanism and Social Change

A significant aspect of the modern movement toward social action has been the new fashion in which the passion for a better society has become indigenous in the Christian Church. To be sure, for centuries the Christian and the Jewish tradition have been characterized by shrewd social analysis and by passionate outbursts against social injustice. The book of Micah in the Old Testament is a bitter and caustic indictment of social injustice. The typical prophets of eighth century Israel are never more intense than when advocating the cause of the underprivileged. The New Testament sees as the goal of the Christian religion first the making of a new individual through the grace of God in Jesus Christ. It also sees as a consummation of its work a new society which it describes as the Kingdom of God and of which it has much to say. The Church of the Middle Ages, when it dreamed the dream of Hildebrand and, after that great priest became Gregory VII, tried to make the dream come true, accepted a profound responsibility for the remaking of society after the fashion of the will of God. The churches of the Reformation tended to turn sharply to the individual, though the work of Calvin at Geneva and of Knox in Edinburgh evinced a profound sense of social responsibility. In England in the eighteenth century the great revival under Wesley and Whitefield had the most far-reaching social effects. The last letter written by Wesley was one to Wilberforce in which he set the seal of his encouragement upon that great fight to abolish the slave trade to which Wilberforce gave his life. It was in nineteenth century England in the Anglican communion, however, that social passion became a more distinctive and masterful element in the witness of the church. Frederick Denison Maurice gave a kind of rich and mystical foun-

121 ·

dation to the sense of social responsibility. Charles Kingsley, a very typical Englishman in his immediate sense of the richness and many-sided values of the life of this world and the spicy, vigorous sense of everyday life, a virile masculine person whom his countrymen felt at once that they could understand, became the voice of a new social conscience. To him religion was to be the lawgiver of the world of industry as well as the heart of a glowing piety. The workers of England recognized him as their great and unselfish friend. In the Free Churches, too, the social conscience was growing. Robert William Dale, that prince of the pulpit who made Carr's Lane Chapel in Birmingham a throne, believed that the Kingdom of God must be made the kingdom of good here and now. He could not conceive of an adequate religious life which ignored its social obligations. He was at the very heart of the movement which wrought such changes in Birmingham that it came to be called the best governed city in the world. The new movement went on apace. At length in the United States of America such thinkers as Josiah Strong and Walter Rauschenbusch and Shailer Mathews had their share in giving to the churches of the republic such a social conscience as they had not possessed before. The day came when the characteristic note of American Christianity was its social passion. Europeans were inclined to call it the *activismus* of the American church.

There was much that was good—much, indeed, that was superbly good—in all this glowing social enthusiasm. And one must say with downright emphasis that without it the American churches would have lost one of the noblest elements of their witness in the world. But as time went on it became evident that the great new day and the brave new church of which men of social passion had dreamed had not come to be. Indeed, often the men most engrossed in social formulas were those least effective in the practical work of the ministry. The churches which had only a social message tended to become arid and dry and dull. They tended to become the victim of what one might call a social scholasticism. They were frequently spiritually anemic.

Just as this situation became a striking element in the life of the Church, a strange phenomenon made its appearance in the larger political life of the world. The mighty social experiment in Russia played curiously with its idealism when it allowed millions of peasants to starve to death. And at last it became an organized fear in the name of brotherhood. In the totalitarian states social passion was made the vehicle of dictators in their rise to positions of conscienceless power. The social hope was becoming blotched and spotted and besmirched in the world. And it was growing singularly futile in the Church. Clearly the time for a new analysis of the whole situation had come. Clearly social passion must be emancipated from relationships which at their best made it futile and at their worst made it evil. And in precisely this situation critical humanists began to speak their words of penetrating and powerful criticism.

Turning now from history to analysis, we may begin by saying that the humanist confronts the apostle of social action in church and in state with standards which are high and demanding, and in their name judges all social programs. The critical humanist realizes that there is no perfect formula which by a kind of magic power will itself secure a social Utopia. When we arrive at the stage of applying formulas, it comes about that good formulas are put

123

to bad purposes by evil men, and formulas which are far from perfect produce an astonishing amount of good when they are applied by men of good will. This does not mean that social formulas are unimportant. It does mean that we must always be on our guard against that preoccupation with social formulas which leads us to ignore the even more definitively important matter of the character of the men who use and apply the formulas.

There is a bit of doggerel jingle which in its own shrewd way goes to the heart of the matter. It runs something like this:

> "We cannot have Utopia now.
> It's a waste of time to plan it;
> For if we had Utopia how
> Would we find the people to man it?
> You cannot work the Utopian plan
> Until you find the Utopian man."

It is at this point that the Christian Church often goes wrong. For one of the most characteristic responsibilities and opportunities of the Christian Church has to do with producing men who can be trusted to put good social formulas into effect. It is the strange and beautiful power of the Church to produce men whose own true lives will make social passion authentic. When it fails at this point, it fails to do its most distinctive work. And it fails—as close analysis reveals—because it falls into one particular fallacy. Let us take time to analyze that fallacy clearly and fully.

The man of social enthusiasm in the Christian Church reads a vast literature which tells the tale of how men have been crushed by a bad environment. Volume after volume he pursues the tale of man's inhumanity to man. Chapter

124

after chapter he follows the story of how men's lives have been cramped and thwarted and brought to frustration by the pressure of circumstances over which they had no control. He reads of little children forced to live in such awful surroundings that Jacob Riis could say of them: "They are not born into the world. They are damned into the world." He goes to the slums of great cities. He visits the regions where sharecroppers live their desperate lives. He studies the organized villainies of unscrupulous masters of industry. And he becomes possessed of a terrible indignation. These things, he vows in his own soul and before God, must be changed. He is gloriously right in his vow. But in his magnificent obsession of wrath against social wrong, he falls into a profound and far-reaching fallacy. Hardly conscious of the steps by which he comes to the position, he assumes that, when a bad environment crushes helpless individuals, if you take away that bad environment these individuals will become good and strong; and especially if you substitute for that bad environment a good environment, the moral problem of the world will be solved. This, as a matter of fact, is simply not true. You have taken only one step toward a better life for man when you have abolished a bad environment. For at once there will spring up in that moral vacuum freed from social evil no end of individuals of such selfishness and hard cruelty that they will make the bad environment all over again. And when you secure a good environment, it by no means follows that you produce a good man. The centers of evil are deep in the individual spirit. And history and biography are full of examples of the fashion in which a good environment has been exploited by bad men. Socrates, that almost perfect teacher, produced something like an ideal intellectual

125

environment for his pupils. And in that environment the poisonously plausible and unprincipled mind of Alcibiades came to flower, just as the rich and noble mind of Plato was maturing. It was Alcibiades who betrayed Athens. A loftier Teacher still, spoke indubitably perfect words in the language of man. And in His school the mind of Judas matured just as the mind of John entered into its high inheritance. The great social fallacy lies in the belief that a good environment will produce good men. Of course we must fight everything which makes environment an evil thing. Of course we must crush that which crushes men. But when this is done, our deepest work lies before us. We must find the secret for making individual men who are good from the central motives of the soul out to the last action of the life. Indeed, if we are going to fight evil environment, we must find these men to do the fighting with anything like success. So the production of the new man—the new individual—is our first task as well as our last. And just this power is the central and definitive power of the Christian Church. When it forgets this, it descends from its throne. When it remembers this, it ascends the throne again. When the social prophet becomes so engrossed with social passion that he forgets to speak to the individual conscience, his cause is lost. And his cause is lost, not because his social passion is wrong, but because that passion must always be directed and implemented by the new individual made strong by the grace of God if that passion is to be effective. Critical humanism may not from the beginning see this consummation of its principles. But from the start it does see that social action always depends on the individual. In the deepest sense the

126

social problem is an individual problem, first, last, and all the time.

Then the whole history of humanism leads it to be on its guard against the sentimental Utopias which have never been submitted to the tests of clear and critical intelligence. The type of man who is sternly realistic in analyzing the evils of the present order, but romantically naive in accepting the premises of the particular Utopia in which he puts his hopes, meets a stern and remorseless critic in the humanist. For the man of critical intelligence knows that you must submit your Utopia to tests just as stern and critical as those which you apply to the present order. And the humanist has a well-grounded fear of the social passion which substitutes undisciplined friendly emotion for moral judgment. The undisciplined humanitarian often turns out in the long run to be one of the worst foes of the under-privileged.

The critical humanist is likely to be regarded as an unpleasant person in any group of romantic social radicals. He is too intelligent. He has an awkward way of puncturing their bubbles of unjustified idealism. But he is really the true friend of the man of social passion. For his unhesitating and clear criticism saves the man of social enthusiasm from follies which would cast discredit upon the very cause to which he is giving his life. The humanist knows that there is no concrete reality named society. Society is an abstraction except as you think of the individuals who compose it. Thus, as we have seen, the humanist knows that you can change society only by changing the minds and actions of the men and women who are its component parts. So the humanist subjects all high-sounding social generalizations to the sharpest critical tests.

This, however, is only one half of the story. And it is of the utmost importance that we give its full significance to the other half. For the humanist's own position has the very seed of social passion in it. In fact, very often it is just his contribution to substitute social conscience based upon an adequate set of principles for social passion based only on kindly emotion. The characteristic humanistic distinction between the human and the subhuman pledges the humanist to seek a life for man worthy of one who belongs to the human level. He is ready to do battle to change any environment whose whole pressure is in the direction of reducing men to things. And he is committed by his most sacred principles to oppose those who treat man as if he were an animal and nothing more. "How much is a man better than a sheep!" might well be his watchword. He knows the awful undertow of the forces in his own life and in the world about him which would pull man down. No one feels more indignation than he against whatever power would make of man an unthinking clod. No one more than he rises in ethical wrath against those who would treat men as if they were merely beasts to bear their burdens. If his criticism of sentimental and romantic Utopias sometimes makes him appear hard and even unsympathetic, it is because he knows that undisciplined and unintelligent sympathy is eventually the foe of those he would like to help. If he refuses to exploit men as if they were merely animals, by the same token he refuses to regard them as merely animals to be kept in pleasant pastures. "Son of man, stand on thy feet," he says to the last and the lowest and the least of men. Sentimental pity does not bring men to their feet. It reduces them to an emotional pulp of receptive weakness. By treating men as men, the humanist summons them to be worthy of their

128

manhood. In other words, the humanist insists upon saving the virility and force and human quality of the underprivileged at the very moment when he is fighting the foes who would crush them. Thus, at the very time when he turns from the methods which would pamper the underprivileged into a state of perpetual childhood, he turns in full armor and with flashing sword against every power which would deprive them of their right to attain full and virile and energetic manhood.

We may indeed say that the tremendous sense of the value of man as man—the distinctive doctrine of the humanist—is one of the greatest of all the forces fighting against human tyranny, against the hard cruelty of the powerful to the weak, against all the forces which would deny to man his true heritage of free personality. When the humanist is sure that he stands on ground which can be defended both intellectually and morally, his social action is as unhesitating as it is brave.

We need also to see that the very realistic and critical quality of the mind of the humanist saves him from that bitter disillusionment which so often turns sentimental humanitarians into soured idealists. The man who believes in the completely curative properties of a good environment is likely to fall into a dark slough of despond when he finds that his social formulas do not work out as he had hoped. So, as Irving Babbitt once pithily said, he begins by having castles in Spain, and when his hour of utter disillusionment comes, he ends by having only dungeons in Spain. The critical humanist knows that when he has won a social battle, a grim battle with the individual conscience lies just ahead. The sentimental humanitarian thinks that when a social battle is won, the fundamental work is done. He

129

takes off his armor and sits waiting to see the Utopia of his dreams unfold. Then when ugly selfishness unmasks itself in the actions of some of his confreres in the very social battle which he has been waging, he is in a doleful state indeed. He has only a social philosophy, and he is completely unprepared for individual treachery. So he enters some cave of unrelieved gloom. He becomes indeed a disillusioned cynic who has lost hope for mankind. The critical humanist is in no such sad and tragic condition. From the beginning he has seen man a free agent at the place of choice between good and evil. He knows that he can choose the evil. He knows that he can like it. He knows that he can want it. He knows that he can make it his good. He knows that he can choose evil in the best environment the world can offer. He knows that the final citadel of evil is not in society but in the secret recesses of the individual spirit. So from social victory he goes on to another and a greater fight.

There is a famous Italian picture of Saint George just after he has slain the dragon. A bitter reaction has set in after all his terrible expenditure of energy. He stands there, weak in the hour of victory. As you look at the picture, you very much hope that another fierce dragon will not appear to challenge him as he stands, for the moment at least, impotent after his great fight.

There is no darker hour in the life of the social reformer than when, after a final victory over some social dragon, he is suddenly confronted by that other fiercer dragon of individual corruption, fire flaming from its nostrils and power breathing in every movement of its body. In his hour of weakness his worst foe has caught him completely unprepared.

130

## Humanism and Social Change

With the humanist it is not so. He engages in social combats with the glad abandon of a great courage. On many a field he fights shoulder to shoulder with the humanitarians against evils which call forth their common hatred. But when the battle is won, the humanist stands tense as he gathers his forces for a greater conflict. The dark evil at the center of individual life looms grim and mighty before him. The first battle was but play compared with the frightful contest which now engages his energies. He has come to the ultimate source of evil. And the evil is a sordid selfishness which, to his complete surprise, has emerged to take its defiant place upon the throne of his own soul. Here he has indeed found evil in its ultimate lair. No social formulas will help him here. No emotional altruistic ideals will make him strong for this ultimate fight. With a sense that the very hour of destiny has come, he plunges into this final battle. No quarter is given, for the end of the fight is the death of the good or evil at the center of a human soul. He is not a friendly man fighting against an unfriendly society. He feels two natures struggling within him. He faces the last terrible conflict in his own soul. On and on goes the fight as our humanist Saint George battles with the final fierce dragon which, coming from without, has so strangely become a dragon within. He knows what it is at last to meet his most dreadful foe in his own soul. And when at length the victory is won, he knows the meaning of those great Latin words: *Vincit qui se vincit*—he conquers who overcomes himself.

There are almost fathomless depths in the regions of thought through which we have been passing. In them tragic and glorious figures appear. Some of them will be met face to face as we go on. For the battling man in his

last great fight finds sources of strength beyond his own
energy and beyond his own will. Here, as we shall see
later, humanism meets religion with its awful sanctions and
its overwhelming powers. At the present stage of the
analysis, we leave the human battler with the glow of victory
upon his brow without lifting questions which will emerge
later as to the nature of that victory. For the deepest insight to which this chapter leads us is the understanding that
man's ultimate battle is the battle in his own soul, and his
ultimate victory is his victory over himself. Society waits
for the victorious individual to make the social dream come
true.

# CHAPTER XI

## *The Three Levels*

HENRY VAN DYKE ONCE PUBLISHED A BOOK ENTITLED *The Ruling Passion*. Its various stories set forth intense pre-occupation with some one desire which had become distinctive and decisive in the lives of certain individuals. So, indeed, life often expresses itself. Men have physical passions. Men have moral passions. Men have social passions. Men have spiritual passions. Men have intellectual passions. And of the intellectual passions, one of the most powerful is the passion for unity. It provides a very important motive for much useful and far-reaching activity on the part of the mind. It seems such a wholesome and altogether inevitable passion on the part of glowing intelligence that it is likely to pass muster without any serious or thoroughgoing criticism. It is unfortunate that this happens so often, for the passion for unity may become an all-devouring passion destroying those distinctions upon which the validity and the permanent meaning of human experience depend.

It is a curious and tragic fact that a mental method may turn the mind into a murderous mother devouring her own offspring. When the mind reaches principles by whose means alone it is possible to understand and interpret life and then, driven by a false desire for unity, destroys these very distinctions, one has a kind of final abdication of the critical intelligence. The desire to rise from heterogeneous diversity to harmonious unity is of course a necessary and right desire. But it is one thing to seek the unity which preserves the necessary distinctions. And it is quite another to lose oneself in the unity which destroys the necessary distinctions. In the latter case the passion for unity has become a false and destructive thing.

The pantheistic monism of India is a very subtle corpus of thought, involving an approach through various equally subtle processes of dialectic. And it comes at last to a place where the distinction between existence and non-existence disappears. It reaches a consummation where the distinction between truth and error vanishes. It attains an attenuated position where the distinction between good and evil is discarded. And all this is done in the name of an intellectual ideal which has used its weapons so remorselessly that intelligence itself is slain. It is done in the name of a conception of meaning which is carved out so ruthlessly that meaning itself is forever lost. Of course, the next logical step would be to see that in this ultimate universe the distinction between unity and diversity, too, would be lost. This would completely reveal the suicidal quality of these processes of thought. Unfortunately, the pantheistic monist usually fails to draw this conclusion from his logic. But he does manage to think his way into a universe where the mind ceases to function, driven by what he believes to be the logical necessities implicit in the use of his own mind.

The philosophy which seeks the absolute has the same quality of destroying elements whose meaning must be permanent if life is not to fall apart. It is really important that philosophers should understand that it is their business to explain life and not to destroy it. Whenever a philosophical principle proves destructive of the very process it exists in order to explain, we may be sure that there is something the matter with the principle. Certain biological developments

134

have set going processes of interpretation which themselves move in the direction of a monism which requires the inspection of the clearest criticism. When these tendencies are supplemented by philosophies of absolutist tendency and by the rich and subtle dialectic of the thinking which comes from India, pantheistic monism becomes a very formidable process of thought. Indeed, it may well turn out that in pantheistic monism there is a greater menace to clear and true thinking and ultimately to good and wise living than in any other interpretation of the problems of existence offered to men in our time.

Critical humanism lives and does its powerful work in the world through making and maintaining those essential distinctions upon which a genuine understanding of life depends. It takes its stand definitely against a monism which would destroy essential distinctions. The only monism in which it can believe—the only unity which it can accept—is one in which these essential distinctions are made permanent as a pattern of thought. Critical humanism is often called—and indeed often calls itself—a form of dualism, because it is willing to do battle with any pseudo unity which would destroy the distinctions which are necessary to the understanding and to the true ongoing of life. But it is not a foe of that true unity in which the validity and permanence of diversity are recognized. And it is not a foe of that true monism which maintains the dualistic distinctions.

Of the distinctions which critical humanism recognizes and emphasizes, the most essential have to do with the three levels. Existence is found on three planes, it is insisted. There is the subhuman. There is the human. And there is the divine. When one first reads about these dis-

135

tinctions, they seem rather simple, almost self-evident. Perhaps the very young student wonders why so much ado should be made about them. But the moment he begins to apply them, he sees that the case is not so simple as it had seemed. He is fairly startled to find how the work of powerful thinkers has a way of coming to failure at last because they forget these distinctions. He begins to see that the words which dropped so easily from his lips at first go very deeply into the texture of existence and life. He approaches his study of these distinctions with a new humility. And now he begins to have flashes of understanding of their far-reaching character. He begins to understand that no philosophy which ignores these distinctions can be permanent. He begins to understand that false passion for unity which leads inevitably to the blurring of the very distinctions which give significance to life. And he sees at last the menace of that pantheistic monism of which we have already said that it is perhaps the greatest danger which confronts the philosophic thought of our time. The pseudo spirituality of pantheistic monism has an allurement which deceives the very elect. The hour when the student detects the fallacy lurking at its heart is a great hour in his life. It is so easy to be contented with a metaphysical unity which blurs essential distinctions, and to miss the moral unity which is based upon living fellowship and leaves all the essential distinctions intact. The student who is too impatient to make an ever-renewed study of the doctrine of the three levels will never understand critical humanism. More than that, he will miss the real meaning of life.

All this comes to a sharp point when we observe the fashion in which a false philosophy of science attempts to interpret every human experience upon a subhuman level.

The result is not an explanation of life. It is an emasculation of life. It would be a splendid thing if another Plato would write a series of dialogues in which another Platonic Socrates would carry on endless conversations about life on the three levels, investigating them in every situation, with the lights and shadows falling in all sorts of ways, and with the devastating Socratic irony constantly playing. It would be a splendid thing if another Lucian would use all the resources of his corrosive wit setting forth the absurdity of all those pretentious forms of thought which in pompous and uncritical arrogance destroy the very foundations of thought itself. So at last we might come to see the far-reaching meaning of these distinctions.

We are ready now to enter upon a more intensive analysis of the meaning of the three levels. Below the human there is the subhuman. There is the realm of mechanical interaction. There is the realm of biological impulse. Physics—indeed, all the physical sciences—have to do with the realms of mathematical interaction. Increasingly we understand that it is possible to discover a series of formulas by whose means we may express and then control the activities which we discover in the physical universe. The new physics has complicated the matter. For sometimes these formulas contradict each other, and yet they work. The classical physics represented a comfortable conformity and harmony of formulas from the smallest atom to the farthest star. The new physics supplements this vast corpus of formulas by a mathematics of its own. But together the classical physics and the new physics represent a vast mathematics of nature, a study of the subhuman apart from the level of animate existence.

Above the level of inanimate existence and still in the region of the subhuman we have the level of animate life. This level embraces all living things which are below the plane of intelligence. It is essentially the realm of biological impulse. The moment life emerges, you have sensation, hunger, and thirst, the sexual experiences, and all the series of energetic activities which set living beings apart from mechanically reacting things. There are all sorts of stages of intensity. But pleasure and pain and appetite are found everywhere. There is, of course, endless debate about the stages of awareness from the higher forms of animal life down to those lowest organisms which seem almost like things. But broadly speaking, the distinction between the animate and the inanimate is clear enough. And both belong to the first level of existence. The worlds of subhuman mathematics and of subhuman appetite together constitute the drama of existence until man appears.

The moment man appears, you have a new series of facts. Now you come upon conscious knowledge and conscious control. To be sure, the human carries over both mathematical organization and biological appetite. But it is distinguished by controlling intelligence. And the important thing about it is that which distinguishes it from the subhuman level and not that which unites it with the subhuman level. Conscious intelligence exercising control is the defining matter in all the higher stages of life. When man appears, the controller has arrived. He turns the world of things to his own purposes. He begins to bend the world of animals to his own will. The master has arrived. And he achieves this mastery not by the size of his body but through the power of his intelligence. The vastness of the physical universe does not overawe him, though he does feel its strange dignity. For it cannot think of him, while

138

he can think of it. Mountains do not discuss the origin of men. Men do discuss the origin of mountains. Man is not permanently overawed by the fact that many animals are larger than he. He pits his intelligence against their size. And when these great beasts are ferocious, he pits his intelligence against their ferocity. His agile, ever-turning, quick-acting mind is on the whole more than a match for the hard energy of things and the fierce power of the creatures of all the jungles. Tempests may overwhelm him at sea, but he builds ships which defy the tempests. Beasts may slay him in the jungle. But he invents weapons which slay the beasts. His intelligence sets him apart from all the creatures below him. He, and not the mountain, is the lord of things. He, and not the lion, is the king of beasts.

The debate about the intelligence of the animals below man is not very important for our discussion. Dogs, for instance, have done rather extraordinary things. If dogs were to develop a written language and write plays like those of Shakespeare, if they were to erect edifices like the Empire State Building and build ships like the Queen Mary, if they were to construct telephones and radio stations, if they were to develop an intricate moral code and write histories of ethics, if they were to discover and classify the laws of nature and use them for their own purposes, we might begin to speak of the humanity of dogs. Until they do these things, we may leave them comfortably upon the subhuman level. For man the controller has his own ways. He has his own thoughts. He has a kingdom which is all his own. It is the kingdom of conscious intelligence foreseeing ends and making them the object of action.

The fact that man in his organism shares the qualities of the world of things and also of the world of animals need not unduly complicate the situation for the critical thinker. The thinker who insists on classifying man by a process of ignoring everything which is distinctive about him simply proves that he is incapable of penetrating thought. The truth is that the man who is mad with a monistic passion dislikes everything which is distinctive and positively hates what is unique. He likes everything which slips back into a pattern of commonness. If man has an organism which in some respects resembles that of a cow, he is filled with delight. Now he is beginning to find another clue to the oneness of all life. If man has intellectual qualities which cows do not possess, he is genuinely annoyed. To admit that man possesses qualities which permanently separate him from the cow can never be tolerated. This would be a break in the oneness of life. This would be a violation of that pantheistic monism which must be the final word in the interpretation of life. So the monist can come to a position which curiously and oddly resembles that cow worship which Mahatma Gandhi so interestingly retains and so naively interprets. Paul Elmer More has called this pseudo passion for unity which denies distinctions that are a very part of the tissue of life "The Demon of the Absolute." It is at least completely unscientific in the most ordinary and accepted interpretation of the meaning of science. For the scientist, we are told in voices which shout from the housetops, faces facts, and when he dislikes them, is especially honest about them; and when they break down his preconceived notions, is especially careful not to misstate them. The man who denies the distinctively human characteristics their rightful place has simply disqualified himself as a serious thinker.

It cannot be said too strongly that humanism is not a

speculation spun out of the inner consciousness of fanciful thinkers in justification of their own weird imaginings. It is simply a facing and a stating of the facts of life. Man has emerged. He does possess intelligence. This intelligence does set him apart from the world of things. It does set him apart from the world of animals. He uses an organism composed of material elements. He uses an organism characterized by biological impulses. But he is not a thing, and he is not an impulse. He is an agent of controlling intelligence. Millions of facts tell this story. They are before our eyes every day of our lives.

It is the pantheistic monist who ignores and then denies facts in the name of a preconceived theory which is the product of his own mind. Facts must go down in order that the theory may survive. The humanist is a son of fact. The pantheistic monist is a son of the speculative imagination.

The distinctive quality of life on the second level stands, then, in its own right. The humanist does not say: In an ideal world there might appear an intelligence controlling things and mastering impulses. He studies his world with eyes completely open and with mind completely awake. And in the light of the facts he finds in his world he declares: There has appeared an intelligence which has controlled things. There has appeared an intelligence which has mastered impulses. This intelligence is man. And man's life is the life of the second level. The human is the controlling. It is the world of mind in action.

There are such vast areas to be inspected and understood and interpreted when we study man doing business with his world and with other men, that the critical humanist may all his life confine himself to this field. He may make it the whole end of his effort to deal with the characteristical-

141

ly human. But if he is as critical as his name implies, he simply must go farther. He must ask questions which cannot be answered by the world of things. He must ask questions which cannot be answered by the world of animals. He must ask questions which cause the world of man to look beyond itself. He must complete his critical humanism by a study of the ultimate sources and meaning of that intelligence which he finds in man. This leads to the third level, which is that of the divine intelligence, which is the final fact of the universe. Of this third level and of the dialectic which justifies our belief in its existence we shall have much to say in later chapters. We content ourselves now by referring to the third level as the completion of that pattern of thought to which the humanist is driven when he attempts to deal adequately with all the facts of existence, of life, and of intelligence.

The dialectic of analysis which we have been conducting has profound relations which emerge only when we saturate our minds in the great and characteristic literature of the civilized nations of the world. We have already seen that the highest sort of literary distinction first came within the reach of man when in Greece, and then in Rome, he began to deal with the specifically human. But a series of expeditions through the literature of the great nations of Europe with the distinctions which this chapter has emphasized constantly kept in mind would be a revealing experience. Relationships would stand forth in sharp antithesis. The adventure of man would be seen with a new clarity.

Let us take an example chosen almost at random. Suppose we join the pilgrims making up the characters of Chaucer's *Canterbury Tales*. Here you have to do with a very famous and not an entirely lofty work of the fourteenth century. Its emphasis is surely secular rather than sacred. Some—perhaps most—of the pilgrims view a journey to the shrine of Thomas à Becket at Canterbury through the eyes of the body rather than through the eyes of the spirit. They are a company of typical fourteenth century people, thrown up from the life of the period, united for a short time by a journey they are taking together. The human interest is the engrossing interest. You never lose sight of these people through the urgency of any other summons. Some of them are good; some of them are bad. Some of them are wise; some of them are foolish. Some of them are spiritual; some of them are sensual. They are all full of that human stuff which makes endless appeal. They feel the tug of many a desire and many a passion below the level of their true life. With some of them the racy animality quite overcomes the intelligence and the moral sense. Some of them live gloriously on the true human level, like the one who gladly teaches and gladly learns. Some of them have eyes not without the flashing of the light of an eternal beauty. You have here the struggle of life on each of the three levels. And the arena is man. In his mind the battle is fought. In his heart the foes contend. In his spirit the battle is won or lost. And it has an impressiveness all its own, one must admit, just because Dan Chaucer is not himself quite on the side of the angels. His eyes are a little too shrewd. His face shows a little too clearly the allurement of the pomps and plausibilities and the sensations of this amazing world. But if he has looked at things from which a saint would have turned his eyes, he has his own honest, if rather distant, appreciation of the eyes of the saint. In the *Canterbury Tales* what we have been saying about the

143

three levels leaves the realm of dialectic and becomes flashing human eyes, tingling human nerves, throbbing human hearts, active human minds, and spirits not quite asleep amid the hot appeals of life.

Or take another fourteenth century document which is as clearly on the side of the angels as the *Canterbury Tales* is on the side of secular men. *The Vision of Piers Plowman* deals with great moral and spiritual facts and great moral and spiritual mysteries. But it quite gives the lie to the contention that the book written with moral and spiritual purpose cannot glow with the fire of true literature. What a picture of everyday men and women in the fourteenth century you find in *The Vision of Piers Plowman*. The human adventure is the great thing. And even when it is the human adventure seen in the light of divine sanctions, it is the human adventure still.

Or take the *Decameron* of Boccaccio. It is all edged about with a grim, if lightly expressed, human irony. These gay men and women who make love and tell tales away in the mountains with clear healthful air, whither they have fled from the plague-stricken city, in their own way tell the story of what men may do with their manhood. Usually it is not a very noble tale. It is hot with the lusts of the flesh. And often man's mind is used only to give full expression to the lusts of his body. But there is always the brave—if never quite successful—attempt to save the life of the flesh from baseness by bringing in the graces of human intelligence. The *Decameron* is an important document to the student of human life.

And so we might go on and on. The humanist is not a grimly mathematical thinker. But he has found a set of principles—he has found some essential distinctions—which, carried through the literature and the history of the world, give endless clues to the true meanings. And if it was Ikhnaton who in the valley of the Nile first thought of God as a supreme conscious person possessing the great human qualities lifted to their highest power, this only shows how the doctrine of the three levels by an inevitable interlacing comes at last to complete the round of existence and to interpret all the facts of life.

In the region of the Tigris and Euphrates valleys, that strange art which pictured in one figure the body of a beast and the face of a man and wings which somehow suggested spiritual flight surely reveals once more man's perpetual moving toward the understanding of that strange bundle of life which makes the sense of the three levels so imperative. Indeed, art even in the most characteristic forms can never get very far from these principles, sometimes asserting them, sometimes trying to deny them, sometimes becoming confused about them, but always returning to them. Even the art which in effect ignores the high levels only succeeds in asserting its interest in the lower levels, and so makes part of the whole picture. And the "Venus de Milo," whose body is somehow suffused by a kind of intellectual and moral and spiritual loftiness, also suggests the fashion in which the highest life must master and interpret all the rest.

## CHAPTER XII

## The Subhuman

EXCEPT IN THE RAREST MOMENTS, WE DO NOT SEE NATURE directly. We see it through spectacles provided by the age in which we live, by some thinkers or school of thinkers, or by some favorite preconception of our own. And much, if not most, of the time we find in nature what we seek. The same places become quite different when set in the frames offered by different periods. For a long time the Lake Country in England was simply a lonely, weird, and unattractive region through which the traveler passed uncomfortably with a sense of undeniable relief when he came to more domestic and friendly regions. The landscape of the district was foreign to his thoughts and ideals and beliefs. It was likely to send little shivers up and down his spine. Then came Wordsworth. And by a magic touch everything was transformed. An exquisite spiritual beauty lay slumbering in every lake. Some glowing sense of lofty meanings was far off and magnificent on every hill and mountain. Some spiritual secret smiled on the bloom of every flower. I remember in the eagerness of my own uncritical Wordsworthian period rapturously going about the Lake Country and visiting Dove Cottage with an almost religious reverence. In this bare and simple little house there had dwelt a spirit tuned to the secret music of life itself. And he had put that music into words which will not die. Of course you cannot dispose of Wordsworth in a paragraph. And there are many ways in which he can teach us, as well as

146

significant ways in which he can mislead us. But at least it is quite clear—and that is the point I am now making—that Wordsworth taught nature to wear garments which he most carefully prepared for her. And if, with his fine religiousness of spirit, at last he prepared for her an Easter bonnet, it was Wordsworth who prepared the bonnet. It was not the secret of nature—all too often we must say—which Wordsworth discovered. It was the secret of the brooding of Wordsworth imposed upon the natural world.

Nature is the material with which we work, the toy with which we play; and we make it the symbol of our dreams, of our hopes, and of our fears. We have used it so long as the warp for the woof of our fancy that it is difficult enough to get at nature itself. If the naturalistic poets have complicated the situation, the natural scientists have not just made it easier. They have taken the logic of their own minds and have superimposed it upon the natural world. But in one way they have been in a better position than the naturalistic poets. If they have found in nature only that which they have sought, they have been forced to test their findings by the laboratory test, and so they have found *something that is there* even if they have not found all that is there. When certain experiments conducted according to the logic implicit in the mind of man work out in exactly the same way century after century, it does at last become clear that the same logic which is integral to the mind of man is inherent in the activities of nature. The scientist has sought what he wanted to find. But at least the perpetual test of his formulas in practical ways proves that in some real fashion nature corresponds to his thought of it. The law of gravitation may be, as one of the most brilliant and provocative of contemporary scientists has said, "a put-up job"; but at least someone else put it up before the scientist thought of it.

Of course one of the greatest sources of our confusion lies precisely in the fact that when we see, we see what we see, or what we think we see, but we do not see ourselves seeing. Just as the eye sees everything except itself, so the mind perceives everything except its own act of perception. And precisely because, when we set about understanding and mastering existence and life, those aspects which are characterized by mathematical relations and which correspond to the logic implicit in our own minds are easiest to fit into the pattern we make and the formulas we use, we concentrate upon them. The elements which express free intelligence do not fit into the impersonal pattern. And so we are apt to center our attention upon the first—the subhuman— rather than upon the second—the human.

This world of hard and fast subhuman relationships is a fascinating region. Its charting has required centuries of time and millions of minds. Sometimes—always, in the last analysis, as science has gradually discovered—it is a world of action. The action itself moves according to perfectly mathematical relationships. One becomes delighted with the far-reaching application of the formulas which express these relationships. The law of the conservation of energy is an example of the almost endless—once scientists would have said quite endless—quality of these uniformities. The tale of the discovery of the characteristics of that vast machine which the physical universe has proved itself to be is one of the most astonishing tales of the use of the mind of man. The history of the physical sciences, when the story is well told, is as fascinating as any romance. And even when the uniformities of the classical physics break down in deal-

ing with new and subtler relationships, it is by means of a
more sophisticated mathematics that scientists deal with the
new problems and cross the great divide, finding new formulas which must also be submitted to the laboratory test. Nobody paid any serious attention to Einstein until the tele-
scopes through which astronomers gazed revealed facts
which answered to his theories. But the manifold formulas by
which the scientists reduce their discoveries to a form easily
handled by the mind of man turn out to be the instruments
by which man can make the world his slave. For all this becomes most exciting when we apprehend the fact that man
can not only understand many things about the world in
which he lives and reduce this understanding to mathematical formulas, but he can also use these formulas to make
the forces of nature do what he wants them to do. Now the
discovery of the dependable relationships of the physical
world and the use of the knowledge of these relationships
for his own purposes becomes the meat and drink of the
investigator. So, indeed, he has been able to build that material civilization of which until recently we were so in-
ordinately proud. The sense of the vast rhythm of natural
law becomes a kind of intoxicating poetry in the mind of
the student of these things who uses his intelligence in ever
larger generalizations. And this rhythm sets itself to the
music of scientific poetry. Here the laws of nature are
turned into song. Alfred Tennyson early saw and realized
possibilities along this line. And some of his most characteristic poetry set natural science to music. Robert Browning
was haunted by the same possibilities. His poetry was
characteristically three-fourths thought and one-fourth music. And he, too, made his age of science the subject of his
verse.

Then there was the profoundly important tendency—going back to those Stoics who first conceived of a law of nature—to make the laws of nature the source of a morality—and even, as in the case of Spinoza, the basis of a religion. In this coherent universe you were delivered from the chaotic, the lawless, the meaningless influx of that which could not be controlled. Very well, then, let a man rule out of his own nature the adventitious and the lawless. Let him even worship that vast harmony of coherent impersonal laws which nature had proved itself to be.

Of course all this was uncritical enough. In a nature where in all the realm of life including that of man there was only impersonal law which could not be resisted, how could man accept or reject this law? You cannot really have morality in a determined world. You have to forget that you have no freedom in order to decide to obey laws which you cannot resist. And by the same token, when Spinoza asked men to make a religion of the vast totalitarian system of impersonal necessity, he was guilty of as astonishing emasculation of his intelligence as ever characterized a philosopher, great or small. Spinoza has often been praised for the vast and at times almost impenetrable profundity of his mind. One is not interested in denying the exquisite interlacing of the various elements of his intriguing thought. But one must insist that he turned his back upon the one insight which would have made his philosophy coherent and authentic, and without which at last, with all its insights at points of detail and in regions of impersonal relationships, it becomes as a whole a piece of intellectual make-believe. You cannot ask an automaton to find spiritual rapture in the free acceptance of a determined universe. And that is just the climax of Spinoza's philosophy. What he regards—

and what his obsessed followers have regarded—as its ultimate spiritual beauty becomes its final and conclusive futility.

Of course—as we have already found it necessary to say, and as we now find it necessary to say again—if the student of nature is to obtain a knowledge of the dependable relationships of nature and is to use them for his own purposes, he must transcend them. He himself must live not in the subhuman but in the human world. The Stoics who talked about a universe which was completely determined and where there was no room for freedom really lived in a human world which transcended their philosophic determinism. And when they asked men to be loyal to this world of necessity, it was the shadow of their own free human life which was falling upon their system. Their actual freedom was making havoc of their philosophy. Spinoza actually lived in a free human world which transcended the vast mechanism of necessity which was central in his philosophic speculations. And when he asked men to make a religion of this vast organism of necessity and to bow down before the beauty of its harmonies, this asking of men to use a freedom which according to his principles they did not possess, to establish a religious loyalty possible only in a free world, was the shadow of his own freedom which was falling upon his determined monism. His actual freedom, like that of the Stoics, was making havoc of his philosophy.

It would be a great mistake to underestimate the significance of the world of mechanical and mathematical interaction. It is the basis of all invention. It makes possible the building of houses and the building of ships. It makes possible the suspension of bridges at dizzy heights over great rivers. It makes possible the building of factories whose workers are forces and not men. It gives men a world to control just because its uniformities enable men to know what to expect under particular circumstances. A chaotic world can never be controlled. In such a world you can never tell what will happen next. Nature in such a world would not hold steady long enough for the building of a house, a bridge, or a ship. Indeed, you must have a world of dependable and sure relationships if you are to have any permanent structure in any region whatever. You must have necessity for freedom to control. You must have freedom to do the controlling. Intelligent action is thus always at the point where freedom and necessity meet.

But the world of mechanical and mathematical reaction can never provide the controller. It is a subhuman world and waits for the master hand of a free intelligence which it is unable to create. There is here a difference in quality which no addition of quantity can obviate. If you add together a million impersonal reactions according to mechanical laws, you will never get one act of freedom, and most especially you will never get one free agent capable of acting consciously on the world of necessity. Here is a necessary dualism, demanded, not by speculation, but by the facts of existence and by the facts of life. And if we ever rise from this dualism to a higher unity, it must be on the basis of free and conscious intelligence establishing order, and not on the basis of impersonal uniformities in some mysterious fashion secreting freedom. The controller and the controlled belong to two orders of existence. And the material which is to be controlled cannot create the free intelligence which is to do the controlling.

When the human controller arrives, he may play strange tricks with his own mind. He may become so obsessed by the uniformities he is controlling that he ceases to believe in himself as the controller. This is a veritable travesty. It is the complete abdication of intelligence. It is probably the ultimate jest about men at which the angels laugh. The clear thinker—who is always a humanistic thinker—perpetually keeps in mind the free intelligence which does the controlling, as well as the subhuman level of existence which is subject to this control.

The second characteristic feature which emerges in the world below the human is appetite. The world of appetite exists quite apart from intelligence. It is found wherever there is life. It is found in all animate creation. Here there is vivid and vital and dramatically energetic impulse. Here are hunger and thirst and all the biological desires. Here are pleasure and pain and all the life of sensation. Here is a region controlled by the laws of instinct among animals. Here is a region especially subject to rational control when once free intelligence has arrived.

It is very important to see that every appetite has a wholesome and fruitful place. The world of appetite is not in itself an evil world, though with the misuse of appetite it may become a lawless world. For every appetite can in one way or another take the bit in its teeth. The very presence of rational control over appetite makes the difference between savagery and civilization. When reason surrenders to impulse, when intelligence surrenders to appetite, you have the great capitulation. At this point we can see in a new way both the strategy and the possible menace of the human position. The possession of free intelligence opens the way to heights undreamed of before. It also opens the way to depths to which an animal could not descend. So it comes to pass that man is either more or less than the beast.

153

For when he puts his appetite on the throne, he becomes not only subhuman but subbestial. When you say to an abandoned sensualist, "You are a beast," you are insulting the beast. For a beast simply obeys his instincts. He does not use intelligence to betray his nature. When a man turns from the path of noble control in the light of reason, he actually begins to use his free intelligence for the purpose of gratifying urges which have now become completely lawless. He betrays not only his body, but also his mind. For he uses his mind for a more subtle and tragic betrayal of his body. So perhaps we actually need a fourth level—the subbestial—in order to classify properly the men who use their intelligence to betray their humanity.

Civilization is always threatened by the invasion of subhuman appetites. And curiously—yet naturally—enough, these invasions always masquerade as movements of emancipation, and their leaders set themselves up as apostles of a new freedom. The situation is complicated by the fact that when men's loyalty to high standards becomes formal and perfunctory, the very words which describe these standards suffer a psychological depreciation. They become formal and artificial. And when the natural instincts rush into this vacuum, they seem particularly vital. For the moment, they seem to have the breath of life, even if it is not the life which is life indeed. I suppose this is what Robert Browning is trying to say in that much discussed poem "The Statue and the Bust" when he condemns the "frustrate ghosts" who did not have enough personal energy to be vicious with virility and whose loyalty to a code—even if a correct code—was quite artificial and empty of any vital meaning whatever. An age which has ceased to glory in its humanity and to rejoice in the human sanctions with vital and virile energy

154

is always waiting unconsciously to be pounced upon by lawless lusts. Obedience is not enough. Only vital and glowing obedience saves morality from dull frustration. And
so it comes about that in an age of formal and artificial
loyalty to high standards the apostle of the lawless following of natural instincts can always use the brave and good
word *sincerity* to describe his position. An unblushing response to impulse, he declares with great plausibility, is more
sincere than an artificial loyalty to what he calls conventional standards. But going to a subhuman level in order to be
sincere only means that one has actually repudiated that life
on a human level which would make loyalty to high standards the only true sincerity. Sincerity consists in actually
being what you are in intent. And if what you are is low
and cunning and morally chaotic, there is not much real
dignity in calling your surrender to the behests of this manifold of evil intent by the noble name of sincerity. There
may be a higher self within you waiting to speak. And if
you listened to its voice you might find another sort of sincerity. On close inspection it will never be discovered that
a betrayal of one's humanity in the name of subhuman impulses is a form of true sincerity. It is always a pity when
men disguise the beginnings of moral slavery as a subtle
form of spiritual emancipation. That men should feel a
spacious sense of freedom at the very moment when they
are fastening the chains upon their wrists represents a particularly ugly part of the human tragedy.

But there is another matter which gives the whole situation an almost bizarre complication. As we shall see very
clearly, it is man's true nature as a relative and finite being
to surrender to something other than himself. The psychology of surrender is a part of man's true life. But here again

155

is a great divide. For he may surrender to that which is higher than himself, or he may surrender to that which is lower than himself. And just because he is made for surrender and the psychological act of surrender corresponds to the necessities of his nature, the surrender to the lower gives a pseudo satisfaction just as the surrender to the higher produces a true satisfaction. A man has a curious and deceptive sense of fulfillment in vice just as he has a true and permanent sense of fulfillment in joyous and triumphant virtue. This accounts for the pseudo spirituality which characterizes certain vices. It may account for the wide-spread practice of sacred prostitution in the unethical naturalistic religions. It may have been a contrast in the thought of Saint Paul when he wrote a sentence which we may paraphrase in the words "Be not filled with intoxicating spirits, but be filled with the spirit of God." For the last fascination of over-indulgence in strong drink is its momentary sense of spiritual emancipation.

In all this we see that the subhuman world of appetite may be made the basis of the misuse of the human and of the prostitution of the divine. All the literature of surrender to the senses is a glorification of the lawless elements of the subhuman. Novels and plays and moving pictures without number vividly express the glow of sensation which comes from the great surrender. When men have become incapable of the delicate and highly integrated mirth of the mind they still respond to the vicarious glow of the life of the senses.

One aspect of the autocracy of the subhuman was expressed in Mrs. Shelley's *Frankenstein,* the tale of a creature constructed by man becoming a giant to make his creator his slave. When Juvenal told the tale of Roman decadence, he was making the victory of the subhuman not the basis of a work of fancy but the substance for an analysis of social conditions in a world which was losing its mind and its soul. Mourning does indeed become Electra when intelligence surrenders to undisciplined sensation. And it is a matter deserving profound meditation and deep analysis that this new Electra—this ultimate study of surrender to the subhuman—should have come from the United States of America.

But this chapter simply cannot close upon this note of realistic pessimism, important as this attitude may be. For it is the business of the humanist not to bury the subhuman under a wave of vituperative words, but to praise it when it holds its proper place and functions according to the true meaning of its own nature. The fact that chemicals may be used to make poison gases ought not to cloud our remembrance of the other fact, that chemicals may be so used as to make the desert blossom as a rose. It is more than a piece of happy symbolism that in the Genesis stories when God has created the subhuman world He calls it *good*. It cannot be too urgently said that only the misuse of the subhuman is evil. The world of things in almost incredible ways may be made the servant of a bright intelligence which moves like quicksilver through the realm of things turning them to its own purposes. And it cannot be too urgently said that all the biological impulses have their place in the good life. Life is meant to be a productive garden, and the true outcome of Eden would have been the casting out of the serpent and the leaving of the man and the woman among the fruitful trees. And even here, something needs to be said which we can say in the language of the Eden story. For the tragedy of Eden was not merely the presence of the ser-

157

pent in the garden.  It was the presence in the mind of the human creatures in the garden of subtle serpents which would whisper affirmative response to the suggestion of the serpent among the trees.  It is the serpent within which gives power to the serpent without.  It is when we corrupt our human intelligence that we surrender to the enticements of the lawless aspects of the subhuman world.  The gibe of FitzGerald's Omar Khayyám at the creator who with the garden provided the snake is a rather weak bit of blasphemy against a creator who could give free intelligence only by the gift of "either—or," who could make possible the victory of moral good only by making possible the surrender to moral evil.  In the last analysis it may well turn out that it is the corrupt mind which brutalizes the helpless body.

So the humanist looks out on his world with a profound sense that in its essence it is good.  The world of things is gloriously good if turned to right uses.  The world of impulses is good if held in loyalty to noble purposes.  To surrender to the subhuman is to turn that which was meant for good to purposes of evil.  And the secret of this great betrayal is found in human personality itself.

## CHAPTER XIII

## *The Human*

IT IS ONE OF THE CURIOUS ASPECTS OF THIS VERY BIZARRE AGE in which we live that it is rather difficult to command an intelligent hearing when you discuss the specifically human aspects of the life of man. Psychology over very large areas has become simply a form of physiology. It studies the aspects of physical and nervous reaction which parallel mental activity rather than the mental activity itself. It is as if one contented oneself with studying the construction of a typewriter and never tried to find the meaning of the letter which had been typed on the machine, and never lifted any question about the intelligence which composed the letter. We probably know more about the typewriters the intelligence uses than has been known by men of any other time. But we know sadly little about the intelligence.

When psychology becomes behaviorism, it inspects activities rather than rational causes; and when it places these activities in the extraordinary energy of certain glands, it quietly slips into the glands the powerful intelligence whose qualities it has never really inspected. One of the outstanding exponents of behaviorism has declared in effect that if "we" really understood the laws of glandular activity, we could do what we would with men. He—like his confreres —keeps using pronouns which have meanings for which his own system finds no place, indeed, meanings which on the basis of his own system would be impossible. What reality —what actuality of any sort—does he indicate by the "we" who discover the laws of glandular activity, who classify them, and who use them? Are there some wise old glands who possess this extraordinary power? And if they have this free and decisive intelligence, have they not already passed far beyond those formulas of impersonal action which constitute the be-all of human activity for the behaviorist?

When the *Gestalt* psychology appears, we hear of totals, of a certain togetherness which seems to promise more than behaviorism could offer. But even here the study and the results are on the physical and not the mental side. The illustrations are likely to be from the region of electrical fields, and you have something like a physical shadow cast by mental action rather than the action itself. You never cross the great divide and behold the work of free intelligence. The students of the subconscious, by definition, are occupied with a study of the regions where the mind is not aware of its own activity. They have what amounts almost to a positive dislike of those regions where intelligence emerges into clear consciousness. The Freudians plunge into a study of psychology with a fascinated obsession in respect of sex. One biological impulse on the subhuman level is made the clue to every essential meaning of human life. We fully expect that one of these days an illuminated Freudian will triumphantly demonstrate that the multiplication table was discovered in the midst of some very subtle and vivid sexual experience.

These various attempts to confine the study of psychology to the mechanical reactions of the thing or the rush of biological impulses have settled down like a fog over the activities of clear intelligence in our time. That we have learned a great deal of real importance in many areas from these long and devoted studies of the subhuman aspects of human experience no competent thinker would wish to deny. We have learned much about the organism man uses in his activities. And we have learned much about the fashion in which the body plays along with the mind. But we have learned very little about that free and controlling intelligence which is the characteristic human activity. And when the various groups of physiological psychologists have declared—as they so often do—that the whole reality about human life is to be found on the physiological side, they have actually prevented their students from investigating the processes of free intelligence. To paraphrase a sentence of Samuel Butler and to use it in a connection which he did not have in mind when he coined its phrases: They have not been content to put blinkers on the eyes of their disciples, but they have actually attempted to gouge out their eyes.

Of course these various forms of physiological psychology have had their ups and downs, and particularly eccentric obsessions have been completely discredited. But the situation has been complicated by the fact that many men of letters whose minds were already dulled by the processes of decadent thought have rushed in to make physiological psychology the basis of their writing, with no profound understanding of its activities, its true service, or its very great limitations. Theodore Dreiser has written powerfully, as in *The American Tragedy,* of people whose mental activities were only the shadows of their physical desires. Thomas Hardy in *The Dynasts* made a mental map of Europe where the reader found everything but free and responsible minds. D. H. Lawrence walked in strange dark paths of the instincts and the biological desires to find substitutes for the clear rational intelligence in which he had ceased to believe.

On page after page of the ninth and tenth volumes of Ernest Baker's *History of the English Novel* you will find reflections of this preoccupation with the subhuman and the decadent, this turning away from the rational. And, curiously enough, Professor Baker gives no indication that he understands the source or the nature of the problems which these novels present. Aldous Huxley is likely to plunge into an ocean of slime and busily occupy his distinguished mind with the analysis of its component parts, and urgently push his potent pen in the making of hard and brittle sentences in which to tell the tale of what he has found. Then he emerges and casts fascinated eyes at the far shining of the bright stars. His hands, however, are still full of the slime. But he is not quite "Eyeless in Gaza."

These are only a few of the ways in which the preoccupation with mental bypaths—so often roads to Avernus—in our time has made the clear and cool and understanding study of free intelligence very difficult.

We have used our intelligence to glorify appetite. We have used our intelligence to study the body, and have turned its bright light away from the mind. We have even used our intelligence to deny the existence of intelligence itself. The second great level of existence—the human—has been almost forgotten. So man in the most amazing ways has betrayed his humanity. It is high time that our minds were turned to a study of the distinctively and specifically human.

We have already had occasion to see that with the arrival of controlling intelligence the world of things suddenly reveals new possibilities. From the first boat made from the trunk of a tree to the greatest ocean liner, from the first use of wheels to the most complicated machinery, from the bending of the wind to human purpose on through the use of steam and electricity and the control of radio activity, the world of things and forces finds its master in the controlling intelligence of man. It is at this point, too, that man becomes the master of appetite and not its slave. The taking of the most primitive urges and the turning of these rushing energies to the higher purposes of creative art—the achievements of poetry and painting and sculpture and architecture and music—all reveal at every point the action of the controlling intelligence of man bending the subhuman to the purposes of the human. The sublimation of biological impulse on the higher levels of moral loyalty and spiritual experience reveals the free mind using the raw materials of sense for the building of the palace of the soul of man. The world of things and the world of appetites belong to the realm over which critical human intelligence is to rule. They find their significance and their ultimate happy place in the great system of existence under this higher lordship. The subhuman finds its meaning and its goal in the human.

It is for this reason that those philosophies which deny the free action of creative intelligence represent not only a failure in insight, but a positive menace to the mental and moral and aesthetic and spiritual and social life of mankind. There is nothing in man's mental life which remains if free-moving intelligence goes. There is nothing in man's moral life which remains if free-moving intelligence goes. Art and literature receive their death blow. For art is freedom making beauty where there might have been ugliness. And literature is freedom weaving words into forms of immortal meaning and harmony. If free intelligence goes, society becomes a collection of determined automata instead of a fellowship of living spirits united in liberty. If free intelligence goes, the subhuman remains inert with no realization of its inherent possibilities. The rush of biological impulse and the call of appetite feel the summons of no goals beyond their own satisfaction. The higher has capitulated to the lower. And life has lost its meaning.

The reply comes back triumphantly that nothing like this has happened. Indeed, the opposite has happened. Things have been controlled by mind. Appetite has been controlled by reason. Men have made high choices under the summons of lofty standards. Masses of men may have taken the lower way. But the men who have given meaning to life and who have made history have taken the higher. You simply cannot successfully deny the possibility of that free control which has been in action for centuries. All denials of the humanistic sanctions can be only verbal. There are too many facts—millions on millions of facts—on the other side. The denial of freedom can never be real. It can consist only of the clever and uncritical juggling of phrases which have lost their contact with actuality.

But it is most important to see these things clearly. Verbal denials can do no end of harm to uncritical minds if men do not see of what essential nonsense these denials are made. The banner of free and controlling intelligence is the one true and important banner for the civilized life of mankind.

We are ready now for a form of words which will express the characteristic quality of life on the second level—which will define the distinctive meaning of the human. You find the human in that functioning of man in which he uses intelligence to choose among alternatives in the light of standards in order to control his world of thought and his world of action, and turn the world of things to his own purposes.

164

## The Human

Man is an agent who uses a free mind to control his thoughts and his deeds and determines this control in the light of standards which he uses as the basis of his judgments. At its highest the human is *critical* intelligence choosing among alternatives in the light of *permanent* standards. Man can be king over nature because he is free. Man is the lord of creation because he can understand. He is master of his world because he can turn free thought into free action.

Whenever you approach human life from the side of free and controlling intelligence, you lift it to the level of its true meanings and its characteristic values. Whenever you approach it from the side of its subhuman constituents, you lower its quality and at last quite rob it of meaning. Man's great cause is his freedom. And the central matter in freedom is uncoerced choice.

Now this choice, as we have already seen, may be used gloriously. And it may be used tragically. And here we come upon the tremendous importance of dependable standards upon the basis of which human choices may be made. If man's great cause is the cause of freedom, the great quest of his mind is the quest for standards. And a civilization is judged by the quality of standards offered to human beings who are poised for choice.

Physics tells the tale of mechanical reactions on the level of impersonal mathematics. Biology tells the tale of satisfactions on the level of appetite which all together secure the ongoing of physical life. Human history is the story of millions of experiments in the use of freedom. It tells the story of the testing of possible standards in the world of action. Its highest gift to man is a series of impeccable standards for the civilized life. It is a characteristic of these standards that as long as they are used with a free and joyous appreciation of their true meaning, they are glorious and up-building things, and when they are used with artificial and mechanical loyalty without true understanding of their meaning, they turn hard and rigid. A man may betray his humanity by refusal to use standards. So he turns his freedom into anarchy. He may betray his humanity by the use of bad standards. So at last he turns his freedom into slavery. He may betray his humanity by a bad use of good standards. So he comes to have the husk without the essence of the good life. To be a human being is a complex and dangerous business.

The man of true culture is the man who has the most complete and critical knowledge of the centuries of experimentation by means of which men have tried to find dependable standards. He knows the tragic experiences by means of which bad standards have been revealed in their true quality. He knows the notable and rich experiences by means of which true standards have stood forth in their essential genius. He is a man who knows the whole tale of what man has done with his freedom. And so he has come to have some genuine understanding as to what he ought to do with his own. The true university is the university of experience.

The studies of the materials man uses have of course a very great importance. The laws by which things react and the impulses which move through the biological world are matters with which man has to do every day. The more he knows of them, the better. Hence the importance of the physical and the biological sciences. But a man may be an expert on any or a competent person in many of the physical and biological sciences and still be an early adolescent in the study and understanding of the essentially human dis-

cipline—the study of man's choices—the study of what man
has done with his freedom. To be sure, a very highly trained
and sophisticated scientist may study either physics or biology as an aspect of man's use of his freedom, keeping the
free mind of the scientist in thought all the while, and so
making his study of the natural sciences a humanistic study.
At their best, Whitehead and Eddington have done this.
But it must be confessed that these are hard trails for the
scientific mind. Most scientists are content to inspect the
uniformities which the free mind studies and to forget to
inspect the processes of the free mind as it studies these uniformities.

At all events, the characteristic humanistic studies have to
do with a direct inspection of what man has done with his
freedom, with the freedom kept in mind perpetually. Here
history—the study of mankind in the large—and biography
—a study of mankind in the small—and literature—a study
of man's fashions of turning his experiences and his dreams
into the music of gracious and, if possible, of immortal
speech—are especially grist to the humanist's mill. When
philosophy rises to the level of an adequate appreciation of
the personal and an adequate criticism of the impersonal—it
is a notable discipline indeed. And as we shall see later,
the consummation of humanism is found in an adequate
theology.

We see, then, that living on the second level is by no
means a light matter. It is so easy to slip back into the level
of things. It is so easy to drop to the level of undisciplined
impulses. It is so easy to follow false loyalties. It is so easy
to become mechanical and artificial in one's loyalty to true
standards and to lose the free splendor of the life of perpetually joyous allegiance to truly creative standards. So

167

the humanist is quite likely to be a provocative person. He is a provocative person because he realizes how much is at stake. He does not tolerate fools gladly. And least of all does he tolerate gladly the folly which he finds in his own mind and heart.

If, like Socrates, he feels that he is something of a midwife assisting at the birth of a new intellectual life, he expects birth pangs, and he is ready to be patient for the sake of the birth. Only in this case the figure is absurdly incomplete. For this is a situation where the midwife has some of the worst pangs!

The training of a man to use his humanity is an endless task. He may begin anywhere. He attains a constantly more complete picture of the human adventure with standards. He himself attains a surer and surer grip upon dependable standards. But, like Tennyson's Ulysses, he is ready for new adventures even as the heaviness of age settles down upon him. He can say with the Latin poet Terence—to use one's own paraphrase—"All that concerns humanity has to do with me."

Suppose our young humanist picks up Quintilian's *Institutio oratoria*. Here he finds first of all a tremendous concern with human speech—just because it deals with methods of influencing human judgment. Here the mind of the man you would like to influence and your own mind working to influence the mind of another are constantly kept before the view of the writer and your own thought as you read what he has written. There is warning as well as guidance in it. For sometimes Quintilian makes suggestions at which your moral judgment draws back. He sometimes illustrates the misuse of human powers even as he usually offers himself as a guide to their wise and reasonable use. But he belongs

168

clearly to a world of men, knowing in what lies man's distinctive power, and very well understanding that the use of that power is the real business of life.

The young student may pick up any characteristic work of Cicero—perhaps the greatest humanist of the Latins. Here again he finds that he is not moving in a world of things. He is moving in a world of people. Agile, brilliant minds are in action all the while. There is truth to discuss, and there are free minds to discuss it. There are right courses of action. And there is brilliant and convincing advocacy of these right ways of action in powerful speech.

The student may go with Cicero to the Athens where he studied. He will not be content until he walks about the streets of the Greek city with the ironic, genial, deadly Socrates. For Socrates had only one concern. He wanted to find out how men used their minds. He wanted to teach them how to use their minds in the right way. From Socrates our student may go to Thucydides, and in clear and deadly words hear the tale of how Athens fell because it turned its mind to the usage of false principles. So forward and backward he may go—always selecting books with a clear sense of critical intelligence as his guide and selecting books whose counsel is darkened in respect of these matters for the use of his own critical teeth. He may see Alexander the Great with the mind Aristotle had given him and the body of an oversensual Oriental potentate. So once more he will realize that life's business is just the terrible choice. By a quick and dizzy journey he may come to the new little republic in America and watch the authors of *The Federalist* as they attempt to set forth principles worthy and trustworthy for the life of a state of free men. He may watch liberty play with license after the fall of the Bastille in France. He may watch the benevolent despots of the eighteenth century—Frederick the Great, Joseph II of Austria, and the others—trying to give the good life without freedom, and leaving the world to learn that there is no good life which is not free. He may read play after play of Shakespeare and find a sense of moral values so keen that the man Ben Jonson loved never needs to tell you that he has a sense of ethical meanings. He may find Goethe living at the place where reason and impulse meet in confusing and baffling fashion, never quite solving the puzzle of his own thought and his own life, often gloriously on the side of the angels, and dying with the symbolic cry for "more light." All about the world he may go, seeing freedom nobly used and freedom betrayed, intelligence busily set about great tasks of penetrating thought, and intelligence abdicating its own throne in an obsession of delight in slavery. And thus, year by year, in the laboratory of life itself he will discover the meaning of manhood, he will find the secret of humanity, and so at last he will become a civilized man holding his head high, whatever the barbarities of the world. And he will find in living experience some great words: truth, honesty, justice, goodness, good will, self-control, beauty, harmony. And each word will enshrine the insight in respect of a permanent standard wrought out in the history of humanity itself.

## CHAPTER XIV

### Nontheistic Humanism

No CRITICAL THINKER WILL ATTEMPT TO DAMN A GROUP WITH an epithet. Even when condemnation is deserved, it must be justified by clear and cogent reasoning. The epithet must be seen to represent the conclusion of an argument, and not a rhetorical substitute for thought. Furthermore, groups of serious thinkers have a way of being gloriously right in some of their positions while they are demonstrably wrong in others. Such a word as "atheist" is a very interesting covering term, but it may easily represent an explosion of emotions rather than a conclusion reached through processes of patient analysis. So we should approach the study of the nontheistic humanists with some circumspection and with an endeavor to see just how they came to be.

The various companies of men bearing the name Unitarian have had a distinguished history and have made very important contributions to Christian thought and life. They have been unabashed individualists and have differed most widely among themselves. Sometimes they have been the unhesitating critics of orthodox thinking who have tended to live by means of their brilliant negations. Sometimes they have had a lofty and positive spirituality of their own, as was so magnificently the case with William E. Channing. Always they have had a deep sense of the obligations of personal character and of the demands of public responsibility. Perhaps their greatest contributions have been to Christian ethics rather than to Christian theology. They have usually

171

been proud of belonging to the advance guard of the adventurous thinkers of the period in which they have lived. Sometimes they have been betrayed by this ambition into making the assumption that the new is necessarily the true. They have been particularly responsive to all the adumbrations of scientific thought, and have sometimes mistaken pseudo science for the science which is truly so called. On the other hand, from within their groups have come clear and unhesitating critics of the obsessions of contemporary thought. And there have even been leaders whose emancipation was so complete that they were ready to consider the truth which might lie embedded with what they believed to be the confusions and the falsehoods of orthodoxy. So it has come to pass that at present you may find among the professors of the Unitarian faith the greatest variety of belief. On the extreme left are those who have ceased to believe in a personal God. On the extreme right are those who are not only avowed theists, but also men of eager evangelical passion.

It is the group at the extreme left which must now engross our attention. In the vivid days of post-Victorian science, before the rise of the new physics, many men came to feel that the universe is a watertight system of impersonal necessity with no room for freedom anywhere. God was politely bowed out of a universe which had no room for Him. The free man dominating circumstances through the power of a conscious decision which had destiny at the heart of it rather quickly followed the personal conscious deity. The guiding wheels of hard necessity alone were left in a depleted universe.

Now thinkers who follow such trails are never consistent. Of course, any sort of unhesitating and honest logic would have left no place for the values which can exist only in a world of free choices. But men are actually so constituted that they cannot give up the values. And as a matter of fact—however illogical that fact may be—the values are here. They have emerged without asking anybody's permission. And they do a thriving business, whatever philosophy of life sits on the throne of men's minds. The presence of values—especially human values—in a determined world presented acute problems to a group of daring and radical Unitarian thinkers. Perhaps they had been more ready to make a god of science than to construct a science of God. At all events, they accepted the nontheistic interpretation of science without hesitation. Indeed, they triumphantly affirmed it. But they had no idea of giving up the values which had given glory to life. So this group of left-wing Unitarians set about a process of interpreting life in which the human values would be conserved in a godless and inhuman world. They were very sincere. They were very earnest. They were sure that they represented the advance guard of sophisticated thinking in a world from which the conscious deity had departed, and in which mathematical interaction was the all-inclusive characteristic of reality. If God has gone, they declared in effect, man remains. And religion emancipated from historic dogmas must consist in the high endeavor to preserve, and indeed enthrone, human values in a nontheistic world. And since the determining factor in all their endeavor was a human factor, and the goal was an essentially human goal, quite righteously they grasped the word humanism and claimed it as their own. They were the true humanists of a scientific age.

Thus it has come about, curiously enough, that in religious circles in the United States when the word humanist

173

is used, it is usually with reference to this little group of thinkers who have ceased to believe in a personal God, most of whom believe in a mechanistic and watertight system of impersonal relationships as embracing all of reality, and who, despite these positions, desire to preserve the humanistic values. These thinkers, however sincere and earnest they may be, and however excellent in personal character and often in public service, are obviously quite outside the central stream of historic humanism. They have turned to their own uses a word which century after century has had quite other meanings. A typical European thinker would be astonished and puzzled to find the word he knows so well turned to the rather narrow uses of their particular pattern. One is not surprised to find that Irving Babbitt spoke with something little short of scorn of this attempt to bend the great word humanism to uses so foreign to the genius of its own nature and of its own history. The truth is that many American thinkers have failed to keep the great stream of Western culture moving in their minds and glowing in their imagination. And so we find it possible now and then to fasten upon great old words a significance before which a more cultivated intelligence would hesitate. Erasmus would have repudiated very quickly the thought that the nontheistic humanists could be considered in any sense his intellectual descendants.

We have seen, however, something of the fashion in which they came to their position, and something of the fashion in which they fell upon the name. That they represent a definite and important tendency in contemporary thought is clear enough. That position must be met and dealt with in very serious fashion. At the moment we are saying only that it is rather a pity that the word humanism

174

should have been connected with intellectual positions so foreign to its own nature and history.

But we must move out to see the whole situation in much larger relations. A significant circle of men belonging to the most various schools of thought and to no schools of thought at all found belief in a conscious God with clearly held purposes and clearly moving volition impossible. They had various attitudes toward the experience which remained in a godless world. But this they had in common. They desired to secure the good life in the world in which they found themselves. Sometimes they were in the historic Christian churches. Here they found themselves in odd and fascinating intellectual straits. If they gave up the word God they must give up their churches. The last thing they were willing to do was to give up the regal strength of organized religion. Some of them, indeed, received salaries from endowed schools founded to perpetuate the tenets of historic Christianity. So the dilemma had some ethical as well as many intellectual aspects. Besides, they very much liked the emotional richness of the word God, if they did feel that they had difficulty with its intellectual content. So they set about the construction of an intellectual usage in respect of the word God which corresponded to their own thought. They did not destroy the word God. They transformed it. A historic thinker would say that they emasculated it. God was now a word used to describe the total human experience which had to do with ideal realms of thought and action. God was the total idealistic experience of the race in its impact upon the life of any generation. He was the sublimest spiritual abstraction of human thought. He was as real as men's hopes. He was as real as men's dreams. He was as real as man's best life. He was man's

175

own idealism turning back upon him with imperial force. Such a God was not a personal intelligence to whom you could pray. Prayer was your communion with your own ideals and the best ideals of the human race. He was not a great companion with whom you could have fellowship. He was your own ideals turned into a deity by the legerdemain of a powerful figure of speech. Such a method of thought enabled leaders in historic churches to use the old words by putting new and different meanings into them, and to set about utterly changing the nature of the church without changing its vocabulary. It was infinitely skillful. It was infinitely adroit. And in the terms of the left-wing type of thought, it carried with it certain humanistic sanctions. Sometimes it seemed to be surprisingly successful. But the broken heart crying in the night was likely to lift a cry to which the minister of the emasculated God could find no answer. For when in dark hours you cry for help to your own beautiful ideals and the beautiful ideals of the race, there comes back to you only an impotent echo.

Many of those who wanted to secure the good life in a godless world had no relation to the historic Christian churches or to organized religion. They snatched precariously at human values in a world which seemed hostile enough to these very values. Usually they refused to follow their own logic to its true conclusion, and tried to believe that the world has a place for the distinctive life of man. Sometimes they were as honest as Joseph Wood Krutch and admitted that human beings would forever be aliens in the world in which they found themselves. But very bravely—sometimes with an almost breath-taking courage—they clung to the good life in a difficult world. One must admit that they were morally splendid, whatever one

176

has to say of the fashion in which they used their minds. In a world of confused thought they clung to whatever was of good report in the life of humanity. They lifted the human flag with their conscience if they did not lift it with their intelligence.

That all the various types of people involved in the attempt to procure and preserve a sense of human values on the part of those who found it impossible to believe in a personal God offered a halfway house to confused people in a difficult period we need not deny. Indeed, we are ready quite eagerly to affirm it. And in the greatest variety of practical ways these dwellers in halfway houses are our friends as we fight the human battles and apply ourselves to the human tasks. Their lives are gloriously better than their logic. And we rejoice and are glad as we think of their lives.

But in all honesty we must admit that there is no place for values in the universe in which these thinkers believe. And in the long run, they themselves cannot avoid the issues of the dilemma in which they find themselves. The implicit logic of the situation always drives such thinkers to a place where they believe more, or to a place where they believe less. They cannot remain static in their world of self-contradiction. On the one hand they move to a place where they accept a view of the universe which makes an honest place for conscious and self-directing intelligence, or they come to the place where they see that it is idle to talk of values in the universe in which they have come to believe. Men who live in houses built right over the great divide have a way for a while of thinking that they can make the most of both regions of thought. But in another sense than the poet meant, East is East and West is West, and sooner or later the thinker living over the great divide must make his choice.

The matter is, of course, complicated by the fact that in our time most people have no intellectual pattern at all. And the temporary advantage of the man who has thoughts rather than thought, who has bright ideas rather than a coherent corpus of harmonious conceptions, is just that he can pick a thought here and a thought there, using each while it pleases him, and having no sense of that intellectual stultification which comes when one is conscious of the contradictions which lie coiling at the center of what one is pleased to call one's thought.

To take an illustration from another field, it is most interesting in reading the ten volumes of Ernest Baker's *History of the English Novel* to watch the author doing work of meticulous skill in detail, but never rising to the height of really first-class criticism, just because he has no pattern of thought. He very easily assumes in one chapter what just as easily he implicitly denies in another as he follows the fluctuations of literary habit and literary conviction. There is a certain hearty hospitality about it all. And this hospitality is made all the easier precisely because the author of this massive work has no stern principles which give a dependable frame to a great house of thought. It all makes him very comfortable. But in the higher regions of thought it makes him very uncritical.

Even more clear is all this in the puckish and irresponsible wit which moves like quicksilver through the writings of Samuel Butler. It is very difficult for him to hold to an insight long enough to get any very coherent sense of its implications. He is all the while changing his base. He is all the while changing his implicit assump-

178

tions. So one minute he is surprisingly on the side of the angels. And the next minute he is as surprisingly on the side of the devils. He is a most brilliant and provocative thinker. And if you go into the jungle of his thought and cut out a clearing and kill the serpents and keep the wild beasts at bay, you can build quite a comfortable house. But it will be wise for you to keep the fire of your intelligence burning brightly beside the house as darkness comes on. The wild beasts will be prowling about. And you can hear their cry in the night.

We live in an age when to many people the vital is the patternless. They are afraid of patterns. For patterns would cramp their style. They do not want to listen to the demand that they should be coherent. For coherent thought works sad havoc with their favorite fallacies. And as long as we have patternless thought we will have endless cities of halfway houses which mistake themselves for cities of journey's end. In such a world it is easy for a time to fight valiantly for the human values in a determined world.

But it is well to scrutinize the scientific situation in respect of these matters. For it has never been a true science, but rather a mechanistic philosophy of science, which has driven men to such positions as those which we have been discussing. A more critical view of the relation of the facts which science inspects to the whole body of reality, and especially a more critical inspection of the free intelligence of the scientist at his work, would have cleared the air long ago. For a penetrating study of science reveals free intelligence dealing with necessary relationships. It does not reveal necessary relationships crushing the life out of freedom. If you have as much freedom as the scientist must have to do his work, you have all the freedom necessary for morals and for religion along the classical lines. Then the new physics has confronted men with a whole body of facts which simply will not fit into the old comfortable mechanistic scheme. Really, the pseudo humanist, as far as he speaks as a man of religion, is all the while trying to reconcile religion with a science which has ceased to exist. As science becomes more critical of its own processes, it leaves open more and more doors which look out in the direction of classical religion. And so far as baffled practical thinkers are trying to maintain the good life in the old determined world whose hard mechanism they have accepted, they are simply fighting dark phantoms which disappear in the clear sunlight of consistent thought. It is not surprising that when pseudo religion unites with pseudo science to produce an interpretation of life, the result is incoherent, and on any critical inspection is seen to be torn by inner contradictions. The great word humanism was not forged in the mind of man for such uses as these.

However, it is well to remember that while we have all the right in the world to call the nontheistic humanist to stern intellectual account, our words of grim analysis of his position are not to be taken as words of moral condemnation. We are not attacking his motives. We are not attacking his character. And we are not denying that he has rendered and is rendering an important service in the world.

The truth is that once you have seen the central fallacy of a position, you are at full liberty to recognize its incidental contribution. Human thought does not leap from perfect syllogism to perfect syllogism as a stag might leap from crag to crag. Much of it is conducted by a pragmatic process of trial and error. And in this process crumbs of truth find themselves deposited in the most astonishing places.

The isolating of human values from a complete pattern of thought and the very attempt to hold them in a scheme which has contradicted their essential nature has been a profoundly significant psychological experience. And in the processes often these values have stood out in a stark reality which has given them a surprising clarity of outline. The inconsistent humanist does not come to the end of the harvest time without sheaves in his hands, even if he has found these sheaves in an alien soil.

The critical humanist must be willing constantly to do business with men who are with him practically, and to do business with them long before they have clarified the processes of their thought to conform to his own true patterns. This is only to say that the man who has reached the goal can afford to exercise all sorts of patience with men who have taken curious paths while they are on the way. This combination of psychological patience with intellectual sternness is, one likes to believe, a characteristic quality of the truly critical humanist.

At all events, those of every school of thought who hate tyranny and despise injustice, who despise the very thought of a life below the human level for any of the children of men, who would make the world a better place for the last and the lowest and the least, as well as a world which gives ample opportunity to those of the highest gifts—those can make common cause in no end of battles which man fights for his manhood in this difficult world. It is a gracious thing that so many men live lives which are better

181

than their theories, and have a logic for action which is much more dependable than the logic of their thought.

In the long run the right logic will secure the right of way. We do well to remember the young materialistic physician in the clever novel *Those About Trench.* He lived in a world which, as he thought, consisted only of physical and chemical reactions. He found it difficult to enjoy the beauty of the face of the girl he loved because he was always making a mental analysis of the color pigments which made up that beauty and the impersonal processes which produced it. He could analyze even the chemistry of a blush. But as time went on he discovered—and this discovery is the substance of the book—that whenever anything important happened, he had to call in qualities which his theory of the universe denied. It was inevitable that sooner or later he would lift the question as to whether it would not be wise to enlarge his universe so that it would be possible for it to include his most characteristic actions.

Sooner or later the nontheistic humanist—or his son or his grandson—will discover that the facts of life simply cannot be included in the small impersonal pattern which he has made for them. First he will face the personality which is human—that constant activity of free and controlling intelligence which gives meaning to the life of this world. He will have to enlarge his pattern of the universe to include these great and indisputable human facts. And once he has broken his old materialistic pattern and has remade it to this extent, great things will begin to happen. Freedom—intelligence—control: these are great words which demand great areas of action. They sweep beyond the human until at last they include the divine. And so the nontheistic humanist will come to his greatest day when at last he sees that his eyes, which have been turned away from God, must turn Godward if the area of his intelligence is to become as large as the area of his life. So the grim denial will be transformed into the great affirmation.

## CHAPTER XV

### The Third Level

ONE OF THE CHARACTERISTIC INSTITUTIONS OF THE FASCINAT-
ing age of Louis XIV in France was a pulpit which, on its
less lofty levels, had qualities of artificiality, as we have seen,
but at its best had qualities of transcending power. In
intellectual acumen, in moral energy, in spiritual dignity,
and in certain royal splendor of expression the great preachers of the period were princes in their own right. A typical
example of an experience where some austere majesty of
the timeless was made real in time is found at the funeral
of Louis XIV in Notre Dame. The cathedral was decorated
as if it had been turned into a mighty pall to rest over the
body of the great king. And the burning glow of the
candles seemed to tell strange secrets of that life which
burns brightly only when it is in process of being consumed.
Beauty and social distinction and high rank and political
power had crowded the cathedral with a company of men
and women who might well be regarded as the microcosm
of the glory of European life. All the pomp and circum-
stance of a richly embroidered age gathered to do honor
to the king who had been the epitome of its grace and the
symbol of its power. The body of the king lay splendid in
rich adornment as if death itself could not rob that royal
form of its imperial grandeur. The preacher to whom this
great hour had come ascended the pulpit. Sophisticated
men and women from all over Europe leaned back, ready
to taste with the appreciation of connoisseurs the distin-

guished phrases of eulogy which would fall from the preacher's lips. A powerful king was to have this last scene at the end of his life signalized by an interpretation of his reign, the majestic beauty of whose sentences would worthily express the quality of the central figure of a great age. The magnetic eye of the preacher, shining with a strange light, pierced into the consciousness of the men and women before him. He pronounced the words of his text. There was a moment of seminal silence. Then he spoke four words. They came with an icy chill, as if blown from the snow-capped mountains of eternity. "Only God is great." Men felt the power of a spell which they could not resist. They looked at each other with startled eyes. They had come to witness a stately spectacle of human pride. And all unexpectedly they had confronted God.

Age after age—in ways corresponding to the life and the thought forms of the period—the men who spoke for God have performed this same miracle. So it was with Chrysostom at Constantinople when the golden words of the preacher were transcended by the sense of the shining presence of God. So it was at the bidding of Saint Bernard when a lawless Europe found itself bending as it became conscious of the high authority and eternal power of the giver of the divine law. So it was when the simple words of Saint Francis of Assisi caused everyday men and mighty princes to feel the fashion in which all men and all things were touched by the power of the divine. So it was when Hugh Latimer made racy, vernacular English the vehicle of a message with eternal sanctions lying under it and speaking through it. So it was when John Donne made of English a prose as glorious as the poetry of Shakespeare, and thus forged an instrument to capture men's imagination

185

and bend their wills so that they would think God's thoughts after Him and gladly do His will. So it was when George Whitefield carried men's hearts away to give them as a loving offering before the throne of God. So it was when John Henry Newman gave a ghostly sanctity to the pulpit of Saint Mary's at Oxford which it had not known before, as his own figure seemed incandescent, shining with the strange beauty of an inner spiritual light. So it was when Robert William Dale made the pulpit of a non-conformist chapel in the Midlands a throne of intellectual and spiritual power. So it was when Liddon stood in the pulpit of Saint Paul's in London. So it was when Phillips Brooks stood in Trinity Church in Boston.

It is possible to look upon all this with the wistful skepticism of a brilliant secular mind, full of aesthetic sympathy for the beautiful patterns of a discarded faith, and a half regretful denial of sanctions which can no more command the mind of man. It is possible to believe that as the great god Pan departed from the ancient world, leaving the classic beauty of many lovely writings in which the old gods walked the earth, so the Christian God has departed to return no more, leaving behind the aspiring beauty of the Gothic cathedral, the singing tenderness of much lovely poetry, and the harmonious grandeur of a high mythology unmatched among the products of the imagination of man.

But can the matter possibly be so simple as this? Can men's highest hopes and their most majestic thoughts be so easily and so casually brushed aside? The skeptic is in his way a lordly figure. But may he not have failed to do his complete work? May it not be possible that the man who is skeptical of skepticism will put his mind to subtler and more penetrating uses than the man who is merely

186

skeptical of faith? May we not too easily have assumed that the cause of intelligence is bound up with a denial of the realm of spiritual vitality? May we not have made the curious blunder of thinking that we surrendered our faith to our intelligence when we only surrendered our intelligence, when we failed to make a critical inspection of the dialectic of faith?

Let us reinspect the humanistic sanctions and follow the great humanistic argument in the light of these questions and see where that high argument leads, and perhaps what specious falacies it discards to perish by the way. Our immediate experience brings us into contact with life on the two levels, the subhuman and the human. We are all the while confronting the physical order. We cannot evade it. We cannot avoid it. And we marvel more and more at the control which man has achieved over nature through understanding and mastering the method of its activities and discovering the formulas which express their mathematical relationships. The engineer builds the George Washington Bridge. The inventor produces the Hurricane type of airplane. In each case the achievement would be entirely impossible but for the possession of formulas regarding the physical world which securely express its dependable relationships. There is a subhuman order which is a kind of externalized mathematics. And by learning the laws of this realm the free mind of man may exercise the most extraordinary control over its activities.

We are also all the while confronting the world of appetite in the lower animals and in ourselves. Here you have vital energy expressing itself in hunger and thirst, in the biological experiences in connection with the ongoing of physical life, in all the rush and restless stir which belong

187

to living organisms. Here is a realm of amazing vividness and intensity, a world abounding in sensations, a world of engrossing pleasure and of tragic pain. The animal world below man is essentially a world of appetite. But here again there are larger and larger relationships. This world of vital energy may be caught up and given majestic and beautiful meanings upon the human level. It may be—indeed, has been—turned to all the wonder of the interpreting of color in great paintings, of the harmonious relations of form in sculpture and architecture, of the harmonious mathematics of sound in great music, of language itself leaping with the rhythm of a high vitality controlled for noble purposes in the great literature of the world. The creative urge begins—as man observes it directly—on the biological level. But it does not end there. It seems never to end. This exhaustless vitality is the inspiration of every art as it is bent to ever more gracious uses on the human level under the disciplines of vital control.

For at every point with the coming of man you do confront this fact of singular and far-reaching significance, the fact of control. Man controls the world of mechanical reactions. He controls the world of appetite. His control is not perfect. But it is real. And in the realm of physical uniformities it is increasing all the while.

Man exercises this control because he can observe and classify. He can stop and think. He can hold a purpose in his mind. He has conscious intelligence. We cannot repeat too often that this controlling power of conscious intelligence is man's peculiar characteristic. It is quite true that he is in one way like the physical realm. He shares its uniformities in his own physical organism. From one angle of observation his body may be called a physical machine. In one way he is like the animal world. He possesses every animal appetite. But in his power to exercise conscious intelligence, to master the physical world, and to control appetite, he is unique. He can discover the laws of physical action and use them. He can erect standards for the control of appetite and for its use on ever higher levels, and he can be loyal to them.

Thus you have existence on the two levels: on the one hand the subhuman world of mechanical uniformities and vital appetites, and on the other the human world of controlling intelligence. This distinction between life on the two levels, as we have already seen, must be kept perpetually in mind for the very sake of the civilized life of man.

But now we have reached the critical point in our whole discussion. We have reached another parting of the ways. It is an experience characteristic of the thought of the humanist, who is continually whetting the instruments of his mind in order that he may be ready to choose among alternatives. In the present case, the most far-reaching issues depend upon the choice. Indeed, it will finally turn out that the validity of everything we have already said is secured or lost by the intellectual choice which we make now. For just at this point the thoughtful man is sure to lift a great question. He has seen the material and vital realms which man controls. He has seen the manifold free activities of man the controller. And this is the question which must arise: What is the character of the ultimate reality of the universe? We breathe deeply as at last we lift this terrible and incisive question, which simply will not be put down. Now at last we question the universe itself, and ask it to tell us its ultimate and distinctive secret. We are ready to storm the battlements of reality. Or, to put the matter

189

in another way, we are ready like a more persistent Jacob to fight through many a night until we find the name which corresponds to the nature of actuality itself.

Very soon we come to see that our previous study and analyses have made possible several alternatives and provisional answers to our question. We may say that the subhuman gives a clue to the character of the final reality of the universe. We may do this in either of two ways. We may find the final actuality of things in a vast mechanical interaction, an all-inclusive impersonal mathematics. Or we may find the final reality of things in a kind of cosmic appetite, the universe being a vast and vital organism, a sort of biology universalized. Or we may refuse to turn to the subhuman in any of its forms for the clue to the universe. We may find that clue in the human. We may find it in free controlling intelligence. From the relative and finite intelligence of man we may rise to free and perfect and transcendent intelligence as the ultimate reality of the universe.

It is at this point of choice that our judgment is now suspended. It is in one of these three ways that we must decide to continue the great journey of the mind of man. If we try to say that the only reality of the universe is mechanical and mathematically determined action and reaction on an impersonal level, we come upon a curious dilemma. How can we now account for the controlling intelligence which is seen wherever man appears? How can we account for the free action which is the most characteristic expression of man's life? How can we account for the conscious activity of man in observing and classifying and using the materials of the world? How can we explain man's power to get back of action to the laws which the action expresses? How can we explain man's use of the logic of his mind to unfold the implicit logic of the world? Can the unconscious produce the conscious? Can the determined create the free? Can the uniformity which does not know that it can be expressed by a formula create the mind which can crystallize the uniformity into a formula and then use that formula for the free control of future action? The more we ask these questions, the more we see that to make the impersonal reactions which we find in the physical world the clue to the nature of the ultimate reality of the universe would be to produce a situation where confusion would be worse confounded. Mechanical uniformities may be the servants of intelligence. They cannot be the creators of intelligence.

In the second place, if we try to think of the universe as cosmic appetite, as a vast and vital organism, a kind of ultimate animal which is the universe itself, using the biological urges as the clue to the final meaning of things, we are once again in a world of curious dilemmas. Appetite is a very real fact in the animal world. The biological urges have a place in organic life which cannot be denied. Vital organisms play their own part in the drama of existence. But the moment man appears, we find that the vital organism is a means to an end. Not the presence of appetite, but the control of appetite is the very genius of civilization. Not the presence of a vital organism, but the control of that vital organism by clear intelligence for purposes which transcend organic life is what matters when we are studying the distinctive aspects of the highest life on this planet. Can the organic, held in chains of biological necessity as completely controlling as those which determine the physical interactions of the inanimate world, create a free intelligence which will use it for its own purposes? Can the appetite whose very genius it is to seek its own gratification produce the clear and cool intelligence which will control it for higher ends and turn it to higher purposes? Can the merely organic produce the intelligent? In a universe which is a perfect biological organism embracing all the real, how could we ever account for the emerging of a masterful and free intelligence which would turn organic life to purposes beyond organic functioning? Once more we would find ourselves in a position which involved confusion worse confounded. We cannot use the realm of biological urges as the clue to the distinctive meaning of the final reality of the universe. The truth— and a most important truth it is—can be put into a sentence. If we try to explain the ultimate universe in the terms of the subhuman, we can never account for the presence of the human.

At this point we may find ourselves confronted by that very subtle form of thought known as panpsychism. It is a characteristic of panpsychism that very deftly it discusses the organic in such a fashion as to include the human; it discusses the world of organic impulses in such a fashion as to include the world of intelligent choices. At first the reasoning of panpsychism seems to be very persuasive. And it seems to be very much on the side of the angels. But in the long run it will be found that it first ignores and then destroys the very distinctions upon which rational and civilized life depends. It is really the very subtlest of all the attempts to reduce the human to the subhuman, the rational to the irrational, the intelligent to the inorganic. For in the last analysis it always makes the

192

lower the clue to the higher, and not the higher the clue to the lower.

On the other hand, if we accept the position that the ultimate fact of the universe is perfect controlling intelligence, everything falls into some sort of understandable relationship. If perfect controlling intelligence is the first reality, we can account for man's intelligence. For intelligence can create intelligence. But we can also account for the world of physical relationships. Indeed, the mathematics of physics suggests a mind which has imposed logical relationships upon the world which it has made. Sir James Jeans has seen this, and has said decisively that the physical universe suggests not merely a mathematical formula, but a mathematician. We can also understand the vital energies of living organisms. For intelligence can be used to account for the presence of vital organisms. But organisms with only appetite cannot be used to explain the emergence of intelligence. We begin to see the far-flung significance of one great principle, which can be expressed both positively and negatively. We can explain the lower by means of the higher. We cannot explain the higher by means of the lower. Only free controlling intelligence, which is the highest and most potent thing one finds as one goes through existence on the two levels, and which exists only on the second level, can be used as a clue to determine the meaning and distinctive quality of the ultimate reality of the universe.

We come clearly, then, to life on the third level. We come to the superhuman. We come to the divine. The last defining fact in our pattern of thought must be that free and perfect intelligence controlling the universe, which can have only one name. And that name is God.

But here it is strategically important that we stop to express and examine a certain insight which carries many implications. For now we see that our only security in believing in the human is also to believe in the divine. For unless controlling intelligence is secure on the throne of the ultimate universe, it has no real security anywhere. A determined universe would inevitably set going processes which would blot out all belief in the freedom of man. The reality of the distinction between life on the two levels requires life on the third level. When humanism follows the logic implicit in its own life, it always leads us to the more than human.

With the meaning of the third level clearly in mind, the whole picture begins to take on a gracious completeness and a perfect harmony. Perfect free and conscious intelligence is the first and the last fact in the universe, and that which gives significance to all that lies between. That ultimate intelligence gives actuality to the physical world and harnesses its activities to the processes of mathematical law. That ultimate intelligence creates the world of animate life, and gives vitality to every organism of the biological world. That ultimate intelligence creates man. His own body sums up the history of the world before and beneath him. His body is a machine. His body is a physical organism with all the urges of biological life. But the Perfect Intelligence gives to man a relative intelligence; the Perfectly Free gives to man a relative freedom. That free intelligence puts in his own mind a logic which corresponds to the mathematical logic found in the impersonal uniformities of nature. That ultimate intelligence gives to man the power of noble control over the vital energies of his own organism. That free and perfect intelligence con-

194

trolling the universe creates man in its own image for the control of his world. So our final insight as to the nature of the human emerges. We may put it into a formula: Man over nature, under God. Or we may express it in another form of words: Man controlling nature, and obeying and worshiping God.

The process by which all these powers unfold in men is a matter of divine method, and not of structural philosophy. The God of perfect and free intelligence can as well work through the processes of what we rather pontifically call organic evolution, as by instant fiat. Intelligence is not less intelligence because it uses processes to effect its clearly held purposes.

Thus we see that the man who is skeptical of skepticism turns out to be very wise after all. The too casual conclusions of a materialistic skepticism do not possess as much intellectual dignity as we had supposed. The mental activity of the man who does away with God—committing a sort of vast act of *deicide*—at the supposed command of his own intelligence turns out to have sinned most conspicuously and precisely against that intelligence itself. It is not necessary, then, to cast into the realm of a deceptive mythology the highest moral and spiritual insights of the race. It is not necessary to throw away the supreme insights of the mind of man at the behest of a series of mechanical formulas which we suppose to be the perfect product of intelligence itself. We cannot ask man to reduce himself to a thing in order to be loyal to his manhood.

So that it comes to pass that we may once more listen to church bells without feeling that our intelligence is insulted. Indeed, we may well feel that our intelligence is insulted if we are asked to refuse to hearken to the pealing of the bells. We have learned that we must look up in order to understand what is below; that we must not look down with so preoccupied a gaze that we become incapable of believing in what is above. Once more we may look upon a cathedral as a crystallization of intellectual insights as well as a repository of moral and spiritual inspirations—which indeed would have no value if they lost intellectual authenticity—and of aesthetic loveliness, whose final beauty, it will now be seen, lies in its truth.

In one of the brilliant novels of Maarten Maartens—I think it is *God's Fool*—a man asks another to take a walk on the sand dunes. At the close of the walk, the man who received the invitation complains, "There was nothing but sand." The other replies, "I asked you to take a walk on the sand dunes. But after all, there is always the sky above."

There is always the third level. There is always the sky above. There is always the free and perfect intelligence which controls the universe. Even when we walk on the sand dunes, we may find the secret of our life in the sky. And our minds as well as our hearts may join in awed acquiescence when we hear the words of the preacher, "Only God is great."

# CHAPTER XVI

## *Theistic Humanism*

THAT MASTERFUL THINKER AND WRITER AND PREACHER DR.
Robert William Dale—concerning whom Sir William Rob-
ertson Nicoll once declared that he had achieved a style
which made him one of the half-dozen masters of English
prose—discussed the matter of theism in a profound and
vital fashion. He declared that the doctrine of God should
be approached through living human experience. It was
a notable assertion, and back of it lay all sorts of significant
assumptions regarding the nature of the world, of man, and
of God, and their relation to each other. All reality must
belong to one great bundle of life if we are to get about
the world without confusion and utter bewilderment. This
does not mean that we should deny distinctions which are
a part of the very texture of existence. It does not mean
that diversity should be blotted out in some sort of abstract
unity. It does mean that the distinctions must be part of
a harmonious system of reality through which one can
move with assurance and intellectual peace.

The apostles of pseudo unity have carried this principle
to lengths which have confused and darkened their own
processes of thought. They have tried to find unity on a
level below the determinations of conscious intelligence.
And so they have thought of the universe as a place where
God first becomes conscious in man, or even as a universe
which in some curious fashion secretes God. Not content
with trying to explain man in the terms of the subhuman,

197

they have tried to explain God in terms of the subhuman. But an impersonal universe which created God as the last achievement of its unconscious intelligence is an even more startling conception than an impersonal universe which, though without conscious intelligence itself, in the vast swing of its endless movement throws off the consciousness of man. A universe which is busy making God is a very fantastic conception, and it is seen to be doubly bizarre when one remembers that the very reason for believing in God is just that in this fashion one accounts for the universe. If the universe can do so well without God that it produces him only as the product of the very last stage of its evolution, we may well ask why it is necessary to have a God at all. We do not have a God whose existence we explain by hurrying off to the universe as an inspired God-maker. We have a universe whose presence and whose characteristics we make coherent and understandable through rising to the height of the conception of the creative God. Our experience of the universe can be made authentic only as it rises first to the thought and then to the living apprehension of God as the creator and the sustainer of the world.

As Etienne Gilson has made abundantly clear, this conception of God the creator is of the most decisive importance. Once we hold firmly the conception of the universe as coming into being as the result of the creative action of the free intelligence of almighty God, we are forever saved from that blighting pantheism in which everything is regarded as an aspect of God and the divine life is so spread about that in the long run it becomes just nothing at all. There is all the difference in the world between regarding the universe as the side of God which is turned toward us and thinking of the universe as the result of the creative and sustaining action of the intelligence of God upon which He has impressed the laws of His own mind, and which therefore tells us something about its author and its preserver. And the conception of God as creator saves us from that subtle and degrading self-worship to which pantheistic monism always descends at last. If God becomes conscious only in our intelligence, how better can we worship God than by worshiping ourselves? But if our intelligence—and all the rest of the universe beside—is the result of the free creative action of the perfect intelligence of God, then we can still look up, we can find a form of worship which is not self-worship. The conception of creation also turns our minds away from impersonal organic processes to personal intentions on the highest level of intelligence. If we think of God as the last secretion of the vast organic processes of the universe, the organic itself tends to take the place of the rational, and God is lost at last in the depth of a sort of vast and universal biology. We approach God not in order to get ourselves deeper into organic life but in order to find a fashion in which organic life may be subjected to some sort of intellectual and moral and spiritual control.

We are often told by apostles of the control of the spirit by the flesh, or of denial of the existence of the spirit in the name of the dominance of the flesh, that the world of intelligence and ethics and spirituality is only a dreamland of the fanciful imagination. The flesh is the concrete. The flesh is the actual. The flesh must rule. And if the existence of the spiritual world is admitted, we are told that it is so exquisitely ethereal, so loftily remote that it can never gain and maintain control over the hard

199

world of material actuality. The answer to all this is complete if we believe in creation as the masterful act of divine intelligence. For if the material exists only because the spiritual has brought it into existence, if the flesh exists only because of the fiat of the perfect Reason which is almighty God, then it is the very genius of the material to be mastered by the spiritual, and it is the very nature of the flesh to be controlled by the spirit. Any doctrine of emanation sets us traveling back toward the organic away from the intelligent, and at last toward the inorganic and the sheer mechanism of a world where, after intelligence is lost in biological impulse, biological impulse is lost in impersonal and unconscious motion. The doctrine of creation by a free and intelligent Deity, which at first may have seemed only a pleasant belief, turns out to be the great rampart which we must man and hold valiantly against encircling foes. And it is precisely the living experience of what these beliefs do, not merely to our thoughts but to our deepest and most important relationships, which at last makes the theistic position impregnable. God the creator is the means by which we emerge from the clutter of things and the clutch of organic relationships and come back to secure control over things and mastery over the world of organic impulse. And God the free intelligent creator alone makes all these things possible.

All this fits into processes of thought whose validity we have already seen, and whose characteristic movement we may once more inspect. A brilliant thinker once declared, "God cannot die while man lives." The sentence was a flashing expression of the insight that belief in a personal God follows naturally from an understanding belief in man. If you come to see that controlling intelligence is the defining human characteristic, you cannot leave this very quality out of the ultimate universe. You cannot find the source of that which is distinctively human in that which is less than human. You can explain man by that which is more than man; you cannot explain him by that which is less than man.

You can put the matter in another way. It is impossible to retain one's belief in controlling intelligence in man without believing in controlling intelligence in God.

At this point the Positivist comes upon us, his banners waving. And very tempestuously he demands that we listen to what he has to say. All this concern with ultimate questions, he declares, leads only to bewilderment and confusion. We become lost in vast clouds of unproductive speculation. Of only a few things can we be sure. We can be sure that we are here. We can be sure that we possess certain powers. Let us use these powers without asking any of those foggy metaphysical questions which only engulf the mind in impenetrable mist. Let us be humanists without metaphysics. Let us be men without a philosophical doctrine of the nature of reality. Then the Positivist rings the changes on the endless mistakes of the metaphysicians, the endless contradictions of the philosophers, the endless dogmatisms of the theologians. Let us leave all this, he says, and come out into the clear light of the common human day. We are men. Let us live like men, whatever becomes of the universe beyond. But that is just the point. Our minds are so constituted that they cannot let the universe alone, and the universe certainly will not let us alone. Positivism is always a half-way house from which one goes on to believe in a conscious intelligent God, or from which one goes back to believe only in an inhuman man. The Positivist is always driven to believe more or to believe less. If God dies, man in his distinctive human quality cannot continue to live. But man does live and does exercise controlling intelligence. Therefore God the perfect controlling intelligence must live too.

The true humanist knows the folly—not to say the intellectual dishonesty—of retaining the name God when one has given up the reality for which that name stands. As we have already seen, there are a good many pleasant idealists of the left wing of the theological armies of our day who would like to preserve all the literary flavor and the moral incentive and the spiritual afflatus of a belief in a personal God after this belief has been cast away. The true humanist is one of the first men to realize that this simply cannot be done. At a certain stage in his development the humanist may not yet see the theistic sanctions which are implicit in his own patterns of thought and essential to the maintaining of his characteristic position. But even at this stage he is too honest to claim the intellectual and moral and spiritual fruits of belief in God without having that belief. If it is true that you cannot gather figs from thistles, it is even more true that you cannot gather fruit where there is no tree at all! But more and more the humanist comes to the position where he says with Professor Irving Babbitt: "For my own part, I range myself unhesitatingly on the side of the supernaturalists." It is inevitable that really advancing intelligence will perceive that we cannot have as man's defining characteristic that which simply does not exist in the ultimate universe. And of course those who believe that man is made in the image of God have no difficulty in seeing that, however dimly, it is only in the image of man so made that the human mind can get a hint of what God is like.

If at this point someone hurls the word "anthropomorphic" into the discussion, the clear thinker is not at all disturbed. In the humanistic sense the word anthropomorphic can mean only that in man at his highest you get a clue as to what God is like. The alternative is that you go below the distinctively human to the realm of organic energy, or the realm of mechanical reaction, to explain the existence of the world. In either alternative you leave out controlling intelligence and go to something below it. You are so afraid of being unduly influenced by the human that you drop into the arms of the subhuman. Such a position is surely palpably absurd. In a very characteristic form it is ready to declare that, while you must not use intelligence as a clue to the nature of God, you are bound to explain the universe in the terms of an impersonal mathematics. The higher is triumphantly ruled out in the name of the lower. This is to say that the ultimate universe cannot be like the minds which we see at work here. It can only be like the matter which is so far below mind. So with a mighty swing of a hammer, which is called a hammer of thought, the subhuman crushes the human.

The fallacy is so obvious that we may be perplexed that men of any sort of intelligence should have clung to it so persistently. The answer is that when men of even very great intelligence give all of their time year after year to analyzing the uniformities of the subhuman world, ignoring the work of their own free minds in the process, they become at last capable of believing only in that upon which their attention has been focused for so long a period.

The problem is in the psychology of the worker, and not in the critical logic of penetrating intelligence.

All this surrender to the subhuman, critical humanism repudiates as the issues become clear. The goal of humanistic thought is perfect intelligence. It is not a universe from which intelligence has been cast out. So humanism and theism belong together.

The action of the creative intelligence of God is the necessary basis for a true belief in the free intelligence of man. The presence of intelligence in man finds its basis and its authentication in the purposive deeds of the divine consciousness, not in the crystallization of unconscious laws, or the strange fruition of conscious reason as a result of the processes of unconscious intelligence. This phrase "unconscious intelligence" itself deserves closer inspection. For it is really an excellent example of the way in which certain schools of thought will put two words side by side whose meanings are completely contradictory, and naively suppose that the juxtaposition of words has somehow harmonized the meanings. The whole point of this movement of the discussion is of course just that when intelligence ceases to be conscious, it ceases to be intelligent. You must trace intelligence back to purposive action. You can never trace it back to impersonal forces unconsciously obeying the behests of an intelligence they do not understand and which has no existence beyond themselves.

That purposive deed which we call creation is followed by all those other purposive deeds which maintain and support the movement and the action of the universe which God has made. God's immanence is not the absence of intelligence. It is the perpetual and exhaustless exercise of conscious intelligence.

## Theistic Humanism

Here the theistic humanist remembers the deist who rather crassly believed that God set the universe going as a spinner sets a top to spinning, and then while the top continued to spin went off to look after something else. It is no more in the nature of the universe to keep going without the constantly sustaining acts of divine intelligence than it was its nature to come into existence without the purposive act of divine creation. This understanding of free intelligence as the source of the motions of the inorganic and the energy of the organic gives existence genuine harmony and forms the basis of what we may with very discriminating thought call humanistic monism. By this we mean that in a world of free intelligence you can unite the dualistic distinctions permanently held in the harmony of a universe whose unity is found in the free control of the divine intelligence. On the impersonal level, the problem of the one and the many can never be solved. On the impersonal level, the presence of truth and error can never be understood. On the impersonal level, you can never account for the distinction between right and wrong. On the impersonal level, intelligence itself is an insoluble mystery. And freedom is a conception which can have no meaning. And as the necessary distinctions fade out of existence, life itself falls apart and there is left only an inarticulate chaos. In a universe created and controlled by the free intelligence of Almighty God we have a monism which preserves all the dualistic distinctions and is never in danger of the palsying blight which pantheistic monism brings to the mind of man.

There are humanists who have spent so much time analyzing the confusions and the frustrations of pantheistic monism that they have come to hate the very word monism.

They call themselves dualists, and let it go at that. One can understand their intellectual wrath. And of course it is quite true that if monism means pantheistic monism, none of us can be monists. We must preserve the necessary distinctions without which existence would fall apart into a meaningless flux.

But it is the very nature of the humanistic interpretation of the universe, when it has seen the theistic implications implicit in its own principles, to reach a position where free intelligence creating and controlling gives both unity and variety to the universe. Because the many are made by the One and controlled by the One, you have unity of control at the very moment when you have definite and dependable variety of existence. If any thinkers so hate the word monism that they find it necessary to look for another word by whose means to express the harmony of a universe created and controlled by perfect and free intelligence, they are welcome to the other word, providing there is no loss of meaning. The main thing to see is that theistic humanism saves us on the one hand from all the poisons circulating in the system of pantheism, and on the other hand saves us from a dualism so extreme that the different elements of existence and of life have no real relation to each other.

All this is moving in the regions of very high and demanding dialectic. To be sure, it is dialectic born of experience and at every step guided by experience, but it leads us into the subtlest processes of philosophical discrimination. It is well for us now to come back to the man with whom we started, for if it turns out that our humanism must be theistic, it is equally true that our theism must be human.

206

If you study the biography of David Livingstone, you discover that in his life of almost incredible adventures and achievements he is always upheld and sustained by his experience of the presence of the Great Companion. In the crisis of a difficult situation, he remembers that Almighty God is a gentleman and lets it go at that. He travels north and south, east and west in Africa until his own feet leave the impress of a mighty cross upon the continent. And all the while he feels that he is guided and upheld by the great God who made the world, and who controls all the forces of its life. He is the friend of the Controller of the universe, and that makes the impossible possible to David Livingstone. When you inspect the extraordinary career of General William Booth, you find that no hard and ugly fact about the slums of London or that larger mass of slums into which man has turned so much of his world was foreign to the knowledge of the leader of the Salvation Army. But he knew a fact behind the ugly facts. He knew a fact behind the bad facts. And that fact was a good fact. It was the fact of the free and perfect God who had not made men to live in slums or to turn their minds into darker slums than those in which their bodies lived, but to use their godlike freedom and their godlike intelligence for the making in the world of something which would correspond to the will of God, to let their minds be fashioned after the mind of God, and to make the purposes of God their own. If you travel back over many centuries and find yourself with Boniface in the dark and mysterious German forests, with a militant paganism of threatening power right across his path, you find that Boniface was aware of something more than the dark mystery of the German forests. You find that he had contact with something more vital than the fiery energies of a cruel paganism. He was aware of God. He was aware of God as the maker and master of the world through which he journeyed. He was aware of God as the maker and master of the men whom he must win. Go back over other centuries and stand with the Apostle Paul on Mars Hill. The stately Areopagus is made the pulpit of more vital words than even Athens had ever heard before. Paul speaks of the structural relation of man to the perfect God who is Lord of all. And it is in the nature and character of that high and perfect God that man is to find the chart of his life. Go out in any one of twenty centuries of Christian history to the homes of multitudes of common and everyday men and women living in a difficult world, their lives harnessed to hard tasks. There is something which makes all the difference. There is something which has put a glory in their minds. It is that the thought of God has taken hold on them. It is that the glory of the free and perfect God has come to possess them. Everyday men and mighty leaders have this in common. Their humanity is secure only in God. Their humanity finds its meaning in God. They are men because they are God's men.

So men find the meaning of their lives in the life of God. In that free and perfect creative and controlling intelligence they have found the goal of their thought and the source of power for their lives. To many of the plain people the phrase "theistic humanism" would be hard indeed. But their experience is richer than their vocabulary, and they would know in the very terms of life the meaning which controls the pen of the philosophic humanist as he writes: "Only in a free God is the life for free man secure."

208

# CHAPTER XVII

## Christian Humanism

ANGRY MORALISTS AND DECADENT POETS AND TEMPERAMENTAL
dramatists have been so busy vicariously repenting of what
they disliked in the Christian religion and in Christian
civilization that it is very difficult to get before the contemporary mind a picture of historic Christianity which is
not a distortion. The type of man who, because he finds
his own favorite vices condemned by Christian sanctions,
has taken a diabolical delight in pointing out the fallacies
and inconsistencies of Christian thought and especially of
Christian action has been the leader in what may be called
the pathological attack on Christianity. When he has been
a man of consummate literary gifts and even of indubitable
genius, his brilliant distortions have won the widest sort
of hearing, and his work has been characterized by what,
for the time at least, has seemed to be a deadly effective-
ness. Precisely because there has been much detailed
truth in what he has said, his work has greatly complicated
the matter of our getting at a true understanding either
of life or of Christianity. Often—to paraphrase words used
by Arthur Clutton-Brock in quite another connection—he
has told little truths in the name of a great lie. He has told
little truths about the inconsistency and folly of Christians
in the name of the great lie involved in his attack on the
Christian Church itself. Really, there is not much to
choose between the type of Victorian Christian who rejoiced
in a mystical experience of religion which he never related

to his economic practices—or, at the worst, to his personal life—and the post-Victorian literary libertine who practices the vices which would disintegrate civilization and at the very moment rejoices in a sense of moral and spiritual superiority because he can condemn the hypocrisies of those whom he uncritically assumes to be typical Victorian Christians.

The moment we escape the vagaries of psychopathic thought, we begin to see how magnificent the history of the Christian Church has been. It has done more than any other form of organized life to keep alive in the world whatsoever has been lovely and of good report. It has kept multitudinous lights burning in the world, even in the darkest ages. It has made foolish men wise. It has made weak men strong. It has made bad men good. It has taught wicked men, with no standard but their own mad desires, to submit themselves to the higher law which would make new men of them and which had within itself the secret of the making of a new world. It has put compassion in the place of cruelty, and justice in the place of oppression. It has crystallized its idealism into institutions which have wrought untold good to the life of human kind. It has produced leaders whose names shine like bright and fixed stars in the firmament of man's mind. No evil has been secure with the conscience of the Church ready to pounce upon it and to set about destroying it. The Christian Church has kept a moral fire burning in the world. It has kept a spiritual splendor hovering before men's eyes. It has turned the thoughts of the most powerful minds to processes of dialectic which have created a Christian corpus of thought which is unsurpassed—indeed, unequalled—among the achievements of the human intellect.

## Christian Humanism

To be sure, the ship of the Christian Church has sailed through stormy seas, and has moved through strange and dangerous waters. Sometimes it has come into port covered with barnacles. Sometimes its masts have been broken and its sails tattered. Sometimes it has been in need of such repair that the repair has seemed like rebuilding. But it has gone on sailing to every port. It has been kept seaworthy in all weather. Its idealisms have been disciplined by all the hard ferocities of the actual world. It has had to deal not only with foes without, but with foes within. It has kept its flag flying. And it still carries to all the ports of the world man's fairest hope.

It has always been a characteristic of the Christian Church that it has produced fiery critics who have turned the fierce light of their examination back upon its own life. The very consciousness that it was flying the flag of the eternal in the midst of time has led it age after age to a critical inspection of its own witness, lest its temporal environment weaken or even corrupt that witness to deathless sanctions. The tendency to use the claim of divine authority to uphold all too human judgments and all too human expressions of selfishness and pride has brought great humiliation to the Church in many a century. Sometimes it has caused the Church to come upon dark hours of penitence. Sometimes it has lowered its flag to the very dust. But the Church has never made the mistake so characteristic of its foes—the mistake of concluding that because divine sanctions can be misused, we are justified in denying that divine sanctions exist. The complacency of the Church has been completely shattered by that divine message which is both its glory and its shame—its glory because of the loftiness and the adequacy of the message, its shame because the

211

Church has been once and again so little worthy of the light which it has held up before the world. It has never been able to refuse to be judged by those standards by which it would judge the world. And so the paradox of the witness of the Church has been the necessity forced upon it by its own nature perpetually to be holding aloft a light which revealed its own failure at the very moment when it revealed the glory of God.

But it has by no means been all a matter of failure in respect of the life of the Church. It has produced saints whose unselfishness has been the glory of the world. It has been the guiding star of public officials whose leadership has uplifted the standards of nations and has changed the life of the planet. It has given new ears and new eyes to the conscience of the world. When truly civilized men make judgments of right and wrong, they speak in a vocabulary which the Christian Church has given them. It has developed new muscles in those who fought against tyranny. It has created a world-wide conscience which condemns the sins of the strong against the weak. It has itself become the very conscience of the world. When men criticize it, when they attack it, they must do so in the name of principles which the Church itself has given to mankind. It has created untold millions of plain men and women unknown to fame whose character has been the strength of nations, whose goodness has been the solid basis of the best life of man, and whose unselfishness has been the hope of a better life for mankind. All this it has done on the basis of a series of facts and a series of interpretations which have made up a coherent corpus of thought which we may call classic Christianity. This corpus of thought is held in common by the Greek and Latin communions, and by the

212

great state churches and by the free churches of the Protestant world. It unites the neo-Thomists in the Roman Catholic Church with the representatives of classic Christianity in any Protestant communion. It is the basis of an ecumenical Christianity which transcends all the walls built up by the different communions. It centers in Jesus Christ. Its fundamental assertion has to do with the Incarnation. Its central spiritual message has to do with the cross. In its name embattled Christians in this bitter and difficult age confront the world.

It has often been said that the central matter in Greek theology was the doctrine of the incarnation, while the central matter in the Latin theology was the doctrine of the cross. At all events, there has always been a stream of thought in the Christian Church which has found the incarnation the very crowning fact in the history of humanity. And the incarnation has been seen to have been possible just because of the inherent dignity of man. Great preachers have felt the strength of this tradition. Phillips Brooks may be said to have belonged to it. One of the texts which brought out his full powers consisted of the words: "Son of man, stand upon thy feet, and I will speak with thee." Phillips Brooks was an apostle of the loftiness of human nature. He believed with all his mind and heart in the dignity of man. And the final seal and glory of this dignity he found in the incarnation. To a man of this type of thought, it is a thing of overwhelming importance that the very structural qualities of humanity are such that God could enter into human life and live the life of a man, and so reveal himself to man. God could not become incarnate in a stone because its nature could not be the vehicle for the expression of the defining characteristics of the

213

divine life. God could not become incarnate in a tree because its impersonal vitality could not express the essential glory of the divine life. God could not become incarnate in an animal because the richness of its organic functioning could not express that purposive will of love which is at the very center of the divine nature and the divine character. God could become incarnate only in man because man alone is made in the divine image. Man can think God's thoughts after Him. Therefore, God can think His own thoughts in human life. Man's free intelligence alone offers an organ for the expression of the free intelligence of God. Whatever the tragedies of sin and evil may have done to human life, it is still true that in its very structure humanity is an organ capable of being the instrument for the expression of the intellectual and moral and spiritual purposes of God. To the Danish theologian Martensen there was the most glorious fitness in the fact that humanity itself came to full flower in the coming of Jesus Christ. In a very real sense humanity was revealed to itself only in that one glorious life. It was only when the Son of God made human life His own that the possible life for men was at last made clear. The human was created with such subtle kinships with that above the human that only the Divine could reveal humanity to itself. You never understand man until you see Jesus Christ walking the earth.

Doubtless this is one aspect of a tremendous paradox. The other aspect has to do with the "otherness" of God, with the startled perception that His ways are not our ways, and His thoughts are not our thoughts. God's life is so far beyond our human life—His infinite thought so far beyond our finite thought, His eternal perfection so far beyond our partly comprehended human good—that when we at-

tempt to understand the beatific splendor of His eternal
life and character, and the effulgent beauty of His perfection, we are struck flat in sheer incompetence. If we
may imitate Luther's famous paradox, we may say: Man
is the one creature made to apprehend God, and yet by his
very nature he is incapable of comprehending God. Only
man can know God. Yet man can never know God. It
is the second part of the paradox which Karl Barth has
emphasized with such tremendous power. Either part of
the paradox alone is dangerous and misleading. The one
makes man overconfident and complacent. The other
plunges man into a depth of debasement which easily
leads to despair. The two together make a great Christian.

It must be said with unhesitating firmness, however, that
the transcendence of God must never be so interpreted as
to discredit the essential nature of man in its structural
quality. When God made man, He made a limited being.
But He did not make a lie. When God made the human
mind, He made an instrument for the seeking and the finding of the truth. He did not make an instrument destined
to the frustration of continually telling lies. If the divine
image had been completely blotted out of human life, not
only would the incarnation have been impossible, but religion itself would have become impossible. There would
have been nothing left to which God could speak. Our
debasement before the grandeur and the moral excellence
of God must never lead us to deny the essential dignity of
human life. It must never lead us to deny the structural
qualities of human worth. We do not dare to turn from
the insight which even Saint Augustine felt so deeply that
he gave it immortal expression when he said, "O God, thou

hast made us for thyself, and our souls are restless until they find rest in thee."

The Cambridge Platonists approached man on the side of his kinship with God. They declared that there was a divine light burning in every human life. The reason of man was the candle of the Lord. The incarnation was the fulfillment of all that for which man wistfully and vaguely longed. The whole story of the interpretation of the Christian religion which centers in the incarnation has been told with complete clarity and splendid and valid eloquence by Alexander V. G. Allen in his famous book *The Continuity of Christian Thought.*

This same sense that human life has so much dignity that God himself could enter into it is of such profound importance that it deserves our most careful scrutiny. It is pivotal for any theology which gives the incarnation its historic place. For it is this structural dignity of man which makes the incarnation possible. But the point at which this position calls for our most searching thought has to do with its relation to the deepest and the most characteristic insights of critical humanism. That free controlling intelligence which we find in man and which the critical humanist constantly emphasizes is just the point of his likeness to God. It is the capacity to choose among alternatives in the light of standards clearly seen and clearly held which makes it possible for God to work in and through man in a different sense from that in which He works in the subhuman world. Long ago Bishop Francis J. McConnell wrote a little book—the smallness of whose size is no indication of its importance—which he called *The Diviner Immanence,* to show how God could be present in saints in a different sense from that in which He was

216

present in stones. He controlled the material. He found fellowship with the human beings who accepted His will.

The great power to confront alternatives consciously seeing them for what they are, to recognize, even to erect a standard by which alternatives can be judged, and to follow loyally that which conforms to the standard—this is what makes a man a man. This is the matter of central concern to the critical humanist. But this is also just that which makes it possible for man to be the organ of the will of God. It is what makes it possible for man to think God's thoughts after Him. But much more, it is just this which makes it possible for God to enter into human life directly. It is this which makes the incarnation credible and authentic. Indeed, it is this which makes the incarnation possible.

This, then, is the most important insight to which we now come. Every step a man takes in the direction of critical humanism is a step toward an intellectual position which by its very nature will tend to make the thought of the incarnation acceptable. Long before the man in the central stream of humanism himself knows that it is true, he is approaching a place where his characteristic beliefs make it possible for him also to believe in the incarnation. It is because man with his free controlling intelligence can become like God, the Perfect Intelligence freely controlling, that God can enter into human life. It is because man can become like God that God can become man.

We have already seen that the humanistic sanctions profoundly considered naturally lead to theism, and that without the theistic consummation humanism itself would at last fall apart. Now we see that the Christian position is the very flower of the humanistic insights. That man is like

God in intelligence and freedom has become clear to the theist. That God Himself has become man is the glorious assertion of the Christian.

But the doctrine of the incarnation itself has the most deep and far-reaching implications. It not only puts the capstone upon the belief in the dignity of man. But it becomes a power by which to crush those dark pessimisms which would crush human nature itself. Christianity, as we have had and will have ample reason to see, believes that man is something good which has freely gone wrong. It very emphatically does not believe that man is something evil which *had* to go wrong. It believes that human nature has been misused—even abused. But it does not believe that human nature in its very essence is bad.

A poison is put at the very center of life by all those beliefs which regard human life as essentially evil. To say that there is something in its very nature evil about the fact of relativity of human life, that this relativity condemns man to sin and indeed makes him a sinner before the first conscious act of sinning, is to miss the Christian position at a most important point. That man has turned his good nature to evil is true enough. That his nature is in its very quality so evil essentially that it could not be turned to good uses is contrary to the whole Christian position. It would of course make the incarnation quite impossible. God can enter a nature which has been grossly misused in order to turn it to right purposes. He could not enter a nature essentially evil. It would have no point of contact with his own life. The only thing goodness can do with that which is essentially evil is to destroy it. God cannot become incarnate in the satanic for any purpose whatsoever.

218

The critical humanist responds with the greatest eagerness to this aspect of the full explication of the doctrine of the incarnation. It not only corresponds to his own deep sense of the dignity of human nature, but answers to his sense of proportion and sanity in thought. It must be confessed that he has his own difficulties with those evangelical thinkers who build up such rhetorical mountains of condemnation when they speak of human sin that at last they have nothing left in man to which God could speak, and certainly have nothing left in man which could be the basis on the human side for the incarnation.

We shall see later the relative justification which this awful rhetoric of human abasement has in the darker facts of life. But it is good for all of us that the doctrine of the incarnation makes it impossible for us to black out all sense of goodness in man in order to do all the more honor to the grace of God. Man is bad enough in all conscience. But there is something left in him to which God can speak. There is something left in him which makes it possible for him to be the vehicle of the eternal good will in glad response to that good will, and there is something left— some structural quality of likeness to God—which makes the incarnation possible. And in all this the Christian humanist rejoices in deep and abiding joy.

The men who think they can find the fullest inspiration for leading the good life quite apart from those sanctions of philosophy which have to do with the ultimate nature of reality, or those assertions of the Christian religion which give final glory to the life of man by seeing it in God, and through God, and for God, and subject to God's personal invasion of human life are really asserting that you can grow the tree of human life without any roots in the nature of things. The truth is, the higher the tree grows, the greater the danger, if it is not deeply rooted. In my walks in the forests in the White Mountain country this summer, repeatedly I have come across trees lying flat, their roots exposed, thrown to the ground by a swift hurricane. Right beside them taller trees with wider branches are still standing. The trees with no adequate hold upon the soil below fell before the storm.

The difficulty with positivistic humanism is just that its roots are never allowed to coil deeply into the earth and clasp firmly some solid strength from the soils and the subsoils of the universe itself. Indeed, positivistic humanism has no roots at all. Sometimes in good weather it climbs high. Sometimes, if season after season is free from tempest, its branches spread widely. But wait until the hurricane comes. Then there is devastation indeed.

And the hurricane has come. The rootless trees all about us are being blown to the ground. The tree which we may well call the Tree of Life stands firm just because its roots go down into the soil of eternity itself.

In the terms of theism alone you may have a free man controlling nature and worshiping God. But it will be a distant God. He will seem to be speaking in the earthquake and the fire. But it will be difficult to hear the voice of gentle stillness. Then with the Christian religion comes the divine invasion of human life. God is no more the infinitely far. He is now the infinitely near. He looks upon us with human eyes. He speaks to us with a human voice. He serves us with human hands. He makes a human body the instrument of His purposes for the good of man. He makes human nature the vehicle of His revelation of Himself to the children of men. And He does this because He has made man with a relative intelligence which requires more knowledge, a relative freedom which demands a larger and more wisely disciplined liberty, a human will which can come to fulfillment only as it becomes one with the will of God. Looking at human life, God has seen a little lake where He could behold the reflection of His own face. Seeing man in action, God beholds something which reminds Him of Himself. That in man which is like God claims the potency of that in God which can transform the life of man. Man's very nature is an inarticulate cry that once for all God will enter it and make clear what that nature was meant to be, can be, will be by the divine grace.

There is a certain tremendous finality in the last words of David in Robert Browning's poem "Saul." The young man from the hills has brought to the distraught king the voice of nature. It has its own beauty and its own charm. But it is not enough. He has brought the voice of humanity. It is kindling and inspiring and at its best very splendid. But it is not enough. Dare David claim more from God for the helping of Saul? Dare he say more for the rousing and the utter uplifting of Saul? It is then that the titanic and overwhelming thought of God's entrance into human life rushes into the mind of David. It is then that he utters his great words and ours: "See the Christ stand!"

# CHAPTER XVIII

## Evangelical Humanism

THE HUMAN DILEMMA CONFRONTS US STARKLY AND BITTERLY and terribly. The fact is beyond argument to whatever school of thought we belong. The world is falling apart, and certain grim forces which in their own way would hold it together would crush personality for the sake of a mechanized world. They would use the freedom of the dictators to rob whole nations of any freedom worthy of the name. Hitler's Europe would be an anvil chorus where nobody would have any freedom but the blacksmith, and his freedom would be freedom to crush a continent. Beyond the political sphere there is incoherence and frustration in man's social life. The new poetry to a surprising degree is a poetry of disillusionment and futility and despair. It knows what it hates. It has discovered nothing to love. It makes an angry gesture as it goes shrieking away in the night. And it calls this gesture art. Whatever power the poetry of disillusionment possesses comes from its reflection of a social unrest which has become social chaos. Institutions like the home which acted as a social cement have lost their stabilizing power over vast areas of human life. In the totalitarian states, both at the extreme right and at the extreme left, the words of social idealism are used as smoke screens to hide a hard and cruel and materialistic selfishness. Because religion has suffered a black-out in countless individual souls, men have assumed that religion has been blacked out of the universe. Men live under a sky where there is no polar star. When their cry goes out into the awful and mysterious silence, they are met with a hard pessimistic assurance that there is no ear to hear, no mind to comprehend, and no heart to understand. Beyond the social and religious spheres man's individual life is breaking apart. It is of the utmost significance that when a man like D. H. Lawrence repudiates the world of intelligence for the world of instinct, takes as his watchword "the body is the soul," and accepts as his engaging preoccupation the experiences of sex with a dark and subhuman mysticism of the glands, he strikes a note which calls forth wide response. Men who have ceased to understand the human are ready to go to the subhuman for an interpretation of life.

So we have come upon almost incredible intellectual and moral, social and spiritual and political disaster. Our solutions have proved to be only a restatement of our problems in other forms, or a repudiation of all thought of true solutions in the hard tragedy of an admitted frustration or the soft tragedy of a slimy sensuality. Our frustration in so many areas of life has dramatized our failure and has given a certain clarity to the elements of our despair. But the problems with which we deal are perennial problems. With all their varied aspects they center in a few matters with which men have dealt in every age. Life asks of men the same questions in every century. Its confusions are varied forms of one central enigma, age after age. It is possible to brush aside the incidental and the irrelevant, however dramatic these may be, and actually to get to the heart of the whole matter. And here again the higher processes of humanistic thought will give us the clues without which we are sure completely to lose our way.

The human mind gives to human beings tasks which are beyond human powers. Here we meet one of those startling insights which may well change all our thought about life. At this point we find both the glory and the tragedy of human life. To belong to a race of men the very structure of whose nature makes it inevitable that they shall erect ideals beyond their attaining is the most amazing and wonderful thing in all the world. The passion for perfection is somehow inherent in the very genius of man. And the perfection which occupies his mind and compels his imagination is so great and glorious that his powers are staggered by the splendor of his dreams. There is much which man can do. There is much which man has done. He has made his mind into a marvelous instrument for the control of nature. He has built structures of subtle symmetry, of delicate grace, of alluring loveliness, and of high grandeur when he has given his attention to architecture. He has turned the languages which he has spoken into instruments for the expression of rare and radiant thoughts. His poetry has taught words to sing. His prose has taught words to march on long campaigns of intellectual investigation. He has built civilizations which have had strength and massiveness and far-flung power. But always at last he has made for himself tasks beyond his achieving. He has dreamed of a perfection he has been unable to attain. He has planned like a god. He has been able to achieve only as a man. And so at the peak of his powerful performance he has stood restless and disappointed.

Then man has confronted a terrible and yet inevitable question. Is he doomed to come upon frustration and failure at the very moment when his mind is most fully awake, most nobly alive, most eager to go on? He cannot go farther alone. Is there a divine friend who will make possible that which man cannot achieve without the help of God? Just when man fails, will God step in to help? Just when the limit of the human is reached, will the Divine expand all the horizons and give to man power for journeys which he could never accomplish without the strength of God?

If at this point humanity turns with ugly bitterness from the thought of the higher regions of help, it enters upon the great descent. Ideas become confused; ideals become hopelessly entangled; and we come step by step upon all those experiences of angry disdain, of the lust for power crashing to defeat at last, of selfishness open and undisguised, or of selfishness hidden behind protecting phrases which capture the vocabulary of nobility for the practice of the ignoble, of restlessness and confusion and frustration which tell the tale of human folly and of human disintegration. But at this point humanity, or any group of human beings, or any one human being alone, can turn toward that outreaching friendliness which comes from beyond the limitations of this mortal life. It is at this point that the strong man at the limit of his strength meets the mighty reinforcements of the grace of God. It is at this point that he hears and responds to the good news which comes to man when at the very apex of his powers his ideals transcend all his capacities.

The divine grace meets him in two ways. First it meets him bringing completion and fulfillment. Every power which the humanist finds in man calls for supplement and final realization in that which is beyond the human. In this sense man's mind is a call for the divine grace. His conscience is a prophecy of the divine grace. His heart is an outreach for the divine companionship. His whole nature lifts a cry which only the voice of God can answer. The man on the heights of life requires the aid of the divine man. The word of man at its best and completest calls for the divine word. Man's life at its fullest calls for the unutterable richness of the life divine.

The profoundest answer to all this is found in that gospel of the incarnation which brings to man the fulfillment of every human power and the completion of every human hope. So along the direct line of its own truest development humanism finds its last word in the Word of God, its final authentication in the Word made flesh. This is the characteristic note of the Greek theology. And here, as we have seen, humanism becomes Christian.

But there are far deeper and more tragic aspects which belong to the whole situation. For man is not always at his best. He meets failures which are far other than those inherent in his own nature when it is exercising its powers at the full. He has misused his intelligence. He has misused his freedom. He has used his power of choice to decide for the lesser of the goods of life, to follow that which is evil instead of that which has any good in it, and even among evils to choose that which is the very worst. He has made a place for treachery in his heart. He has told the lie which corrupts the soul. He has broken his own life and has put poison into the social organism. He has used his intellect to destroy goodness and truth and beauty. With demoniac skill he has made the worse appear the better reason. His profoundest problem does not have to do with the relation of the finite to the Infinite. It does not have to do with the supplement of incomplete powers and the completion of partly realized potencies. Man's pro-

226

foundest problem has to do with the moral disease which has rotted the very fibers of life; with evil which has deliberately crushed the good; with treachery which has pounced upon the innocent and the weak with lawless cruelty, which in the individual life has betrayed man's human destiny and has made the soul the dwelling place of coiling serpents of evil; with a corruption of the very sources of goodness in the soul by the dethroning of motives which are good and the enthroning of motives which burn with destructive power.

By a strange paradox the humanist never rises to a loftier height than when he tells the truth about these things. When he refuses to tell the life which would make evil seem good, when he turns from the complacency which could be obtained only at the expense of truth, when with an almost deadly candor he faces the treachery in his own soul and in the soul of humanity, his desperate and courageous honesty is a kind of final vindication of humanity, a proof that humanity has not sold all its good for evil. It can still tell the whole bitter truth about itself. Therefore it possesses something upon which God can act. It has a quality to which God can speak. It has not become so evil that it is completely incapable of responding to the divine. It is yet a subject for the mighty surgery of the grace of God. Its eyes can look to the sky though its feet are caught in the mire. It is ready at last for the greatest word which God has to speak to man. Humanism is at the very end of its journey in this hour when it receives the full message of the grace of God and humanism itself becomes evangelical.

This frank facing of man's moral tragedy has always been the prelude to a new appreciation of the profoundest forces of the Christian religion. Such a book as Professor Edwin Lewis' *A Christian Manifesto* gains its ringing power from its refusal to turn from the grimness of the human tragedy or to be satisfied by any superficial solution of the human problem. In varied ways, and not without some understandable confusion of thought, Kierkegaard shouted to Europe that the deeper nature of the human tragedy must be faced. Berdyaev, who is so much stronger in diagnosis than in clear prescription, has powerfully insisted that a veritable searchlight must be allowed to fall upon the devious ways of human evil. Emil Brunner has refused to construct an anthropology which is based upon a superficial optimism.

All these—and many other speakers and writers in these days when we have been driven from our bowers of easy content near the crater of the human volcano—have helped to prepare us for a new understanding of the deeper elements in the Christian gospel. And in the meantime, smoke and fire and lava have poured from the human volcano as it has come to wild eruption once more. And now man is surely ready as he has not been ready for centuries for the awful majesty and the unbelievable tenderness of the word of God.

The most tremendous experience which comes to man is his in that hour when God meets him with forgiveness for his sin, and the surgery which will remove the treachery from his soul. It is when God finds man in all his moral failure and spiritual treachery and brings to him the power of a great deliverance that the problem of life is really solved. Now man sees that the tragic note in his own life—so grim and so terrible—simply must be answered to by a tragic note coming from the very center of the life of God, if the human tragedy is to be turned into creative hope. It is the suffering God with the marks of the nails in His hands who meets man's last and most overwhelming need. It is God who makes the sign of the cross in a fashion which makes all the world new. The work of the figure upon the cross is the final catharsis beyond anything of which Aristotle even remotely conceived in his *Poetics*. The suffering God who comes to man when man cannot go to Him is the world's hope. It is He and He alone who saves man from frustration and despair.

This high paradox of the hour when humanism itself becomes evangelical is what Saint Paul would call a Christian mystery. But it is not a mystery in the sense that it is something foreign to man's life and experience, which is somehow thrust upon him in mechanical fashion by an arbitrary God. It is something toward which all man's deepest moral—and even immoral—experience points, something upon which man can seize because of its relation to the very texture of human life. The writing more profoundly aware of human pain and human bitterness and human frustration has always been moving in regions where there was an occasional flash of its meaning and there was always nearness to the mood where its word could be heard. Tolstoy is always asking questions which only evangelical religion can answer. Dostoievsky is always dealing with experiences into which only the suffering God could enter with true surgery and with emancipating power. Russia has not been conspicuous in finding right answers. It has been terribly tenacious in asking real questions.

And even the most bitterly lawless expressions of the new poetry in their own inverted way reveal the nature of that problem which only the suffering God can solve. Even

229

when they are only a wild expression of symptoms, they are full of very definite significance for the man who knows how to make a dependable diagnosis.

Long ago Professor James Denney, in that powerful and memorable book *The Death of Christ,* made it clear that there is one point at which the very center of the Christian religion must be found. And that point was revealed in the title of the book, just as its contents amply vindicated this position. But of course the matter goes far deeper than any brilliant study of New Testament materials—as important as this study is. The call for the cross comes from the very deepest movement of the life of man. Man finds himself at last alone. His selfish choice of evil has pushed him to a spot where human fellowship is impotent and divine fellowship is impossible. At last he realizes that the very nature of the evil which he has made one with the very central meaning of his life is the essential contradiction of all that lives in the life of God. The great Master of life can be aware of him only to crush him because He must crush the evil which he has made the very soul of his soul. God can come to him only with arrows bright, ready to fly in deadly execution from His terrible bow. All this is perfectly clear. It is the sentence man imposes upon himself in his hours of sharpest moral awareness. And the disintegrating dark energies which have moved from his life into the life of the world confirm the justice of the analysis and the rightness of the sentence. And if one may put it so, the central desperate element in the situation is not so much that God is not willing to forgive man, as that man cannot allow God to forgive him. In the final hour of his kingly moral awareness the humanist frankly faces the nature of the evil he has embraced, and in defiant

230

faithfulness to a moral beauty he has defaced he refuses to allow God to be too friendly with him. And we must see that no casual deity whose easy friendliness was offered to man with no light of the torture of evil in the divine eyes and no burning pain of the agony of God in the presence of deadly evil in the divine heart could ever speak to this desperate humanist whose very hopelessness is a tribute to some indestructible loyalty to the moral ideal against which his treachery has sinned with utter finality.

And now he sees—to use Gilbert Chesterton's great phrase—the God upon the cross. He sees the supreme arbiter as the supreme sufferer. He sees the supreme judge as the one who can make His own the lot of the supreme culprit. He sees God turning the glittering arrow which must find the last citadel of evil at His own heart.

This is just the one thing for which the desperate humanist is not prepared. To find God taking his place in the prisoner's box is unthinkable. There is no logic—none of the hard intolerable logic of mechanical punishment which is the only logic he knows at the moment— there is none of this logic in it. But perhaps there is a higher logic. Perhaps on the personal level that is possible which is quite impossible on the level of impersonal criminal mathematics. Perhaps on the personal level God can make His own the bitter burden of the unworthy. Perhaps on the personal level there is such a thing as a love which will not let evil men go. Perhaps as a highly spiritual experience God Himself can take the place of the personality— of the race of personalities—defiled by treacherous selfishness and in His own divine agony may create the moral and spiritual force of forgiveness and peace and the power of a new life. So at this last great moment of supreme need

231

and of utter moral and spiritual appropriation, it is the distinction between the world of personal experiences and the world of subpersonal mathematical relationships which makes it possible for the honest man to accept the mighty ministry of the cross. For what would be perfectly impossible on the level of impersonal judicial mathematics is perfectly and gloriously possible on the level of living personal experience. God has made man's sin His own in order that the righteousness of God may be the divine gift to man.

All this requires and will doubtless one day receive a loftier and more majestic interpretation than even that which men's moral struggles and the strange ways of the ethical life received at the hands of Aeschylus, Sophocles, and Euripides. The supreme poem of the passion of God is yet to be written. And when it is written, the whole humanistic dialectic from man's first choice among alternatives to his last choice of the God who speaks to him from the cross will march to a music like that to which Dante set the theology of the Middle Ages. As Saint Thomas Aquinas learned to sing in Dante, so the modern evangelical humanist will sing in the great poet who is to be.

In the meantime it is our humbler task to recognize that we have reached the goal of this particular discussion in what we believe is the veritable goal of human life, in the strategy of the cross as the central and determining fact of the Christian religion. There are many implications for the searching of eager minds and the inspiration of honest lives. And some of them we may set forth. There are many relationships, of which not a few belong to the more formal aspects of theological treatment, except in so far as all true theology is at last grist to the humanist's mill. And of some of these we may think. But we will stand

232

at no point of a stranger or more tragically glorious beauty than that from which we see the figure on the cross speaking the word of forgiveness and creative hope which brings man after the long experience of his travail to that journey's end where his mind is full of the very light of God. Now he sees that as human intelligence finds its goal in action after decisive choice, so the very God of all brings all His perfections to the mighty focus of a great decision for the rescue of man and brings that decision to the ineffable act upon the cross where all that God is of goodness and of love, of righteousness and of redemptive power speaks in one perfect deed. And the rhythm of the human and the divine is made complete when the deed of acceptance in man's soul answers to the deed of God's redemptive love.

# CHAPTER XIX

## Humanism and the Christian Church

THE CHRISTIAN CHURCH HAS AT ALL TIMES BEEN SUBJECT TO a very difficult and sometimes a very bitter paradox. Or perhaps we may best say that its life and its witness have been characterized by a series of paradoxes. It has been an institution in time whose very reason for existence was found in its claim to represent sanctions which came from eternity. It has existed in a relative world, and yet it has asserted its foundations in absolute meanings. It has lived its life in an imperfect society, and yet it has declared that it represented the demands of perfection. In the very nature of the case it has shared the limitations of the temporal, and this has affected the adequacy of its witness to the eternal. Inevitably it has taken upon itself qualities of the relative, and this has depleted its power as the representative of the absolute. It has taken to itself qualities of the imperfect society of which it was a part, and this has often compromised and even betrayed its upholding of standards which belong to the world of perfection. Disconcerting and even ugly as these paradoxes are, they inevitably emerge in any institutions in which the temporal and the eternal, the relative and the absolute, the imperfect and the perfect meet. As a result, the Church must maintain its life by means of a perpetual repentance of its own inadequacies at the very moment when it is upholding the divine decrees. This very paradoxical nature of the Christian Church helps us to approach in more sympathetic fashion the story of its

234

relation to the stream of humanism and to the humanistic sanctions and the humanistic goals. Indeed, the paradox of the Church can exist only in a world such as the humanistic dialectic reveals. In an impersonal world you have either static imperfection or definite static perfection. The vital movement where the imperfect sets out on the journey toward perfection is possible only in a personal world such as that which humanism perpetually declares to be the world in which we live.

We are now in a position to see more clearly the relation which has obtained between the stream of humanistic influences and the Christian Church. If we remember the statement made more than once in these studies that humanism existed as a fact centuries before a word was found to describe it, we may say that the Christian Church emerged in a period of decadent humanism. That bright confidence in man's intelligence which characterized fifth and fourth century Athens had lost its brilliancy by the first century A.D. The spirit of belief in man and in man's power which Greece had given to the world had come to fine flower in Athens. It had deeply influenced the spirit of Rome. And it had come to a secondary kind of flowering in the brilliant Hellenistic days in Alexandria. But all about the world there was a sense of frustration and of wistful moral and spiritual longing by the time the men of the first century A.D. looked out upon life. Their minds were molded by the great works which were the product of the humanism of Greece and Rome, but with all of this there was a sense of disillusionment and often of tragic defeat. Man was soon to use his humanistic skills to express his cynical disbelief in humanity. By the second century A.D. the mood of intellectual scorn was ready to become some-

thing like a cult, and was corrosively expressed in the ironic
dialogues of Lucian. Yet all the sense of the significance of
man as man and of the importance of his mental, moral,
and spiritual experience which Athens had brought to
the world prepared the way for the Christian religion. In
particular the fashion in which Plato had moved from
ideas in the mind of man to perfect ideas in the ultimate
universe—its very texture and its very reality—and finally
to the conscious intelligence in which these ideas found
their home, represented a dialectic which in its own way
Christianity was to use century after century in moving
from the human to the divine. The One who was called the
Son of Man had His own profound relation to the deepest
insights of the humanistic spirit. As we have seen, it is
a humanism fully conscious of its distinctive meanings and
of their implications which makes it possible to believe
in the incarnation. And Jesus always turned men's minds
away from the subhuman to the human and then on to the
divine. When the Christian religion as a living experience
crystallized into theological forms, it was the Greek culture
and its humanistic literature and philosophy which gave
to the Alexandrian theologians the thought forms which
they sorely needed and without which they could not have
done their work. Humanism was always present as a subtle
and informing spirit in the Greek theology. And even
such a great Latin theologian as Saint Augustine was first
of all a humanist. Indeed, to the very end of his life there
were important humanistic elements in his thinking. The
appeal to man's reason which was so important in the
massive volumes which came from his pen can be made
only on a humanistic basis.

It is true that many Christian thinkers feared the influence of the Greek and Latin literatures. This is not hard to understand, for these literatures all too often told the tale not only of the decadence of humanism but of the decadence of man. Too often they represented that very evil from which the Christian religion was to set men free. The tares kept growing with the wheat. But there was wheat in the Greek and Latin writings. And this wheat was necessary even for those theologians who were afraid of the classic heritage. Their minds were molded far more than they knew by the very masterpieces whose influence they viewed with anxious fear.

As far as the Middle Ages possessed a culture, it was a by-product of the humanistic spirit of Greece and Rome. When great thinkers like Anselm appeared, the old cultures gave them their thought forms, while the Hebrew and Christian scriptures gave them their beliefs. That belief in the human reason which was so important a part of the thinking of the Middle Ages was a gift to the Christian Church of the humanism of Greece. Later through the consummate work of the scholastic thinkers in logical dialectic it became the basis of modern science, whose pursuits it made possible. The supreme theological masterpiece of Saint Thomas—the *Summa*—depended upon Aristotle for its logic. It turned Aristotle into a Christian theologian. And in it, in a sense, the humanist became a Christian.

It is also true, to be sure, that the movements of the Middle Ages which tended in a direction which a later period would have called rationalism also grew in part out of humanistic inspiration. Abelard's *Sic et non* is characterized by an inquiring, half skeptical attitude which had actual humanistic roots. If you believe in the investigating,

237

judging quality of man's mind, you must expect its activity to take negative as well as positive directions. And so it was even in the Middle Ages.

In the Renaissance at its best humanism became a Christian philosophy. In the Renaissance on its secular side—Leonardo the Florentine had an essentially secular mind—humanism became engrossed with the investigation of the subhuman. In the Renaissance at its worst—on the naturalistic side—humanism turned pagan. In the Renaissance in its cool and appraising mood—as in Erasmus—humanism was the critic of the Church, but the critic could remain the son of the Church even while doing his most critical work.

The acerbities of ecclesiastical controversy have often prevented men from seeing that during the period of the Protestant Revolt, and especially at the time of the Council of Trent and the Counter Reformation, and during the centuries which have followed, the Latin communion has never lost its hold upon humanistic sanctions. Such men as Jacques Maritain and Etienne Gilson represent a venerable and a lofty tradition. It must also be remembered that on one side the Protestant Revolt was a humanistic movement. It always used some weapons forged by humanism in its great fights. The Reformed theology had profound humanistic connections. Calvin was a humanist before he was a theologian. The French church of the classic period, both in its Latin and its Protestant form—especially, indeed, in its Latin form—graced its Christian devotion by beauties won from a stately Christian humanism. Then—by another odd paradox—eighteenth century skepticism owned a humanistic parentage. It was the product of a self-conscious arrogant humanism which tore human life from its roots in religion and then often offered detailed criticisms full of justice and importance, but it was a movement which had the seed of its own death in it. When the period of Revolution came, it also felt influences which originated in humanistic sources. The watchword "the rights of man" has its own humanistic connections. But the leaders of the revolutionary period drank most of all the wine of a heady human romanticism different enough from the cool, clear drink with which the true humanist satisfied his palate. Nineteenth century science was so busy with subhuman nature that it became very much confused about the humanistic insights. The Marxian dialectic took the desire for human betterment implicit in humanism and attempted to implement it by means of a thoroughly subhuman philosophy—a materialistic and inverted Hegelianism. It is not strange that when Marxism became a political program it tended to lose its human spirit in its mechanistic organization. Even at its best it must be confessed that it turned more toward humanitarianism which is humanism become romantic and emphasizing comfort instead of freedom, rather than to genuine humanism, which is thoroughly critical and values even comfort only when it is secured without the loss of freedom.

From the period of the Reformation the Protestant churches were influenced in various degrees by the old humanism, the hot romanticism, the new mood produced by the natural sciences, and the uncritical humanitarianism which was the product of socialistic thought. During the latter part of the nineteenth century, Christian thinkers held no end of peace congresses with a natural science little disciplined by the humanistic insights. And in the twentieth century the Church in many parts of the world was tempted to forget—or at least to cease to emphasize—its distinctive message in the devotion it developed to dreams of a new social order based upon an impersonal social formula rather than upon a company of transformed persons. Until the day of messianic science and all the pseudo sciences, and the day of all-engrossing social passion, a humanistic culture dominated the intellectual life of the Church and of the world. This was particularly true in the Latin communion, which taught humanistic culture to speak in a stately ecclesiastical voice. Wherever the evangelical revival went in Protestant churches, there were groups who were characterized by an unfortunate distrust not merely of a decadent humanistic culture but of humanism itself, and who thought of evangelical religion as the substitute for humanism rather than as its inevitable completion and consummation. Such men as Alexander Whyte and Peter Forsyth in the British tradition represented an evangelicalism which was more critical. The spirit of evangelical humanism was already alive in them. In another line of ecclesiastical development, the humanistic light which the Cambridge Platonists brought to seventeenth century England was never without votaries in the churches. And in our own time neo-Thomism has given to Christian humanism many-faceted lights in the Latin communion.

The relation of the sanctions of humanism to the thought and life of the Christian Church in the world today is of decisive and urgent importance. It is not too much to say that every point at which the world has gone wrong is a point at which it has turned from the characteristic insights of humanism. And it is not too much to say that every point at which the Church is to put the world right is a point at which it is necessary to return to humanistic sanctions. The totalitarian state—whether at the extreme right or at the extreme left—is a subhuman institution. And if the mad ambition of the totalitarian state were to be realized, the result would be a subhuman world.

The leaders of the totalitarian state use every power of human intelligence which they can command for the production of a mechanical efficiency before which all human values will go down. They use human reason in order to construct the machines which will strike down the men. They represent the vastest and most monumental attempt of humanity to commit suicide. A humanistic Christian criticism would teach the makers of machines to use them for the preservation and not for the destruction of human values. Such a criticism would make the machines the servants and not the foes of men. Such a criticism would refuse to allow man to destroy his humanity as the last triumphant gesture of his control over the physical world.

The question of the control of the machines for the execution of truly human purposes involves a vast and far-reaching interrogation. It turns itself at critical periods into another question which may be phrased thus: When men of bad will make and use powerful machines for the enforcing of their evil purposes, have men of good will the right to make and use machines to return the attack of the evil men and to baffle their evil purposes so that they are brought to naught? If men can use machines to project the purposes of evil, have men the right to use machines to thwart the purposes of evil? Is all the destructive power of the machine to be turned against the good by bad men, and are good men to stand helpless, never having the right to use the power of the machine to defend themselves against the conscienceless attack of evil?

True humanistic—and, indeed, critical Christian—thought comes with an unhesitating answer to these questions. And the answer may be put in this fashion: Whenever you have evil minds dominating mechanical forces, you have tyranny and the breaking of every human right and the overthrow of every human value. Whenever you have goodness which refuses to use its intelligence to make and master machines and to hurl them against attacking evil, you have impotence and defeat coming upon the forces of goodness. When you have goodness which is not afraid to use physical force against attacking bad will, you have the securing of some sort of decency and of some sort of order in the world. Indeed, in this last case the authorities representing good will may often maintain their position by the use of potential rather than of actual physical force. When the men of bad purpose know that the men of good purpose will not hesitate to use the power of a mechanized world for the forces of good and are ready to do just that, increasingly they will be brought to terms by a threat which they would ignore if they believed it was merely verbal, but before which they will draw back when they know that it is authentic. You cannot fight bad will with words which you are not willing to follow up by decisive acts.

The humanist—the Christian humanist—does not discount the glory of goodness as the result of the use of freedom in right choice on the part of a living person. And by the same token he does not discount the tragic importance of evil as the result of the use of freedom in wrong choice on the part of a living person who knows perfectly well what he is about. There is an evil which is the result of ignorance. And it can be conquered by the forces of education and gracious unselfishness. There is an evil which is conscious and deliberate and deeply personal. You cannot conquer that evil by asserting the moral invincibility of the friendly smile.

The critical mind of the Christian humanist must of course deal frankly and honestly with the attitude of our Lord toward these great matters. And here he will have no reason to falter or to hesitate. In all His teaching, both explicit and implicit, Jesus perpetually declared that only a willing and uncoerced allegiance was of value in the kingdom of God. So the incarnation with the life of the Church following the achievement of Jesus was first of all an adventure to secure voluntary loyalty. It was an adventure of revelation, clearing up ignorance by a glorious setting forth of knowledge of God. It was an adventure of loving unselfishness, showing how far love would go to secure the willing response even of those who were unworthy. Here there was no place for the use of physical force of any kind. Here there was the cloak given when the coat was asked. Here there was the left cheek turned when the right cheek had been struck. Here was the following of the path of unselfish love to the uttermost limit of the cross. So far love could go. So far divine love did go to secure the glad loyalty, the willing and uncoerced obedience of men. Here we have a great and powerful part of the Christian religion. Here we have the method of securing that brotherhood of unselfish good will which responds to the sacrificial and unselfish love of God. Here we have the justification of the creation of men by means of the creation of the beloved community.

But this is just half of the Christian religion. Jesus was always utterly realistic in confronting the dark nature of personal evil. He set that royal value on personality which we

243

have found to be essential to the humanistic sanctions. He understood all the negative as well as all the positive nature of this royal form of decision. He knew that while men could accept Him, they could also reject Him. And implicitly—and again and again explicitly—He declared this in the most unhesitating fashion. He wanted to meet men as a friend. He offered to meet them as a friend. He went to the cross to prove His friendship. But if men in the awful strength of their personal power rejected His friendship, the men who refused to have Him as a friend *would have to meet Him as a judge*. And His picture of this ultimate judgment was completely realistic. There was no hesitation and there was no evasion. In the ultimate universe Almighty God would use the grimmest and the sternest force to deal with those recalcitrant persons who made evil their good and turned from every outreach of the love of God. There is such a thing as recalcitrant evil. And in the ultimate universe it will be dealt with by that righteous overlordship which will restrain its evil impulses by sheer omnipotent power.

Christianity is the religion of love on the cross. It is also the religion of judgment on the throne. To speak of the love alone—as so many sentimental Christians do today—is to emasculate Christianity and to leave it soft and morally impotent in the presence of recalcitrant evil. To speak of the judgment alone is to harden Christianity and to make it something grim and implacable. To speak of love on the cross and of judgment on the throne is to give the full Christian witness to the whole of Christian truth. But if there is personal evil in the ultimate universe—and this Jesus clearly taught—which can be restrained only by the sheer omnipotence of God, by the same token there is evil in this present world which can be restrained only by a good will which is not afraid to use force where force is needed. To say that we can do by tenderness in time what God can do only by the use of force in eternity is—to put it mildly—greatly to overestimate human powers. Love on the cross and judgment on the throne must characterize man's moral life in time as well as the ultimate adjudication of eternity. Without this, evil would run amuck—without this, evil will run amuck—in a world where goodness constantly must hold its own against the grim assault of powerful evil.

But the Christian never forgets the love even in the exercise—the necessary exercise—of moral judgment. And he is kept perpetually humble by a knowledge of the awful responsibility of making even those ethical judgments without whose active support the world would fall into complete moral decay. On the other hand, he is saved from that ethical softness and that betrayal of the great spiritual and the great human values which come to those who make merely sentimental love unpurged by critical processes of analysis an absolute of such a character that moral judgments become impossible. Not even in the name of love do we dare to risk moral frustration.

But the love which judges and yet saves us is to inspire in us the love which judges and yet goes to great and glorious lengths to bring God's salvation to others.

The teacher who castigates the school bully and then in the happiest fashion does all he can to make him his best friend is a homely and intimate illustration of a far-reaching principle. Tenderness must not drive out virility. But virility finds its crown in the tenderness of the victor. Our last word when persons who uphold dark evils are conquered is a word of friendly peace—once their malignant

245

desires are brought to definite frustration. We can go only so far as to restrain the evil which would blight human life. Then we turn to win those who have practiced that evil to better ways of living. We must—and how gladly we do—leave the ultimate judgment of the evil persons, who would never respond to the outreach of love, to the all-seeing eye and the all-understanding mind of God. This alone we know—and this is enough for us to know—that only that personality which so makes evil its good as to be eternally incapable of responding to the compassion of God is lost to the pursuit of that divine love which not only put a cross upon a green hill far away but keeps a cross forever in its heart.

The Christian humanist is happiest in the carrying out of his positive tasks. His knowledge of his own unworthiness makes him shrink from even necessary judgments. And in a very characteristic activity he is pursuing irresponsive evil with the tenderness of a good will whose glory it is to find the human equivalent of the cross of Christ in the endeavor to win men to the willing acceptance of the love of God.

Life itself is to be interpreted in the terms of the largest sense of the royal quality of that creature who stands poised between alternatives, always making decisions in the light of permanent standards. These standards have now become more than the result of the inspection of vast and varied centuries of human experience. They have been confirmed and amplified and far transcended by the revelation which has come to us from God Himself. They rest at last upon the words of God and the Word of God and the acts of God. These principles become a living fire of glorious inspiration in the relation of human persons with the divine person, in all the fashion in which we see the face of God in the face of Jesus Christ.

There is such a thing as a Christian culture. And here Christian humanism shines in its very brightest light. For Christian culture at its best is the Christian victory made splendid in Christian architecture, made glorious in Christian poetry, capturing all the glow of color for the expression of its mysteries in Christian art, and filling every process of human expression with its own beauty, its own finality, and its own power.

In an age whose characteristic art expresses the dismemberment of man, which has descended from the human to the subhuman to find a rhythm untouched by intelligence, which has found its sharpest words to tell the tale of its own disillusionment, its frustration, and its despair, which has found a momentary false illumination as it has turned to the world of sense undisciplined by the world of spirit—in such an age it seems almost too good to be true that the most actual realism is that which confronts the reality of the good and living and perfect God, that the profoundest depth of probing understanding finds a divine love which pursues man to his last lair of disillusionment and despair with the hope of a good life and an eternal hope, that man's ultimate song is not a song of death but a song of life, that it is cynicism which is failing to come into contact with the reality of things and which becomes not only confused but dishonest at last. The suicide of the despairing artist whose only words have been lucid words of disintegration and bitter gloom is only the symbol of the frustration of his dark creed, of his failure to grasp reality itself. The death of the martyr, his eyes shining with the love of God, is the symbol of the endless victory of the Christian Church; and the life

247

of the everyday man who in the light of eternity finds his way among the fogs of time is the last beautiful tribute to the power of the God whose face the Church sees in the face of Jesus Christ, very God but also *very man.*

# CHAPTER XX

## The Beloved Community

THE CRITICS MUST ALWAYS EXPECT TO BE CRITICIZED. SO IT IS not surprising that critical humanism has lived its life in a constant barrage of hostile discussion. The critical humanists have by no means objected to this. They have never themselves hesitated to be caustically provocative. And they have rather rejoiced in the type of provocation on the part of their foes which has given them the opportunity to clarify their own position or to make a counterattack of even more deadly character than that to which they have been subjected. They have remembered the Moslem watchword, "Paradise lies in the shadow of the crossing of swords." And they have been willing to declare that often the realm of truth is found beyond the clashing of the swords of the mind.

Probably the most cutting of the criticisms which lance-like have been hurled at the critical humanists is the assertion that they are a group of intellectual aristocrats constantly moving away from the richness and the fullness of the conscious life of man. They have worked out a dialectic for sophisticated patricians which must always leave the plain man cold and untouched, and which, when the attempt is made to force it upon him, will turn his indifference into hostility. The heat of life has gone out of it. It has lost its contact with that fertile soil out of which human life has grown, and which must perpetually enrich man's life if it is to keep its virility and its primitive energy. The critics may even go so far as to say—if they are willing for a moment to use the vocabulary of the humanists for purposes of attack—that the humanistic thinkers have never understood that it is constantly necessary to bring in the subhuman in order to save the human from frustration. In the name of the widely diffused richness of the life of common men —and in the name of that rush of creative vitality which moves through all animate life and to which man must again and again return when his cold mathematical mind has betrayed him—they protest against that which they are ready to declare would impoverish the very lives which it endeavors to control. In fact, some of them are ready to insist, it is not by control of the rich energies of life but by surrender to them that man finds his fullest being. The padlock of the passions, some of them loudly assert, does not mean the emancipation of humanity. It means only that man himself has been put behind the bars.

The best reply to this onslaught against critical humanism is just to allow its votaries to take the way of their own enthusiasm and see what happens. Before long it begins to be evident that just as the unexamined life is the uncivilized life, so the uncontrolled life is the life on the road to disintegration and frustration and despair. Modernistic poets have often taken very much the position we have been describing. Their poetry has been like hot lava edged with flame and dark with smoke, erupted from the volcano of their inner chaos. When one of them at the end of his own tether committed suicide, it was a member of his circle of thought who admitted that he had only taught and exemplified another method of damnation.

As a matter of fact, when the critical humanist insists upon *vital control,* he is by no means either cold or hard or lacking in warmth. For he emphasizes the vitality as well

250

blame his personal weakness upon social institutions. He is inclined to dream of a society which will relieve him of the necessity of self-discipline and will make unnecessary the practice of self-control. This "escape mechanism" by means of which the individual avoids responsibility for his own personality by social dreams and by revolutionary action is soundly condemned by the critical humanist.

To the humanist, the central matter of life is always the exercise of free intelligence by the individual in the light of permanent standards. Indeed, he sees clearly enough that just as a matter of fact there is no social action which is not accomplished by an individual or by individuals. If you want to carry out a social reform, the first thing you would do is to secure an individual of outstanding personal power and of aggressive qualities of leadership. This individual enters the world of action. He enlists the help of other individuals. And the reform is carried through triumphantly by individual men. Social action itself is, at first, at last, and all the time, the action of individuals. There is no transcendental entity called society which will go on working while all the individuals sleep. Society is only an abstract term which has no actuality apart from the action of individuals.

So at the very moment when the critical humanist sees the corrupting tendencies of a social passion which is made the substitute for an honest facing by the individual of the central problems of his own life, he sees that social action itself is effective only when carried out by individuals who have already achieved some sort of personal self-mastery. Then the searchlight of a very far-reaching criticism is allowed to fall upon the type of mind which dances about irresponsibly, now caustically honest in analysis, the next moment

253

idyllically naive in childlike and unintelligent faith. The critical humanist sees the pathetic intellectual futility of the mind which is corrosively realistic in analyzing the evils of the present order, and rapturously romantic in expecting the happiest result from a social order which exists only in the land of dreams and whose formulas are never subjected to the tests of effective criticism.

By the time he has said all this and has said it with caustic power and provocative energy, the humanistic critic of romantic Utopias is likely to be regarded by idealistic young thinkers hurrying to create a new world as the very incarnation of the spirit of social reaction, the defender of wrongs which ought never to be defended, the upholder of a rotten and falling social structure, the last voice of a decadent past which would enlist the urbanities of a classic culture to defeat the onward march of mankind. As a matter of fact, however, the critical humanist has not yet uttered his last word. He has done all this destructive work with an essentially constructive purpose. He does not want rotten timbers in the house of his social thought. But this is just because he wants that house to be solid and permanent. As a matter of fact, it is the social thinker who grows angry at the first suggestion of intelligent criticism who rushes out to build his house upon the sand where it will be overwhelmed by the inrushing sea. The critical thinker wants to build the house. But he wants to build it upon a rock.

For the social hope will not admit of defeat. The conception of the beloved community where each man finds richness of life in devotion to the good of all the others, and the others find added quality in life because of their devotion to him and to his good, has elements of challenge to which men must listen, and incorporates demands which men of good will cannot ignore or cast aside. That this beloved community can never be produced by legislation goes without saying. Legislation alone, if seemingly successful, would produce only the external union of unsocialized individuals. That the beloved community cannot be produced by revolution is as clear as anything can be to the critical thinker. Revolution produces by dramatic force a community of mechanical co-operation with seething unrest beneath the surface. It is far enough from the beloved community. Indeed, in any social organization one individual who misused his intelligence and followed evil instead of good would bring hatred into what was in theory the beloved community. And neither legislation nor revolution can insure the beloved community against the presence of a great many such individuals. The irony of a good deal of so-called social action consists in the presence of selfish and evil-minded leaders who use the formulas of brotherhood as a smoke screen under cover of which to accomplish their purposes in what is still a very wicked and unbrotherly world.

The social hope has a very difficult fight in a world like ours. We may now well ask ourselves what are those forces which may be trusted to advance its true interests and which will not use its watchwords, only afterward to betray it from within. When with this thought dominating our minds we turn to the Christian religion, we discover that wherever it is fully and vitally active it is all the while producing individuals who are capable of becoming members of the beloved community. And we soon come to understand that wherever there is a group of such individuals there is a sense in which the beloved community is already present. The production of such individuals is the supreme matter in human life.

When the number of individual men and women who already have the beloved community in their hearts is very few, and their circles of fellowship far and scattered, they represent shining little centers of light in a dark world. They keep man's fairest hope alive. But they do not yet have much influence upon the great world. Sometimes their witness against the hostility of evil forces can only be the witness of martyrdom. But as they grow in number they become increasingly a force in the life of which they are a part. More and more they become responsible for the lives and the practical relationships of every sort which are accepted as a standard in the society in which they live. When at length they have increased to that point where they have the balance of power, they can do much. When they come to possess a majority, they can do more. When they have a great and decisive majority, they can do most of all. Laws and social orders are effective only as these individuals put their own character into the making and the enforcing of these laws and the establishing of these orders. At all these points there is a very definite possibility of self-delusion. The critical humanist is needed all the while to subject messianic social dreams to cool and clear analysis, and to remind the leaders who think that institutions can make men of their tragic mistake.

It is always particularly necessary to keep an eye on the small groups of impatient and undisciplined idealists who by subterfuge and force would dominate a majority which they really despise in the name of their favorite messianic social formulas. They are always tempted to regard themselves as intelligence officers in a great social war, and to claim exemption from the operation of the code of truth and honest dealing which ordinarily obtains among gentle-

men. The man who is false to every one of his principles as a matter of practical strategy in order to secure the
triumph of these very principles is a very curious phenomenon, and never more curious than when he carries on his
baffling activities within the councils of the Christian
Church! The temptation to get by overshrewdness and by
wily strategy what one cannot get by honest persuasion is
perpetually present. In all societies which recognize democratic principles it is important to remember this. There
is a truth in the political liberalism, which men too often
speak of as discredited, that may be expressed in these
words: A passionate minority can never force an uncon-
vinced majority into a messianic age of its own contriving.
And even when the minority is not only passionately sincere
but also nobly right in its ideals, it can never use the methods
of the beast to force an unregenerate majority to follow the
ways of the angels. The practices of idealists who are unethical in their methods have corrupted the life of many institutions and have left their stains upon the history of the
Christian Church.

But the beloved community remains indeed the city of
God which must forever haunt the humanist who has found
the final fulfillment of his life in the Christian religion. He
knows the menace of false hopes. And he knows that only
as individuals enter its portals one by one does the beloved
community become real. He works with good cheer. And
if the light of the revolutionist does not shine in his eyes, it
is also true that the bitter taste which comes to the idealist
turned cynic as he drinks the cup of disillusionment is never
felt upon his tongue.

The soured idealist is actually a human phenomenon of
the utmost importance. He dreams vast and varied dreams

which he never subjects to the tests of critical intelligence. And his gregarious and romantic idealism leaves him particularly open to attack. One by one he sees his dreams fall lifeless beside him. At last he becomes the very living presence of a deflated idealism. He turns hard and cynical. He repudiates a hopefulness which he now is assured can never find standing ground in such a world as ours. All his old enthusiasms turn bitter upon his tongue. His only satisfaction is in raucous cries of pain and in an ugly rejoicing whenever noble words and noble phrases are discredited. He hates all ideals because his own ideals have betrayed him.

The Christian humanist begins to exercise his critical faculty the very moment social hopes emerge, and at every stage in the process of their acceptance as a program of action, and continues to exercise his critical intelligence in all the activities which follow. He anticipates disillusionment from afar. And so his idealism and his critical reason march together down the highway of life. Then his sure sense of social demand grows, not out of mere romantic dreaming, but out of an analysis of the nature of man himself. The very study of human nature which prepares him for bad choices gives sound basis for his belief in good choices. And his social hope is not the by-product of a glowing or even fevered imagination, but the soundly buttressed conviction that humanity can never rest in a social achievement below the level of man's true life. Man must achieve a social life which is worthy of his humanity. If the humanist can have no easy hopes, he can have no tempestuous emotional despairs. He is at least as far from an uncritical pessimism as he is free from an uncritical optimism.

Then because he is a Christian who has found the fulfillment of his humanism in the Christian religion, he has a hope whose final support is found far beyond the structure of human life in the very character of the God whose face we see in the face of Jesus Christ. When the darkest hours of his own experience and of the experience of the age arrive, he does not become a soured idealist. Because the house of his assurance is built upon the character of God, no human storm can dislodge it. He has the veritable experience of dwelling in a habitation resting securely—if one may use the great old phrase—upon the rock of ages. So, as his disciplined intelligence saves him from romantic dreams, his Christian faith gives him secure hopes. And thus he goes forth to work loyally for the realization of the city of God among the hard actualities of the city of man.

And he does go forth to work. He does not use his caustic criticism as an excuse for accepting freedom from difficult responsibility. He does not allow his belief in God's power and God's governance to be made an excuse for escape from the most difficult action on his own part and on the part of other men. He knows the meaning of the paradox of believing as if God is to do everything, and acting as if only man can do anything. He has a complete distaste for the spiritual dilettante who makes the richness of his mystical experience with God a reason for being freed from all practical relations with the life of men. He regards the soiled battle flag as a nobler emblem than the mystic rose which has never been carried into the ugly fight. And yet he knows that the fight without the mystic rose is bound to come to frustration and to defeat at last. So he comes upon another of those great paradoxes which are at once the strangeness and the glory of Christian thought and of the Christian life. That all in all he must look for a fulfillment of his social

259

hopes beyond the borders of time we shall see in the next chapter. That these ultimate hopes are never to be made an excuse for avoiding immediate responsibility we ought clearly to see just now.

The Christian is not responsible for the results of the social struggle in any period. He is responsible for putting on his armor. He is responsible for entering the army. He is responsible for sharing in the long marches and the terrible thirsts. He is responsible for striking his deadliest blows against the evil of the world. It is only after he has put every last ounce of his power into the struggle that he has a right to rest back on the thought of the providence of God and of the ultimate fulfillment which will bring realizations never found within the borders of time.

With all this, the Christian humanist knows that he has a responsibility to his own life, for the sake of its contribution to the life of mankind, as well as for the sake of doing well with God's good gift of human personality. A man never serves society by being less of a man himself. He never uplifts mankind by lowering his personal standards. He never really aids in bringing in the beloved community by becoming an unlovely person. This does not mean that he is to become the self-conscious pursuer of an isolated excellence. It does mean that he is to attain by the grace of God a certain self-respect which will at last give the final quality of authenticity to his social passion. Indeed, the integrity of his own life will be his final security against betraying his social ideals by making them the mere instruments of selfish personal plans. Individual honesty and courage and faithfulness—the whole integrity of the individual life—represent the final security of the social achievement.

260

As a member of the great community which is being formed by the grace of God, he will need a house of silence as well as a house of communication. It is easy to be socially friendly and to have very little to give to other men. There is nothing more empty than the chatter of endless words never enriched by something which comes from the depths of the individual spirit.

> "The man who idly sits and thinks
> May sow a nobler crop than corn,
> For thoughts are seeds of future deeds,
> And when God thought a world was born."

The house of silence will contain a library. Here in the silence of brooding understanding our Christian humanist will have fellowship with the best that has been thought, the best that has been said, and the best that has been done in the world. And in volume after volume of poetry he will touch the best that has been felt in the world. So he will come to action in the age with a certain aloof understanding which means that he brings to the problem of the hour the wisdom of the ages. So his house of silence will have become a house of understanding. And in this house of silence he will not only meet the great human past. Here he will live over again men's life with God in other centuries. The Old Testament scriptures will make real the religious experience of Israel, which in so many ways may become his own. Forever the gospels will tell him the tale of the great consummation, and forever the letters of Paul will tell him the tale of the great interpretation. These things will become the very breath of his spirit. Here in his house of silence he will meet the vast and varied experiences of the Christian Church century after century. This is the story of his own family. Here is his own family tree. Saints and prophets and martyrs and Christian men of thought and Christian men of action will come out of the tomb to keep company with him in his house of silence. And here, in the greatest hours of all, the Jesus of history will become the living Christ of personal experience. We drop the curtains over that sacred hour, but we know why the Christian humanist comes out of the house of silence with a shining face.

So he brings a full Christian manhood to the world of action in its busy and turbulent hours. He fights as one who sees beyond the battlefield, and so he fights best, and so he never comes to despair if the fighting goes badly on a particular day.

In all this, in increasing and beautiful fashion, he finds fellowship with other men and women and with little children as the days go by. And often a golden light falls upon his friendship. And it seems as if the beloved community were already a reality in this transient world.

## CHAPTER XXI

## Humanism and Immortality

VERY OFTEN YOU UNDERSTAND THE NATURE OF PRINCIPLES BEST when they have been turned into poetry. The philosopher frequently allows his principles to lie so coldly in his mind that you scarcely know what they would do if they were put in command of human life, or where they would lead if they became the inspiration of man's ultimate thoughts about life and destiny. But the poet extorts from a principle all its vital qualities and all its emotional possibilities. He makes it a part of living experience. Those views of life which flatly reject the insights of humanism have been eagerly accepted by no end of the modernistic poets. And what was entered upon as an experience of emancipation has had a curious way of turning into a black blight of pessimism which is worse than slavery. D. H. Lawrence was ready to declare that his belief was in the blood, that the flesh was wiser than the intellect. But so he did not find a glad rejoicing in life. He became weary with the world. He became utterly sick of it. He found everything tainted. His inhuman ecstasy of the flesh could not quite hide that loathing which followed. Robinson Jeffers declared stoutly that humanity was a mold from which to break away. And so utterly did he come to despise genuine human life with its vital orderliness that he could think of unnatural crime and inhuman science as a way of escape. He comes to the emancipated insight that drunkenness and killing are not enormous evils, and then with the psychopathic revulsion so

263

characteristic of his type of pseudo emancipator he looks with utter loathing at man the corrupter, and with ugly cynicism full of bitter energy repudiates the thought of resurrection for man. And, as if afraid of the thing he repudiates, he cries out half in fear and half in anger, "Dead man, be quiet." So he comes at last to a hatred of conscious existence. The dialectic in experience is definite and sure. A man begins by repudiating his human heritage. He goes on to glorify the subhuman. He turns from the human with loathing. Then in the bitter reaction of sated subhuman emotions he turns from all conscious existence with anger. He comes to abhor the very vital forces whose nature he has misunderstood and whose energies he has so often misused. The dialectic of subhumanism is: pseudo emancipation on lower levels, the deification of the blood or the thing, the dark pessimism of utter frustration, and the hard quiet of the sated senses in nihilism at last. Clearly subhumanism has so emptied life of noble meaning that the thought of immortality can rouse only a sickly feeling of angry scorn.

On the other hand, there are doubtless those who would claim that humanism has to do only with man's life on this planet. They are very keen about emphasizing human values here and now. They appreciate the present life. But they draw back at once if it is suggested that we should attempt to draw aside the curtain and to look beyond its activities. By all means let us make the most of this life on high human levels, they would say. But let us be guided by those hesitations which emerge so naturally when we are tempted to try to look beyond its experiences. Already we have seen that while the critical humanist may thus limit himself, there will be something in his essential position

264

which will inevitably tend to move beyond man's life in time. More and more he will feel that he must find a reality in eternity which answers to the distinctive quality of human life in time. He will find the authentication of the human person here in the Divine Person who gives security to the qualities of free intelligence in His own life in eternity. But if you find the justification for believing in the human in the divine life beyond time, is it not possible that you will find the fulfillment of the human also beyond the borders of this all too relative world? Of the humanist also may not the French proverb be true, "To understand earth you must have known heaven"? Or, if this is putting the matter too bluntly at the beginning of the argument, is it not already clear that to understand time you must approach the life of time with insights coming out of eternity?

At all events, we want now to lift the question of the relation of the principles of critical humanism to a belief in immortality. We have already seen that all subhuman views of existence and experience make belief in immortality impossible. If you explain the universe in terms of mechanical and mathematical reaction, there is no place for immortality. If you explain the universe in the terms of biological impulse, there is no place for immortality. It is of the very nature of naturalism to create doubts as to an afterlife, and at last to make belief in a life beyond death impossible.

But by critical humanism man is seen emerging from nature. And he is seen so emerging not as a matter of speculation on the part of the humanist. The humanist merely insists upon calling attention to facts which the man caught in the clutches of naturalism ignores. Man has emerged. The critical humanist sees that this is the defining fact about man, and he makes it the basis of all of his thinking. The fact of man's controlling intelligence is not only the decisive fact in his experience. It is something so new, so startling, so differing in quality from the aspects of existence below man that at first we have only the vaguest sense of the regions into which it will lead us. The free movement of man's mind in choosing among alternatives introduces us to a new world of actuality. The existence on this planet of a creature exercising critical intelligence is a fact which lifts us completely above the level of mechanical interaction and biological appetite. In a sense man's control of things in time already transcends the temporal. In a sense man's control of his appetites in time also transcends the temporal. The truth of the matter is that the moment you accept the principles of critical humanism, whether you know it or not, you are moving in the direction of a belief in immortality. For critical intelligence has to do with values which transcend time. It has to do with standards which transcend time. And since critical humanism is only dealing with the distinctive facts which it finds in human life, this is only another way of saying that man lives his characteristic life in time all the while by using that which transcends the time limits. The "universals" which are a perpetual—if often implicit—part of man's distinctively human life simply could not appear on the subhuman level, and inevitably they point to a third level above the human. Long ago in his powerful volume *Nature and the Supernatural* Horace Bushnell made it abundantly clear that you cannot study the life of man with understanding without finding the supernatural here and now. In a sense this very much simplifies our problem. For now we see that we do not have to go to some far-off realm of ethereal speculation quite apart from human life in order to find something beyond this life to which a man can relate his final aspirations. It would be hard for us to believe that something which has no relation to the structure of a man's life and the quality of his activity now is yet the very fulfillment of his nature and the expression of his ultimate destiny. But if, the moment man reaches the distinctively human stage, he lives his life in time by perpetually transcending the temporal, here we have a fact of the most tremendous significance. For now we see that when man's mind moves in the direction of the thought of immortality, he is moving in the direction of the veritable fulfillment of his nature, and not a distortion of his nature, at the demand of lovely and ethereal dreams.

The truth is that man's exercise of free and controlling intelligence in time is just as amazing, as astonishing, and as completely bewildering a fact as the resurrection and the life immortal could ever be. No "miracle" of which we read transcends this miracle of everyday experience. We have a crass way of thinking that because a theory is familiar there is no mystery about it, that because we meet it every day we quite sufficiently understand it. At this point the truth is quite the opposite. If we were to fathom the sheer glorious mystery of one man poised between alternatives and using his free intelligence to reach a decision in the light of clearly held standards, we would never have intellectual difficulty with the conception that man's real life utterly transcends the limitations of time. To put it sharply, if we believe that man's experience goes sweeping beyond his physical death and there transcends the temporal order, we find this belief possible, because man has already gone completely above and beyond that order in his characteristic experience and his characteristic activity in this very relative world.

The argument has a moral as well as an intellectual aspect. The moment you find yourself in the realm of free human intelligence loyally choosing among alternatives in the light of permanent standards, you are already in the region of values which deserve to persist beyond death. Somehow death seems an incongruity—and an impertinence—in the presence of these values.

As long as man has nothing in his experience which deserves to continue beyond death, it would be hard to persuade him to believe in immortality. In *After Many a Summer Dies the Swan* Aldous Huxley ironically professes to find a man and a woman who live on from one century to another, lost to every interest except the throb of the distinctive biological process. Clearly immortality on any such terms would be the ultimate absurdity. One of the reasons why the belief in immortality has waned in our time is just because so many of our activities are petty or worse. The projection of the machine age, without control in the name of high standards, into a perpetual ongoing, repeating ceaselessly the meaningless jargon of whirring wheels, would be turning eternity into a nightmare. There is something like the ultimate combination of tragedy and comedy in the thought of an eternity spent in the manufacture of automobiles followed by the ceaseless driving of purring machines from one place which has no meaning to another which is equally meaningless, from vacuum to vacuum forever and ever. As long as you have discovered no values which deserve to go on beyond death, annihilation is a boon and not a curse.

But the moment man comes to have in his experience that in whose presence he cannot think of death without distaste and a sense of incongruity, something very important has happened. The courage which faces death in the name of an invisible loyalty; the love which reaches beyond the bright world of the senses with a devotion which has something of the infinite in it; the awareness of an eternal truth, an eternal goodness, and an eternal beauty which can bend even the intractable world of sense to their uses; the experience of clear intelligence emerging from the world of things and the world of appetites; the experience of fellowship on the personal level—all these belong to a realm the ugly symbol of the skull and crossbones cannot reach. Already they belong to eternity when we experience them in time, and by the same token they must persist in eternity when the life of time has passed away.

And these realities are never in a world of abstraction apart from conscious existence. It is only when they are real in the experience of conscious persons that they are truly actual. To say that they persist as impersonal abstractions after they are lost as living experience is to talk nonsense. That which does not exist in consciousness does not exist at all. Even George Eliot's "Choir Invisible" has to have an audience of later conscious personalities to which to sing. It is odd that she never understood that that choir might still enjoy singing. This connection of all intellectual and moral and spiritual experience with consciousness is the pivotal matter. To be capable of experiencing an eternal value in consciousness is to have a consciousness which by its very nature and the quality of its experience belongs to eternity and not to time. If it is only a creature who can experience eternal values who can believe in immortality with any sort of authenticity, it is also true that such a creature must believe in immortality the moment he is conscious of the nature, the qualities, and the implications of his own experience. Critical humanism sees man in the midst of the experience of dealing with values which are eternal.

We see, then, that life on the level of free and controlling intelligence simply does not belong to the order of experience in which death is triumphant. And this we see, also, is a good deal more than a matter of logic. It is a matter of living experience. When year after year men are making decisions and are having experiences on the human level which rise clear from the murk of experience whose final meaning is found on the level of things, more and more the eternal hope tends to become clear and authentic. It was not by accident that John Wesley died saying, "The best of all is, God is with us." The saints and martyrs have found within their own souls the very shining beauty whose glory they saw resplendent on the hills of light. When a man sinks to the level of things, and of things never shot through by a meaning beyond themselves, of course he cannot believe in immortality. When he rises to the level of personality and high loyalty and noble spiritual love, the whole question appears in a new fashion. The high meanings bend even the material world to their purposes here and now until the material itself wears the livery of the spiritual. Things are put in their place as the servants of mind. And it becomes possible to think of minds. And it becomes possible to think of minds as high adventurers through an eternity of experience on lofty levels. The world of critical humanism is a world in which immortality can become a living theme.

But we have already seen that the free and controlling intelligence which the critical humanist finds in man is likely to become for him a clue to the nature of the reality to be found in the ultimate universe. Now when this happens and he comes to a belief in perfect controlling intelligence as the final fact of existence, the desire for fellowship with that Perfect Intelligence becomes a real and an important motive in a man's life. It may now become his dominant and controlling motive. A life lived in fellowship with God becomes the supreme life. Here is a beatific experience which is the very transfiguration of life. It begins here. The biographies and the autobiographies of the saints tell the story in awed but haunting phrases as if they have set about the impossible task of expressing a perfect joy in imperfect speech, and a timeless splendor of glorious experience in the all too inelastic and incapable language of time. The experience of fellowship with the divine does indeed begin here, and it edges human life with transcendent joy even in the midst of this relative world. But the very thought of this fellowship sweeps beyond death. Fellowship with the eternal cannot be a merely temporal experience. It requires —it even demands—eternity. So that belief in which critical humanism finds its intellectual completion becomes a spiritual experience which sweeps majestically beyond the tomb to the timeless fulfillment which belongs to the exhaustless resources of God himself. *When God begins to talk with man, it must be a long conversation.*

And now we can see that it is not only true that the characteristic human powers have aspects which transcend the temporal order; it is also true that in eternity man must find his supreme motives for life in time. It is here that humanity finds escape from the unethical otherworldliness which would avoid the responsibilities of life in time through a perpetual brooding meditation in respect of life in eternity. The passion for God is at best incomplete and at worst is false unless it is an ethical passion. Devotion to

God means devotion to the will of God. And that means a glorious passion for getting the will of God done in whatever world of experience you find yourself. When someone who was impatient with the great Dr. Dale because of his public activities in Birmingham wrote to him, "There are no politics in heaven. Sad, sad that your thoughts are not there," he replied in effect that there were no wrongs to right in heaven, and that as long as this world was so unlike heaven, he must fight to make it a more heavenly place.

The heart of the matter is put in Longfellow's "Golden Legend." The monk in his cell was visited by the effulgent glory of the presence of the living Christ. And just when he was rapt in the ecstasy of the completest self-surrender to the vision and the splendor, the convent bell rang. It was his daily summons to the gate of the convent, where the poor in their dire need waited for bread. Hesitating but a moment, the monk went off about his duties, leaving his cell bathed in radiance, while he spent an hour ministering to the poor. When a little sadly he returned, to his unutterable surprise he found the shining vision still filling his cell with supernal glory. And he heard the voice of his divine Lord:

> " 'Hadst thou stayed, I must have fled,'
> That is what the vision said."

The beatific vision never comes as an escape from life here in this temporal world. It comes as man's supreme preparation to live in time with motives which are found in eternity.

So in many ways—for we might pursue the matter much further—humanism lives in the region in which a belief in immortality emerges and becomes real and authentic and secure. And when the critical humanist meets the Christian religion with its mighty affirmations regarding the resurrection and the life to come, he is ready to receive them, to welcome them, and to move into a region where he holds them with triumphant assurance.

So the humanism which has already traveled to the green hill far away and has received its darkly glorious message with reverence and awe and glad acceptance, now journeys to the empty tomb; and the best you can say of a truly understanding humanism is that it is prepared to find the tomb empty.

The study of all other faces prepares us for That One Face. There are the faces of wistful aspiration. They are longing for fulfillment in that which is found in the human face divine. There are the faces drawn with suffering, and torn by tragedy and pain. They are ready for the face of one who was despised and rejected of men, the man of sorrows and acquainted with grief, the man who could transform sorrow into singing joy. There are faces dark with the tragedies of selfishness and sin, heavy with the dullness of sensuality, and bitter with the utter loneliness of stark despair. They look up upon a face tender with the beauty of a great forgiveness, and glowing with the promise of a new life. There are faces hardening into the coldness of death, and eyes flashing with the last gleam of earthly light. And they fall upon the triumphant face of one emerging from the tomb who greets them with a great shout: "I am the resurrection and the life."

It all fits together. Humanism is not humanism until it meets the answer to all its questions in Jesus Christ. It is only a hint of a possible glory until it sees itself in Him.

Dante wrote the only account of heaven to be found out-

273

side the New Testament apocalypse which does not turn
out at last to be an anticlimax. And he brings us finally to
the perfect bloom of the rose of love and fire, the perpetual
burning of a cleansed and deathless passion which, having
been purged of all that is unworthy, can burn forever without consuming or being consumed. Here perfect beauty and
perfect truth and perfect righteousness and perfect peace and
perfect love are a perpetual fire of eternal bloom. And in
order that we may never forget the control of the perfect
over the imperfect, of the divine over even that which is below the human, we are told that it is this same love which
moves the sun and all the other stars. Only in some such
flaming symbolism can the eternal fulfillment be expressed
in mortal speech.

And this last word lifts us completely from the frustration which comes with the thought of a static perfection,
cold and distant and without the vigor of intense life. For
the fulfillment is not found in the absence of passion, but in
the eternal vitality of a passion as deathless as the life of
God. So the humanist finds the goal of all his pilgrimage
in a rapture in which discipline is transfigured in eternal
love.

## CHAPTER XXII

### *The Humanism of Irving Babbitt*

DR. PAUL ELMER MORE USED TO TELL A DELIGHTFUL STORY about how he once gave to a friend from India a letter of introduction to Professor Irving Babbitt. Off to Cambridge and to the distinguished Harvard professor the man from India went. On his return from New England Dr. More held a little dinner party in honor of his friend. In the course of the dinner he asked the man from the Far East what he thought of Professor Babbitt. Instantly the face of the man from India became very serious. There was even a touch of awe in his expression. "Professor Babbitt," he replied rather definitely, to the surprise of everyone at the table—"Professor Babbitt is a saint." Then turning to Dr. More with a charming twinkle in his eye he said, "You are not a saint. You are a philosopher." The story is particularly pertinent here because Professor Babbitt was one of those men who give one the sense that their lives have touched some source of vital spiritual energy beyond the terms of their thinking and their writing. This sense of a loftiness of spirit beyond his formal thought and its brilliant expression came home to the man from India. And so he called Babbitt a saint.

My own first meeting with Professor Babbitt was under rather interesting circumstances. In the midst of a busy pastorate in the great industrial city of Detroit, where the spire of my church in Grand Circus Park, looking down so many converging streets, was a sort of moral and spiritual challenge to the city, I had read pretty much everything written by Professor Babbitt. From the first page of the first book I knew that he wrote in a language which I could understand. His characteristic principles were grist to my mill. Indeed, my own mind had been moving in the direction of these distinctions ever since the time when as a very young man I had written a wretched novel—now fortunately inaccessible to mortal eye—called *Instinct Versus Intellect*. Just at the time when I was most taken by the corpus of criticism which Professor Babbitt had given me, I was lunching one day in London at the National Liberal Club—a place of no end of happy memories—with the editor of the *London Quarterly Review*. When he asked me for an article, I immediately suggested a discussion of Irving Babbitt, who was not then too well known in England. He accepted the suggestion, and when the article was sent in, gave it the place of honor in a particular number of the *Review*. Only a few months after, I received a letter from Irving Babbitt asking me to let him know of my next coming to Boston. So it happened that a little later we were lunching together at the Harvard Club in New England's metropolis. I had looked forward to the interview with some anxiety. Meeting your heroes in the flesh is always a precarious business. Sometimes you cannot get out to them. And sometimes they cannot get out to you. But on this occasion all went well. From the first sentence there was the give and take of minds which do not have to waste any time with preliminary fencing. We talked for two hours at fairly lightning speed. I have not the least idea what we had for lunch. My own vitality was quite used up by the demand of these fascinating hours; and when later in the afternoon I went out

276

to Somerville to give a lecture, I perpetrated positively the worst public address of my career, going over a frame of thought which may have been clear enough, but with no movement whatever of living energy, and not a single flash of the fire of the mind.

But the experience was worth what it cost. It was not merely that Professor Babbitt was a kind of incarnate personification of erudition. It was not merely the incisiveness of his mind, which moved like lightning. It was the sense of moral energy and even of spiritual power which came from his mind to one's own as he talked. He was a great figure of a man. His shoulders suggested that he was a kind of Atlas bearing the weight of a world of thought. And he was in complete possession of his mind. The world might be disintegrating. But there was no disintegration in the mind of Professor Babbitt.

He was a gift of the Middle West to the life of the republic. And he came to his time of testing when he was a student at Paris at the period when the symbolist movement was at its height. There were so many brilliant ways of going wrong at that time and in that place that it seems most extraordinary that he kept control of the critical forces of his intelligence and insisted on following the central stream of a true humanistic thought, turning neither to the right nor to the left. His long years as a professor at Harvard belonged to the time expressing what Van Wyck Brooks has called New England's "Indian Summer." The creative force of Puritanism in the form in which New England had known it was spent. The gregarious liberalism which represented the weakest side of Emerson's thought was already revealing its aridity and its incapacity in the matter of meeting the demand for positive

277

and kindling inspiration. Harvard itself was not particularly friendly. It had ceased to have permanent principles and was inclined to rely upon a combination of technical scholarship, the intellectual adventure of playing in a patrician fashion with every form of thought and every kind of life, and a social arrogance which did not take time to seek to analyze the sources of its consciousness of superiority, and was quite incapable of that moral repentance which is the first step toward delivery from intellectual impotence. So for years Professor Babbitt rowed against the stream. But the sheer force of his masterful intelligence and the overwhelming impact of his erudition more and more completely won their way. Even the gregariousness of President Eliot's regime could not prevent his getting a hearing. And in his last years he was a regal figure whose classes very well felt the imperial quality of his intellectual leadership.

During these years men themselves destined to come to places of leadership were among his students. Even when they did not make his point of view completely their own, their mental outlook was essentially affected by his keen mind. T. S. Eliot never became quite a part of the Babbitt tradition; indeed, it may be that he never completely understood it. But without his hours in the classes of Professor Babbitt at Harvard he would not be the T. S. Eliot we know. Walter Lippmann wandered far from the paths of critical humanism. But you cannot peruse his columns or read his books without feeling the impact of his great teacher at Harvard. Stuart Sherman—in spite of his tragic capitulation to the criticism of the flux—did work always modified by Babbitt's influence, and he did his most distinguished writing when he was still carrying the humanistic banner. More thoroughly a part of the tradition were Professor Norman Foerster—who has actually viewed contemporary education with the alert eyes of a critical humanist—and Professor G. R. Elliott, who has produced works of critical judgment of distinguished insight and power. And there are many others. Able men in the Latin communion of the Christian Church have taken the humanistic criticism of Professor Babbitt with the utmost seriousness. European scholars have not failed to understand its significance. In Harvard itself, Professor Louis Mercier carries on the tradition and relates it with keen understanding to the thinking of the neo-Thomists.

Irving Babbitt was a critical humanist who was contented to spend most of his career battling for life on the second level, and only rarely casting his eyes toward the third level. His great battle was for the human as against the subhuman. In the main, he left the discussion of the third level to others. He was ready, however, at the very maturity of his power to say that he took his own stand unhesitatingly on the side of the supernaturalists.

Very clearly Professor Babbitt saw that contemporary civilization all about the world was rushing from the human over the abyss to the subhuman. He saw this in the days of messianic confidence in a materialistic science. He saw this in the days of men's assurance that within their still unclouded industrial prosperity were all the principles necessary to give comfort and contentment to the world. He saw this in the days when men were willing to exercise democratic privileges without developing the intelligence which is necessary if democratic controls are to be made wise and effective. Before the bubble burst, he saw what was coming. In the days of unclouded and superficial optimism, he wrote works whose clairvoyant understanding and whose forecast of the contemporary debacle are amazing enough as we read them now. It was not a matter of academic interest merely to Professor Babbitt. It was a struggle to save civilization itself. He saw everywhere the relinquishing of discipline and the surrender to expansive emotions. This way he felt lay madness and at last despair. And so with all his cool and clear intelligence as the years went on he became more and more a general commanding soldiers of light who were all the while fighting the invading hosts of darkness. In a world which was surrendering to things and appetites, he lifted the flag of critical intelligence. His erudition was amazing. It was quite unsafe to quote any authority against him. You were sure to find that his knowledge of that authority was more complete than your own. He had the literature of the ages at the tip of his tongue. From this vast survey he justified—as in a sense he gathered—those dependable principles in the light of which decisions should be made. To him the central matter in life was controlling intelligence choosing between alternatives in the light of permanent standards. He saw in all the subhuman realm of experience the perpetually renewed opportunity for control on the part of man. He was not afraid of energy and vitality. But he felt that both energy and vitality must be controlled. So over against Bergson's *élan vital* (vital impulse) he put *frein vital* (vital control). He was all for vitality. But he knew that apart from control by critical intelligence in the light of permanent standards, vitality is a delusion and a snare.

At this point Professor Babbitt was often—sometimes

perversely—misunderstood. The apostles of the flux were having their way in such an utterly irresponsible dance of thought and expression that the very idea of subjecting their unleashed energies to control of any kind roused them to something not unlike fury. And so the war—which on the side of Professor Babbitt's critics was very much a war of ugly adjectives—began. He went on his work with something like Olympian calm, and with complete self-control. But he proved clearly enough that you do not have to be impotent because you are a gentleman. He could strike hard blows. He did strike deadly blows. And only the complacency of an ignorance which mistook anger for insight was undisturbed when he turned defense into brilliant attack. It was really not enough to fill a hall with complacent and uncritical minds when he spoke, and then to vote him down by means of the franchise of the incompetent. He never denied that democracy must justify itself at last by producing the aristocratic virtues. He never denied that one man of critical intelligence was more important than an army which insists that it will not use its mind about the essential matters. And so the advocates of a gregarious and uncritical democracy distrusted him. Some of them came to hate him.

It was equally true that the advocates of an uncritical and mystical naturalism found him a difficult person with whom to deal. He never denied the qualities of literary excellence in Wordsworth, but the members of the Wordsworth cult were disconcerted when he forced them to face the complete nonsense which was revealed upon a discriminating analysis of such lines as:

> "One impulse from a vernal wood
> May teach you more of man,
> Of moral evil and of good,
> Than all the sages can."

So by the trick of a plausible jingle Wordsworth had declared that an oak tree is more significant than Socrates or Plato or Jesus. But more than this, it is the very nature of moral evil and of moral good to be related to free intelligence choosing among alternatives. By definition *moral* evil arises when freedom has been misused through the choice of the bad. And by definition *moral* good arises when freedom has been rightly used through the choice of the good. What can the sap rising in a tree teach you of intelligence, poised between alternatives and busy with the decisively important matter of choice? The morals of the vernal wood always turn out in the long run to be the morals of the jungle. So the uncritical complacency of an age which had almost forgotten how to use its mind with cool intellectual discipline was perpetually disturbed by the critical studies which came from the pen of this Harvard teacher.

In two great modern figures Professor Babbitt saw the menace of the subhuman. One was Jean Jacques Rousseau. The other was Francis Bacon.

With his brilliant command of French literary history Professor Babbitt knew how inevitable it was that after the starched and stiff conventions of the seventeenth century there would come a reaction. The period had been one of pseudo classicism. You may say that it had been a period of pseudo humanism. It had given to artificial conventions a loyalty which belongs only to permanent standards. It was an outstanding illustration of the hu-

282

man tendency to give first-class loyalties to second-class distinctions. Jean Jacques Rousseau represented the reaction from all this. And as a reaction he was an important and wholesome influence. But from mechanical and artificial convention he went the full length in the opposite direction to entire surrender to undisciplined emotion. Rousseau became the apostle of a movement which can be represented by the phrase "obey that impulse." Now to be delivered from artificial restraint into the despotic power of lawless emotion is not much of a deliverance. The artificial restraints produce human sticks who call themselves men. The lawless emotions produce hectic and fevered animals who go through the world crushing everything in the name of impulses which are subjected to no standard above their own immense appetite. The body takes the place of the mind. Sensations take the place of judgment. Impulses take the place of the sanctions which are inherent in the intellectual and moral and spiritual life.

So Professor Babbitt set himself to fighting all those influences which have put upon the throne of the modern world expansive emotion which is unchecked by intellectual insight and which is undisciplined by loyalty to permanent standards. With every variety of brilliant analysis and exposition and corrosive irony he made himself the great critic of romantic and undisciplined emotion in the contemporary world. The Rousseauistic claim that men should surrender to the vital rush of appetite without question and without criticism he met with masterful denial and with brilliant attack unhesitatingly continued through a long period of years. It used to be said laughingly that before he retired at night he always looked under the bed to see if Rousseau was hidden there. That can hardly be

283

true, for he knew perfectly well what multitudinous beds would be necessary to hide all the conscious and unconscious disciples of Rousseau who were menacing the civilized life among contemporary men.

If Rousseau represented the surrender to appetite, the earlier figure, Francis Bacon, represented the surrender to things. Bacon believed that the great task of man was to be found on the level of the control of the forces of nature. He never saw the significance of control on the human level. He saw the importance of the control of things. He never saw the importance of self-control in loyalty to moral standards. And it is significant that just the failure of insight at this point led him into those ways of moral confusion which produced his own dramatic and tragic fall from a position of the highest power. He had a romantic belief that the achievements of what we would call practical science, applied to every physical fact and relationship, would produce a world of comfort and of the good life. The modern world has followed him almost to the abyss. Our great depression in the midst of plenty was the very result you might have expected from the subhuman scientific Utopianism of Francis Bacon. And the mechanized warfare of the totalitarian states bent on crushing the free life of the world, and the mechanized "peace" in the totalitarian states bent on crushing every minority and the freedom of every individual in any fashion to think his own thoughts and to live his own life, are the natural result of that messianic belief in things and that perpetual disregard of intellectual and moral and spiritual standards which lurk unnoticed at the heart of the Baconian Utopia. When Dean Church declared that Francis Bacon failed to observe that "nature and man are different powers and are under different laws," he went to the root of the matter. When Sir James Alfred Ewing lamented that our control over nature had not been equaled by our control over human nature, he spoke in the midst of the debacle which the influence of Francis Bacon helped to produce. This confidence that a subhuman science can produce a good world met in Professor Babbitt a constant and unflinching antagonist.

It goes without saying that he regarded the instrumental philosophy of Professor John Dewey with complete hostility. This disagreement he unhesitatingly and vigorously expressed. Perhaps there was no possible meeting of the two minds. When a man has cast away all belief in essential principles and all acceptance of dependable standards and has substituted for these a pragmatism which deals with each individual situation out of relation to everything else, the difference is indeed about first principles. And when the apostle of an uncritical pragmatism perpetually assumes implicitly and uses unconsciously general principles of the very type whose existence he explicitly denies, the situation becomes more baffling. It is not insignificant that the instrumentalist always depreciates and underestimates the importance of the study of the history of culture. Down that road he will find foes with whom he will not know how to cope.

It is a matter worth noting that Professor Babbitt's best pupils often began attending his classes only to find that they very much disliked him and his weapons and everything for which he stood. They came with minds trained in the fashions of every sort of subhuman culture. Some were held in the chains of deterministic science. Some were caught in the clutches of an uncritical primitivism. Some were pragmatists who had learned to distrust all general

285

principles. And so there were men not a few who fell by
the wayside. But there were those who persisted and gradually learned that the very logic of human life itself was on
the side of the contentions of Professor Babbitt. Slowly the
coverings fell from their eyes, and at last they came into a
sense of that human freedom of which this teacher never
lost sight and of those standards which to him were meat
and drink.

Professor Babbitt was always willing to use the flashing insights of those fragmentary thinkers who would have golden
moments of understanding which they quite failed to make
commanding in their thinking. No one knew better than
he the limitations and the incoherent elements in the
thought of Ralph Waldo Emerson. But he never tired of
quoting Emerson's great words:

> "There are two laws discrete,
> Not reconciled,—
> Law for man, and law for thing;
> The last builds town and fleet,
> But it runs wild,
> And doth the man unking."

Here for one good hour Emerson had stood upon the
heights of critical thought, and Babbitt was glad to remember this and so to pay tribute to the sage of Concord. Indeed, once and again he surprises you by his power to find
good grain in fields where many tares are growing.

For many reasons Professor Babbitt was content to fight
for the human values without saying much of divine sanctions. He was always ready to declare that it was so important to make man human that it was safe for him to be busy
about that, putting aside for the time the questions involved

286

in the study of divinity. He was also profoundly offended by an uncritical religiosity which never subjected its own sanctions to intellectual analysis and was contented with a romantic emotionalism of its own. In this sense he was even in a heightened moment of scorn able to shake his fist at a church and bitterly to describe it as "the foe." But increasingly as the years went by he saw the place of the superhuman in fortifying the human. He saw and said that while religion might get along without humanism, humanism could not get along at last without religion. It is important that when Professor Mercier read to him his book *The Challenge of Humanism,* in which humanism has a completely Christian outcome, he found him entirely friendly. One day toward the end of his life, venturing perhaps too casually into this realm, I told him I was glad that he had stuck to the human level, because many men who were not willing as yet to consider religion seriously would be won by him to an acceptance of the great human values. Dr. More and some of the rest of us were busy with carrying the tradition to its Christian consummation. And to this he made no objection. He was always ready to be interested in any movement of thought which could be used in his battle with the lower forces which threaten man's life. In our last interview he brought up the subject of Karl Barth!

There were regions in which Professor Babbitt decided not to move. Within the limits he set for himself his achievement was consummate and his contribution will not be forgotten.

# CHAPTER XXIII

## The Humanism of Paul Elmer More

VAN WYCK BROOKS' "NEW ENGLAND: INDIAN SUMMER" IS IN certain ways—the most significant of them quite unsuspected by the author—a volume of first-class importance. Beginning at the periphery, one may say that the most casual reader will be impressed at once by certain qualities of grace and charm. The writer has the patience of the indefatigable investigator, and his sympathy is as rich and varied as the types of men and of thought which he is describing. He has a disconcerting way of getting inside the people of whom he is writing and looking at you out of their eyes. He likes the people. He likes wandering in unsuspected places in their minds. And New England has captured his imagination and has even caused his heart to beat more quickly. He has himself attained a culture rich and varied and many-sided. And he tells his tale in sentences which have the sap of life in them and in phrases which echo with the very sounds of the life which he is describing.

In *The Flowering of New England* he had told of the days of the giants, when men did great deeds and flung out great words in the name of commanding causes and of insights which they believed held in their heart not only the future of New England but the future of the world. Then came the days of increasing disillusionment and of waning vitality. There were still brilliant men and powerful women. But the creative faiths had lost their hold. The human spirit had lost contact with something mightier than itself. And

288

so the summer with its glorious harvest was succeeded by the Indian summer when the leaves of the trees took on beautiful color just before they fell, and the bronze glow of light and the mellow warmth were precursers of the cold of winter and the retreat of all the forces of life. The age of gold was followed by the age of silver. The journey was *away from* the supreme values. Mr. Van Wyck Brooks might have called this book *The Decadence of New England* or *The Frustration of New England*. Perhaps in few periods have so many first-class minds failed to reach quite first-class achievements. There is the sputter of light—the blaze which gradually fades out. And then there is the un-lighted night. The New England of the giants of faith in God and belief in great causes gradually becomes the New England of Santayana's *The Last Puritan,* of Marquand's *Wickford Point,* and even of *Mourning Becomes Electra.*

Mr. Van Wyck Brooks does not draw the lines as sharply as this. But he is honest enough. And you feel the waning vitality all the while. You see the men who have ceased to believe in great principles turning to the passionate pursuit of facts in the physical world. You see the Yankee turning his practical skill to shrewd business enterprises without the light of the vision of the Puritan in his eye. You see men who have lost belief in the sanctions of religion turning with al-most pathetic eagerness to the pragmatism of William James. You see people who live in an age when the optimistic pan-theism of Emerson is becoming worn and discredited try-ing to find mechanical formulas to express the ongoing of the processes of life, and sometimes believing for a moment that they have found such formulas as did Henry Adams. You see men who have lost their sense of the majestic quali-ty of historic Christianity finding peace without the loss of complacency in the pseudo spirituality of Christian Science. You see gifted young men seeking all over the world for something which was once clear and commanding in the soul of New England but which has now been lost. To be sure, it is all part of the experience of a larger world where multitudes of men have also lost their polar star. But it is all particularly striking in New England, where so much has been lost. You are looking upon a people whose memories have become greater than their hopes.

Van Wyck Brooks is a literary and social historian rather than a powerful critic or a commanding philosophical thinker. And so he assembles a mass of materials which he never quite uses. With meticulous care he tells of the waning of faith, the loss of inspiration, the substitution of secondary for primary motives, and the stopping of the clocks in the fascinating little world whose life he portrays. He accepts the grim skepticism as final. He has no creative loyalties to offer for the loyalties which have been lost. Wistfully and with many a flash of the color of autumn in his style, he tells his story. Just because he shares the disease which he is describing, he speaks with a more gracious and tender understanding of those whom that disease has already brought to the tomb.

The story itself is one of the most tragic importance. Sometime it will be told even more effectively than Mr. Van Wyck Brooks has told it, because it will be told by a critic who understands fully the character of the disease and the nature of the remedy. For just here in New England something else was occurring in the very days of the decadence which was to lead on to such dark frustration and such bitter disillusionment. In the very period when men lost their hold on commanding principles and so were los-

290

ing their way in no end of matters, a man of the most cutting qualities of critical mind was subjecting the whole process to thorough analysis and, beyond his destructive work, was amassing principles of indubitable firmness and strength. It was a fateful moment at Harvard when Irving Babbitt began to speak within its walls. It is a story centuries old—this tale of the prophet for whose witness neither the time nor the place is ready. And so Irving Babbitt did his supreme work in an atmosphere of indifference, sometimes of reluctant admiration, and often of downright hostility. But it was increasingly evident as the years went by that Professor Babbitt had found something which saved him completely from the decadent diseases which were attacking contemporary New England. With a mind more amply fortified by cosmopolitan learning than that possessed by any of the men who refused to follow him, with a critical faculty more devastatingly active than that revealed by any of the men who thought that intellectual honesty had made it impossible for them to have positive beliefs, with a secure grasp on living principles in whose reign lies the security of the civilized life, he went on his way. When his university itself became the home of brilliant Philistinism, he kept his head high and went on with his work, his inner serenity undisturbed.

In his student days at Harvard, Irving Babbitt had a friend whose intellectual interests became closely entwined with his own, whose life paralleled the life of Babbitt in many ways, and who ultimately spoke an even more commanding word than that which was uttered by Babbitt to a decadent New England, to a republic drifting into ways of spiritual confusion, and to a world set upon paths which led inevitably to disintegration and despair. If Irving Bab-

bitt summoned men to follow permanent principles in days
of mental anarchy, Paul Elmer More, when he had com-
pleted his own long pilgrimage, spoke to men in the name
of a historic faith which had proved itself when subjected to
the most searching tests, and lifted its voice to speak the only
word which would turn men from intellectual decadence
to intellectual power.

Dr. More was born in Saint Louis. He went through the
public schools of his native city, and received two degrees
from Washington University. In some ways his years at
Harvard must have been pivotal in his earlier career. He
did not find himself easily or quickly. He repudiated the
Calvinism in which he had been brought up, and for a
time took refuge in the romanticism which was so easily
accessible to a young man of the period. He was a vora-
cious student. He became easily familiar with the masterpieces of Greek and Latin literature. He made himself at
home in Indian thought, especially in the literary and philosophical tales which Sanskrit tells. He came to know European literature. He was especially at home in the literature
which uses the English language as its vehicle. So he came
to the place where he could see pretty much any problems
in the terms of the whole European experience of thought
and action and expression.

At the moment I am writing in a little study among the
trees on the hill at Randolph, New Hampshire, looking out
on Madison and Adams of the Presidential Range. Here,
indeed, the mornings of much of this strange summer of
1940 have been spent writing this book. Only a few miles
away is Shelburne. There the other day I visited the little
red cottage in the Androscoggin valley—empty now—where
Paul Elmer More lived with his dog and his books and his

pipe and began to do the work which year after year was published in the *Shelburne Essays*. So the critical work of Paul Elmer More has its inevitable and its permanent relation with New England.

Like Babbitt, he came to see the necessity of permanent standards. He, too, saw that man lives at the place where controlling intelligence has the opportunity to dominate the subhuman realm. He liked the term "inner check" to describe the moment when man began to exercise control. He got the term from Emerson, who, as we have seen, had hours when his mind was turned away from pantheistic gregariousness toward critical insight. Doubtless the similarity of the "inner check" to the *daimon* of Socrates made a definite, if unconscious, appeal to him. He, too, entered upon a vigorous battle for the human in a world which was fast becoming inhuman.

The *Shelburne Essays* describe his experiences with a vast body of literature. To read the first series is to attend a kind of university in eleven volumes. He sees every problem in the light of an amazing background in literature and history. So the great standards emerge. So he sees the age in the light of the ages. So he himself becomes a notable critic in the central stream of humanistic thought. He writes of authors and of movements with understanding sympathy and with penetrating critical power.

The mind of More—like the mind of Babbitt, perhaps even more than the mind of Babbitt—was securely rooted in American life, though it came to have equally secure rootage in a most cosmopolitan culture. On the one hand, he was never a self-conscious or parochial American. And on the other, he was never baffled as were Henry James and Henry Adams by losing one culture without ever complete-

ly finding another.  He was so simple and natural and unconscious in the exercise of this American quality that he
moved to the farthest reaches of other cultures and other
forms of life with no sense of disloyalty and with no sense
of strain.  He had a right to inherit everything human.  And
the inner pith of his mind included the American quality—
as naturally as it appropriated the most cosmopolitan interests and insights.  He never wore his Americanism as a
heavy chain.  And he was never like a tree whose leaves
became thin and anemic because they had no deep roots in
any particular soil.  There are cosmopolitan expatriates who
in the end do not have citizenship in any land, not even the
land of their adoption.  There are men whose lives are so
honestly rooted in their own soil that they can appropriate
the best coming from every culture and from every land
with complete sincerity, thus making their cosmopolitan culture the very flower of their national inheritance, cross-
fertilized by the riches of every land.  Such a man was Paul
Elmer More.  His ultimate standards were human rather
than national or racial.  But it was the humanism of a man
who had first put his feet upon a particular soil.  He never
gave you the sense of being like a kite fluttering far in the
sky, moving about very wildly in the far winds because no
stout thread connected it with a masterful hand in some particular spot.

In all the reading and thinking whose harvest was so ample in the first eleven volumes of the *Shelburne Essays,* Dr.
More was very much alive to the realities of ethical experience, and very much outside the sanctions of religion.  This
sharpness of ethical sense gives the clue to a good many
places of turning in his thought.  A gregarious romanticism
put lawless impulse in the place of creative loyalty to high

principles, and so More in his own way and at his own time broke with romanticism. Any position which blurred the action of clear intelligence and confused the sharpness of necessary judgments became an object of suspicion and at length of scorn. With singular penetration which was the product of a continual investigation he became able to appropriate the meaning of a man or a book or a movement and then to apply unhesitatingly the knife of surgical criticism. This combination of understanding and critical analysis became even more characteristic as the years went by, and perhaps is never seen to better advantage than in some of his later essays, like that on Marcel Proust.

It was doubtless the deepening sense of the pivotal importance of the mind's power to make distinctions which saved him from surrender to the plausible allurements of pantheistic monism as he made a deeper and deeper study of Indian thought. To be able to say one thing definitely at a certain level of thought, and to contradict it with equal zest at another level, and then to take an entirely different position at a third, and at last to reach security in a world beyond truth and error, good and evil, existence and non-existence—this constituted for him the ultimate surrender of the integrity of the mind. The opposite position he characterized by the word dualism. If life is to have genuine significance and if everything is not to disappear in a meaningless flux at last, there must be real distinctions. And they must be permanent. So he was always suspicious of philosophical terms like unity which he felt opened the way for the dissolution of necessary distinctions. His own thought all the while moved toward a coherence in experience in which the necessary distinctions are forever conserved. So— to forget terms for a moment—he was never afraid of unity

295

if it did not dissolve into meaningless flux those distinctions upon which all true life rests, and he never advocated a dualism which would make a coherent interpretation of experience impossible.

At the end of the first great stage of his experience and study, Dr. More was a humanist whose humanism centered in the thought of intelligent control and who believed unhesitatingly in permanent standards.

But all the while he was becoming a convinced Platonist. These principles of his mind have security—beyond the relativities of man's fitful life. And so Plato's doctrine of ideas made a deep appeal to him. He came to a full conviction that the values for which he contended must be forever secure in the ultimate universe. Man finds his true humanity in loyalty to standards whose relevance—whose commanding power—he can perceive, but whose source is beyond his own relative life. But in what way do these ideas —these principles—exist and have their security? Here More followed his master, Plato, in the journey whose completion the great Athenian signalized in the *Laws*. He came to see clearly that the security of the ideas cannot be found in the realm of the unconscious. He came at last to the unhesitating conviction that it is in the life of a conscious God that the ideas, the principles, the values which meant everything to him have their source and maintain their power. In God these values live. So his Platonism became theistic. So the very distinctive principles of his humanism led him to a stout affirmation of the existence of a conscious God.

It is just a little diverting to remember that there were among More's contemporaries self-conscious intellectuals who thought that a belief in God was quite impossible to men of their emancipated enlightenment. Henry Adams' sneering reference to theism will stand as an illustration. The truth is, of course, that it was the lack of capacity in sheer intelligence which debarred such men from a brilliant dialectic which led to a theistic conclusion. Historic religion of the theistic type—whatever its faults—at all its hours of fully conscious power has been characterized by a dialectic of consummate brilliance and strength. To return to More. His arrival at a definite theistic position made further questions not only pertinent but inevitable. The most penetrating of these questions may be phrased in this fashion: If controlling intelligence exists perfectly in the life of God and relatively in the life of man, can God refrain from making His thought the possession of creatures so like Himself? If the ideas by which men must live if they are to find their true life are forever alive in God, must He not make them known to these creatures, whom He has so made that they are able to think His thoughts after Him? Dr. More is now ready for the deepest words of the Hebrew prophets. It is their great claim that God has spoken, that He has given them the words which they preface with the great declaration, "Thus saith the Lord." He has now a quite new approach to the great prophets of Israel. He comes predisposed toward belief in a God who *speaks*. The question is: Was the message of the great prophets of Israel set to a note so lofty that it is worthy of the claim they made for it? After the most searching study More's reply is an unhesitating affirmation. Such a God as the one in whom he must believe ought to speak. Such a God as the one in whom he must believe has spoken. And here we have a record of his words. And now More is a believer in revelation with a definite appeal to history. His brilliant speculation has come to the world of fact. And the two meet in happy harmony.

Having traveled so far, he must go farther. Is the God in whom he believes one who has merely spoken? Or is He also a God who *has come?* Most seriously he makes a study of the gospels, the New Testament documents, and of the processes of Christian thought up to and including Nicaea and Chalcedon. Here again he has a fresh approach through the character of his personal pilgrimage and the quality of his own dialectic. The thinker who finds his belief in the human coming to inevitable fulfillment in his belief in the divine—mind answering mind—will not only find it a part of clear and coherent thinking to believe in God's speech with men. He will be ready to come with a friendly mind to the thought of God's life with men. So More came to a completely secure belief in the incarnation. All these processes of thought are perpetually buttressed and authenticated by an ever renewed study of Greek philosophy, of Plato, of the New Testament, and of four centuries of Greek theology. These results he published in the six memorable volumes dealing with *The Greek Tradition.* The one volume *Christ the Word* gives the key to all the rest. Dr. More has now come to be not merely a theistic humanist. He is a Christian humanist, holding with complete assurance the central assertion of historic Christianity that the Word became flesh. He has found the great goal of his thinking in Christ the Word.

The whole story of this approach to and final acceptance of the sanctions which are interpreted in the classical forms of Christian thought is told with careful and closely reasoned dialectic in *The Sceptical Approach to Religion.* Here there is even more than a hint of a movement in More's thought

298

advancing from a belief in the incarnation to the great adventure of God in suffering and death as the final divine participation in the experiences of men. The argument is all the while conducted with forms of thought as clear as crystal and with the steadily controlled processes of the most critical intelligence.

Dr. More's last word—a very personal word, though its form is made objective by means of the pleasant fiction that it is the writing of an Oxford don—is found in the little book *Pages from an Oxford Diary*. Here More tells of his long journey. Here he says more clearly than elsewhere what he has come to perceive regarding the light which falls upon the cross. And as his very last word, this far-traveled skeptic declares with a quiet passion which has an impressiveness all of its own, "If I were young, I would preach."

The tale of the intellectual and spiritual pilgrimage of Paul Elmer More is in its own fashion an epic of keen intelligence fighting its way into the world of religion. The stalwart humanist using the weapons of his own craft becomes a Christian humanist at last.

This pilgrimage and its consummation are seen in a strangely lurid light against the background of intellectual and moral and spiritual frustration in New England, which has had so profound an influence on the life of the whole republic. It was the author of the *Shelburne Essays* and of *The Greek Tradition* who spoke the word which could not be uttered by the masters of distinguished disillusionment who believed that they sat on the intellectual thrones of this hemisphere, if not of the whole world. His mind was even more critical than theirs. His attitude was even more skeptical than theirs. His erudition was unequaled among the most learned of them all. He was as instinctively a patrician of the mind, an aristocrat in the realm of the intelligence. And yet he came to understand the commanding and creative word which none of them could speak.

The contrast between the moral and spiritual satisfaction which crowned More's quest and the selfish disillusionment to which the distinguished mind of Henry Adams came is of the greatest significance and deserves a detailed study which we cannot give it here. Henry Adams never found anything in the universe greater than himself. Paul Elmer More, with all his proud intelligence, bowed before truths which were greater than he, and so he came to the noble humility which supplemented his clear intelligence when at last he confronted the fact of God. He came to see what a vital and creative belief can do for men. In one of his most revealing letters to me he said, "It is the great believers who do the big things."

His later volumes of criticism were ripe with the fullness of his erudition, at times surprising in their qualities of patient sympathy, and sharp enough in their cutting surgery. In a world moving into disintegration and confusion—for what happened in New England was only an example of what was happening in the larger life of men—he found his way to intellectual security and to inner peace. And so he spoke the word which, either in the forms in which his own clear mind expressed it or in other forms drawn from the bitter conflict in this grim day, must yet command the mind of man as he is driven to turn from himself and the futilities and tragedies of human life, when it has no center beyond the human, to the great Companion who yet holds the secret of our peace, the secret of our power, and the final satisfaction of our intelligence as well.

# CHAPTER XXIV

## Evangelical Humanism and the Christian Pulpit

AT EVERY GREAT PERIOD IN THE LIFE OF THE CHURCH THE Christian pulpit has become an intellectual throne. In the words of the preacher the mighty corpus of Christian thought became a glorious inspiration for life in the world of men. In Christian worship theology became lyrical and went about the world rapturously singing. In the pulpit the sanctions of theology became magnificent proclamation. In decadent days worship became formal and the pulpit became arid and lifeless. And in the attempt to secure some sort of rehabilitation in such degenerate periods the pulpit held the mirror up to contemporary life and tried to find a hearing by reflecting back upon a confused humanity its own fervors of the moment and the inadequate solutions which it was inclined to substitute for eternal truths. So the pulpit lost its mastery. It substituted "Thus saith the age" for "Thus saith the Lord." It became a bright chameleon reflecting the colors of its environment. It lost that imperial note without which the pulpit has ceased to express the very genius by which it lives. No wonder, then, that Paul Elmer More at the end of his long intellectual and spiritual pilgrimage, when he had found a secure and authentic journey's end, wrote "If I were young, I would preach."

A humanism which finds its goal in the Christian religion will inevitably claim the Christian pulpit as its own. It is here that the Christian criticism of life will most fully and

decisively and characteristically express itself.  And so, we
dare believe, will come that renaissance of preaching which
will not only bring new power to the church, but which
will also bring new life to the world.  The brilliant ma-
terialisms, the pretentious secularisms, and the confident
idealisms whose hopes have a consummation without God
have had their day.  They have brought bitterness and
confusion and disintegration.  The dark and hot voices
which would go to the beast to learn the meaning of the
life of man have led only to ugly frustrations of their own.
The solutions in a pantheism leading to a Nirvana which
is a black-out of all the distinctions that give meaning to
life have an appeal only for the utterly weary who, because
they have really given up the battle, try to believe that an
eternal silence is better than any speech, an eternal meaning-
lessness is better than any meaning.  They build a tomb at
the end of the human enterprise and call it the ultimate
peace.

We have heard all the falsehoods.  We have heard all
the voices of brilliant confusion.  We have heard all the
half-truths which betray truth itself.  Now the time has
come to hear once more with the new vitality of its relation
to this new age the great historic voice which sees the human problem in the terms of the Christian solution, and
which utters with complete assurance the imperial message
of the Christian religion.  And it is just here that the disciplines of that humanism which moves by meticulous dialectic from man to standards, from standards to God, from
God to Christ, and from Christ to the cross will do their
most effective work.  Through these disciplines men may
be prepared to speak that good and commanding word with-

out which our age confronts the darkening shadows of the night with no expectation of the light of another dawn.

The distinction of life on the three levels is one which is of the most critical importance for all of a preacher's thought and utterance. The lure of the subhuman is felt by the preacher just about as much as it is felt by any other man. Those wild and shrieking poets who are rushing back to the beast in angry repudiation of life on the human level have made themselves the vehicle of forces which he quite well understands. There is no voice in the manifold confusion of this lost age which does not speak to something which is alive in his own organism. So it is all too easy for him to hang suspended at the point of some psychopathic reaction of angry critics of the world in which we live and mistake the rush of energy released in this mood of anger for an important contribution to the religious life. The great danger which confronts religion is always pseudo religion rather than irreligion. For the moment you reject a particular religion you have to invent another to take its place. No person is more tempted than the preacher to substitute the electric lights for the stars. The contemporary mind is always lifting its favorite idols and saying, "These be thy gods, O Israel." No end of preachers piece out a Christianity whose sanctions they have never understood with bright flashes of rich emotion hot with the qualities of contemporary life. So the pulpit surrenders to the very age whose life it must conquer if it is to do its real work in the world.

The situation is complicated by the fact that there are elements of truth in most falsehoods. And a man may spend his life extracting little truths from the big falsehoods which betray mankind. He wins a precarious hearing by so ministering to the complacency of a confused and bewildered age. But nobody goes to him in a supreme hour of moral darkness. And no one goes to him in the bitterest hour of spiritual loneliness.

The subhuman world of the senses is always attempting to capture the throne. And it is perfectly willing to accept the help of the preacher. It requires some critical insight firmly to reject on the one hand the hot decadence of the sensual and on the other the cold asceticism which has never understood that the senses as good servants will always have their place in the house of man.

But if it is true that the senses are always attempting to proclaim slave insurrections which would disintegrate human life and that at this point the preacher—as a critical interpreter of life—must always be on his guard, it is also true that by a strange and recurrent folly man is always tempted to put the mechanics of life in the place of free intelligence. And here, too, the interpreter of life must be perpetually watchful. Pseudo science in all its forms comes at last to the interpretation of human experiences on the level of impersonal mechanics. On this level of thinking men seek impersonal formulas for psychology, quite leaving free intelligence out of account. On this level of thinking they make sociology a subhuman science, reducing it to impersonal terms. On this level theology itself is denuded and becomes a kind of mechanism of values in a world where there is no real personality, either human or divine. On this level it is possible to have a theory of education which studies the laws of glandular action in order to find mathematical formulas of human behavior.

There are so many ways of going wrong that the young preacher—not to speak of the older—is likely to become be-

304

wildered. He can in one period of his life follow a type of so-called religious education which substitutes surrender to impulse for the guidance of impulse through loyalty to high standards. He can turn from this only to fall into an impersonal behaviorism in which little machines are taught how to react. He can be so filled with hatred for the wrongs man has committed against man that he falls a prey to the lure of social theories which rob man of his free manhood in order to give him a comfortable bodily life, or to political theories which unblushingly surrender freedom in the name of efficiency. The greatest menace the Christian pulpit faces today—outside that perpetual temptation to selfishness and hypocrisy which hounds good men in every age—is found in the cluster of pseudo solutions to human problems, to some of which we have referred. The preachers who surrender to them—and some men of the pulpit are versatile enough to surrender to all of them successively and to most of them simultaneously—are all the while emasculating their message as they try to interpret life in subhuman terms. Their churches become dull and cold. Their congregations become thin in quality and small in quantity, and a subtle lethargy settles upon their parishes. They make charts and they plan projects, but they never rise above the world of things and the world of undisciplined emotion.

The preacher who builds all his work upon a clear discernment of the meaning of man's controlling intelligence as he decides among alternatives in the light of permanent standards is constantly advancing toward a position of greater solidity and power and actual leadership. Very quickly he turns from any solution which would betray man's freedom, would destroy his intelligence, or would break down the vigor of the personal life in the name of any sort of totalitarian claims whatsoever. He has an Ithuriel's spear by means of which he can judge all the pseudo sciences. He has a virility and a strength which often mystify those who do not share his insights. He knows that unconsciously many of his congregation think of men and women as puppets living in a determined world. He knows that in the name of every value human and divine he must break down this tragic misapprehension. So day by day and night by night he bombards his congregation with tales from biography and history and literature telling the story of men who have freely chosen hard tasks and have lived with steady loyalty to demanding standards. By and by his people begin to believe in human freedom. By and by they begin to believe in human responsibility. By and by they begin to understand that in a world with such tremendous human powers "life's business is just the terrible choice." The men who listen to him come to have a sense of human dignity which lifts life into a new and glorious meaning. The dark and corrosive pessimisms are struck lifeless as a true sense of the significance of the human adventure comes home to men. They come to understand that the preacher is not summoning puppets to choices which they can never make. With all authenticity he uses the words, "Come now, and let us reason together." With all assurance he demands, "Choose you this day whom ye will serve."

The preacher who is a critical humanist sees the documents of the Old Testament and the New in the light of the vast body of enriching literature in the world. Only when you come to these documents with a mind bright with the light coming from the literature of all ages and dark with the sense of human tragedy which broods upon all the great books of the world will you see them in their true majesty.

## Evangelical Humanism and the Christian Pulpit

The preacher who is a true humanist comes to the age ripe with the wisdom of the ages. The great voices of Greece and of Rome, of the ancient world and of the Middle Ages, of England and France and Germany and Italy and Spain and his own young republic speak in his own voice. Against this background the voices of the Hebrew prophets break with sudden thunder. And the voice of Jesus is the mightiest voice of all.

He comes not only to think of God as conscious perfect intelligence, but to measure all his thought and feeling and action and the thought and feeling and action of the world by that divine and perfect intelligence which is the ultimate fact of life. The very word God comes to life in his mind. When he utters the word it is as if in the actual utterance it bursts into flame. That flame burns up many things and it illuminates brightly everything which remains. The preacher comes to know that you can see things truly only as you see them in relation to God, you can think of things wisely only as you think of them in connection with God. And he comes to see that the only feelings which are dependable and permanent are related directly or indirectly to the experiences of living men with the living God.

But up to this point he is only standing at the open door of the temple and looking at the beauty within. Now he sees God coming into the world in Jesus Christ. And a new glory comes to humanity as he realizes that the Son of God could look out of human eyes and speak with a human voice and live a truly human life. All men's experiences are caught up into a new meaning as his belief in the incarnation enables him in quite an astounding way to see man's human life from the standpoint of eternity, and even his daily experiences in the light of the supreme fact of the God-

307

man. Now his pulpit glows with a veritably divine light. He is perpetually making real in his high summons the words spoken to the prophet Ezekiel, "Son of man, stand upon thy feet, and I will speak with thee." Never again will he judge human life—never again can his congregation judge human life—by the depths to which man has sunk. If you want to know the high possibilities of the human, you can find them—and then only can you find them—as you behold the Human Life Divine.

The tragedy persists, however. It too is actual. The preacher cannot evade it. He cannot avoid it. He must face it with complete honesty and with an almost terrible candor. He must behold man's weakness. He must behold man's sorrow. He must behold man's treachery. He must behold the black blight of his sin. And he must see all this against the white and radiant glory of the life of God, until for himself and for his fellow men he cries at last, "Against thee, thee only, have I sinned, and done this evil in thy sight." And now he is ready for a greater hour than he has yet known. This is the hour when he first begins to sight the far-flung significance of his faith in the suffering God.

During the last period of the life of Paul Elmer More, he accepted an invitation which I gave him to come to Madison for dinner with one of my seminars, and to attend its evening session. I sent to Princeton for him, and a memorable evening followed. The paper at the seminar—though I had not forewarned Dr. More of this—was an account of the processes of his own thought and of his intellectual and spiritual pilgrimage. The student who had written the paper had done a competent piece of work, and in the discussion which followed I was very proud of the fashion in which the students carried on quite as if Dr. More had not been present. Then they began to question him, and he replied to their questions with completely urbane friendliness. At last, with the typical unconsciously irreverent bluntness of theological students, one of them blurted out the one question I had not foreseen, and certainly the one question I would have censored had it been possible: "Dr. More, what do you think of the cross?" The journey Dr. More had taken had been so long. Its goals had been at each stage so secure. His affirmation of the truth of the incarnation had been so tremendously effective, that I would not for the world have lifted prematurely the next question, though I knew perfectly well what the next question was. But the student in my seminar had flung it out sharply.

There was a quiet moment. Then Dr. More replied with complete courtesy, and with a candor which was utterly revealing. He admitted that for years he had disliked the very thought of the cross. He disliked the sentimental and unintelligent hymns which were written about it. He disliked the unethical way in which preachers often referred to it. But as he had gone on with the intellectual journey which on the whole had been truly reflected in the paper to which we had just listened, it had become evident that if one once believed in Christ the Word, one must at least consider going farther. Would it not be necessary that the sword which so tragically pierced the life of man should pierce the very heart of God as he lived among men in Jesus Christ? And thinking along these lines he had come to believe that perhaps the cross was the central—the most important—matter of all. As we listened in sharp attention it seemed as if we were watching the ship of the skeptical humanist as it made its ultimate port. Later, as we have

309

already seen in considering his very last little book—destined to become a Christian classic—Dr. More made this position conclusive and expressed it in words which were abundantly clear.

The hour when the Christian preacher sees these things is indeed an hour of transcendent importance. For now he enters the very central stream of historic Christian thought and life. That in Jesus Christ God feels the piercing sword of man's pain, that He bends under the burden of man's woe, and that on the cross He takes His place on man's side in the midst of the tragedy brought to man by the treachery which lurks in his heart and poisons his life—this is the most tremendous conception which can come to the preacher. No wonder Charles Hadden Spurgeon declared, "I build my study on Mount Calvary." And when all this glows with an ineffable radiance and a conquering power in the words the preacher utters, something transforming happens to the men who listen. When it all becomes first living experience and then living speech, the pulpit reaches heights of power of which the preacher never dreamed. It is the evangelical humanist to whom a pulpit becomes a throne.

And all this drives the preacher into powerful ways of interpreting human need, its satisfaction through the grace of God, and the necessary expression of the new life in the most varied aspects of human service. The evangelical humanist is kept free from idyllic and romantic Utopias. He is forever too much of a realist to be betrayed by them. But he does have the full inspiration of the true hope of the kingdom of God. There is an inevitable social outcome to all true experience of the grace of God. And the only social prophet who need have no fear of reaction and of cynical disillusionment is the evangelical humanist. He knows the evil which is in the heart of man. He knows the tragic fashion in which man may misuse his freedom. He also knows the glorious way in which man may use that same freedom, and most of all he knows the glory of the grace of God. And so he faces the future unafraid.

*He is unafraid not because he refuses to believe in the human tragedy. He is unafraid because he can see beyond the tragedy.*

Once more today mankind stands at the crossing of the ways. There is a choice beyond which lies transcendent achievement in civilized and in Christian living in the near future. There is a choice which will plunge the world into another blackness like that of the Dark Ages. The evangelical humanist does not know which choice will be made. But whichever choice decides the immediate future of the world, the ultimate future is secure. Because all values are held securely in the mind and life of God, they must have their ultimate triumph. In the meantime, the evangelical humanist fights every inch of the ground. He fights to secure the right decision now. And when the right decision is not made, he continues to be a witness where he cannot be a controlling power. He may conceivably once more be driven to the catacombs, but the truth for which he stands cannot be slain.

Indeed, the preacher whose central message has to do with the suffering God is of all leaders best prepared for days when the suffering in the life of God must be answered to by suffering in the lives of men. Because he believes in a divine Golgotha, he is never taken completely unaware by a human Golgotha. And even in the darkest hour he does not forget the empty tomb.

# The Christian Criticism of Life

There are clouds on the summits of Mount Madison and Mount Adams as I write. The very outlines of the heights which day by day have been so sharply limned against the sky are blurred except for one clear point. But there is a difference between clouds and mountains. Even as I write, the blurring clouds are shifting. But the mountains remain.